"At its core, this is a book about vegetables and how to treat them in the kitchen with the love and respect that they deserve. However, there is a deeper parallel story here, told through Hetty Lui McKinnon's personal journey of love, loss, and grief—and how transformation through healing and grace makes us evolve as people and teaches us how to be better humans."

—NIK SHARMA,
James Beard Award–nominated author and photographer of *The Flavor Equation* and *Season*

Tenderheart

FOR MY DAD WAI KEUNG LUI/ A TENDERHEART

Grief and love are sisters, woven together from the beginning. Their kinship reminds us that there is no love that does not contain loss and no loss that is not a reminder of the love we carry for what we once held close.

—Francis Weller, *The Wild Edge of Sorrow: Rituals of Renewal and the Sacred Work of Grief*, 2015

Tenderheart

A Cookbook About Vegetables and Unbreakable Family Bonds

Hetty Lui McKinnon

雷瑜

Photographs by Hetty Lui McKinnon

Alfred A. Knopf   New York   2023

Images on pages 21, 460 and 510 by Shirley Cai, copyright © 2022 by Shirley Cai.

Library of Congress Cataloging-in-Publication Data
Names: Lui McKinnon, Hetty, author, photographer.
Title: Tenderheart : a cookbook about vegetables and unbreakable family bonds /
Hetty Lui McKinnon ; photographs by Hetty Lui McKinnon.
Description: First edition. | New York : Alfred A. Knopf, [2023] |
Originally published in Australia by Pan Macmillan Australia Pty Limited, Melbourne, in 2022.
Identifiers: LCCN 2022030021 | ISBN 9780593534861 (hardcover) |
ISBN 9780593534878 (ebook)
Subjects: LCSH: Vegetarian cooking. | Cooking (Natural foods) | LCGFT: Cookbooks.
Classification: LCC TX837 M47725 2023 | DDC 641.5/6362—dc23/eng/20220817
LC record available at https://lccn.loc.gov/2022030021

Cover photograph: Hetty Lui McKinnon
Cover design by Daniel New

Manufactured in China
First American Edition

Contents

Author's Note

An individual's memory is shaped by time, personal experiences and evolving perspectives. The vignettes that I write about in this book are drawn from my own unique memories. And while these recollections are often different from those of my siblings and my mother, our collective memories interweave to create a vivid picture of the man we once knew.

For much of my life, I only dared to remember. Even decades later, it still felt too raw. But I am so grateful that food (and vegetables) have given me the courage and language to do so. Writing this story has helped me heal, as though writing about my dad has given him life again. Some may see this as a book about loss, but I see it as a story about life, an exploration of love, human resilience and unbreakable family bonds. Here, in this playful and assertive collection of vegetable recipes, I can celebrate the mark he left on my life. I am grateful to have found my father again in this book and I am honored to share my memories of him in such a joyous way.

A Book About Vegetables . . .
and So Much More

This book is about vegetables but, for me, there can be no story about the significance of vegetables in my life without telling you about my father, and the enduring legacy of the fresh, tender world he created for his family.

I only knew my father for a short time. He slipped away quietly on a Sunday afternoon on the last day of 1989. As the world outside prepared to celebrate the dawn of a new decade, our world fell apart. I was 15 and my life would never be the same again.

My father's name was Wai Keung Lui, but in Australia he was known as Ken. Born in Guangdong, China, he came to Sydney, Australia, as a teenager during the mid-1950s to study business. He learned to speak his special version of English, heavy-accented, with many endearing language quirks. As a young man, he lived in Sydney's Chinatown, above a grocery store. The inner city of Sydney is now home to sought-after, urbane neighborhoods, but back then it was where postwar immigrants landed, crammed into tiny terrace houses or apartments. He eventually joined the urban sprawl, moving to a house in the southwestern suburbs of Sydney, next door to my Goo Ma (Aunt Betty) and Goo Jeung (Uncle Benny). My Yee Goo Ma (my dad's second eldest sister) and my Paw (his mother) lived on the same street, in the house "on the corner." In 1967, he married my mother, and it was in this house that my siblings and I grew up, where my father would see out his unexpectedly short life.

My memories of my father are suspended in time, a disrupted dream without an ending. Every memory I have of him is through the lens of a child. He was tenderhearted—generous, caring, affectionate, kind and playful. Solidly built with a booming voice, he looked and behaved as the model immigrant—polite, well dressed, respectful and gregarious. His charcoal hair was neat, perfectly slicked with Brylcreem; he wore button-down shirts and meticulously ironed slacks to work, saving his three-piece suits for our weekend visits to Chinatown. He took photos constantly, filling album after album with images of family celebrations and outings, turning the laundry room into a makeshift darkroom. On our first family holiday to China in the early 1980s, he traveled with a camera bag the size of a suitcase. Through my child-eyes, he embodied strength; he routinely carried boxes of vegetables and sacks of rice on his shoulders. For years after his death, I dreamed of this image on repeat, my dad entering the house like a hologram, a sack of rice stacked upon his broad shoulders.

My dad woke at 3 a.m. every morning. In darkness, he dressed swiftly and met my Uncle Benny outside, traveling together to work at Flemington Markets (now known as Sydney Markets), the largest wholesale fruit and vegetable market in Australia. During the week, my dad worked for my Uncle Benny, who oversaw a banana wholesale business. On the weekends, he worked part time as a waiter at a Chinese restaurant.

In many ways, his job at the markets defined him. He became known as a supplier of fresh produce not only at work, but among our family and friends. Every day, he came home from work with trays and boxes of vegetables and fruits, ready for our family meals, but always enough to share with others. Crates of mangoes for our elderly neighbor Earl who lived two doors away, oranges and apples for our family doctor, boxes of cherries as gifts at Christmastime, peaches, plums and apricots for aunts, uncles, cousins and friends. There were bananas, too, in excessive quantities. My older sister Letty recalls that, as a small child, she walked around the neighborhood distributing fruit baskets to the neighbors.

For my mum, he brought home gai choy (Chinese mustard greens) for pickling, fresh gai lan, ong choy, choy sum and bok choy for nightly stir-fries and juicy iceberg lettuce for braising. Mammoth, plump heads of cauliflower and broccoli, hefty daikon, tender cabbage and shiny eggplant sat in deep cardboard boxes left around the kitchen, dining room and laundry room. As a child, I didn't see living among cartons of fresh produce as anything but normal. We snacked on fruit all day, often making ourselves sick on it (there was a notorious cherry overconsumption incident, which my mother still laughs about today). One summer's day, I ate an entire basket of apricots in one sitting; they were the best apricots I'd ever tasted—plump, sweet, floral and tenderly firm—spoiling apricots for me forever. I am still constantly searching for the apricots of my youth.

My father had an indulgent side. On Fridays he brought home live mud crabs from the market, their shells trussed in pink string. He left them in a large bucket in the kitchen, their death row. I would prod at them, childishly taunting them in their final hours of life; they responded with snapping claws and flailing legs. At the deft hands of my mother, they would soon lose their lives, wok-tossed with ginger and shallots, a succulent, irresistible dish.

My father's job meant he kept strange hours, which filtered into our daily lives. Due to his early start at work, he was always home when we arrived back from school. "After-school snack" was an official meal in our house because this was my dad's time to shine—he relished the opportunity to purchase or prepare more "Western" foods for us. From our local bakery he would pick up meat pies, sausage rolls, finger buns, custard tarts or apple turnovers. But my siblings and I agree that our favorite afternoon snack was his salad roll, which he filled with iceberg lettuce so finely shredded with a cleaver that we wondered if he was hiding some secret ninja kitchen skills. My dad was the type of person who, if we told him we liked a particular food, would inundate us with it; once my sister told him she liked orange juice, and for weeks he bought her an entire bottle of orange juice every single day. It was my dad I turned to when I wanted to try cheese; he brought home packs of Kraft singles, which were like gold to me, and later introduced me to blocks of cheddar. My dad possessed a child-like wonderment about life in the West and a palpable excitement about the world, which I sensed was too often suppressed by his predestined duty as an earnest Chinese man, bound by tradition and responsibility.

My father went to bed at an early hour, so we rushed through evening activities. We ate dinner while the sun was still up. At around 5 p.m., we would hear my mother bellowing through the rumble of the kitchen exhaust fan—"hong toi" (set the table), "sik faan" (the Cantonese term for dinnertime, which translates to "eat rice"). Dinner in our house was a noisy affair. My father liked the hectic sounds of the television while we ate, so, to the soundtrack of the nightly news, we devoured our dinner swiftly and neatly. My parents didn't allow a messy table and every grain of rice needed to be accounted for. At the end of every meal, like clockwork, my father remained at the table, peeling himself an orange. On occasion, I would stand beside him, hoping to snare a segment or two.

Losing a parent or carer (or any loved one) as a child, or before we fully understand who we are or who we will become, changes us in a profound, uncomfortable way. The reverberations of loss echo throughout our lives, in ways that we don't expect. It's a crack that keeps opening, a knife that keeps twisting. It is a dull ache that lingers in our soul. I have carried this memory of my father as the generous "fruit and vegetable guy" close to my heart my entire adult life. It is a memory that fills me with pride. When I stopped eating meat as a teenager, I felt comforted by this choice, a quiet contentment in centering the vegetables and fruits that sustained me as a child. When I started my food journey at Arthur Street Kitchen, vegetables naturally served as my main source of inspiration, sparking a deep and enduring passion for creating big-flavored, vegetable-centric food for my community. Every day, vegetables and fruits are a tangible force, shaping the way I think about food, how I cook for my family, the recipes I share with the world and, indeed, the recipes in this book. Today, my endless love for vegetables is one of the ways I honor my dad's legacy, by cooking them every day, with detail and care.

Mum and Dad on their honeymoon, Gold Coast, 1967 (taken on self-timer).

Loss, Life and a Legacy
That Lingers

I have often felt estranged from the person I was before my father died. So much of my "living," my big moments, happened in the years following—graduating from university, getting married, having children, my career in food, moving around the world. Memory is fragile. It is not easy to hang on to the voice, the touch, the laughter and the mannerisms of someone no longer with us. But living away from home, geographically distant from my mother and my siblings, has taught me that our past, our legacy, is not always something we can hold on to physically, but it already lingers deep within us.

Food has always been emotional for me. It is tied to my identity, my heritage, my family and my community. It represents the experiences of the generations before me, and it is a legacy for my children. In food, I find my home, and in this vegetable life I have found a way to stay connected to my dad.

Through my parents, we saw the many sides of food. Where my mum held on tightly to tradition, my dad offered us gateways to the West. My dad was a *foodie* before the term existed, often introducing us to new ingredients and foods that were not common in a Chinese immigrant household. In my early teenage years, he began taking the family to "fancy" restaurants. On weekends, we got dressed up and dined at The Summit and Sydney's Centerpoint Tower, both "expensive" revolving restaurants serving Western buffets high in the sky, offering 360-degree views of the city. We visited hotel restaurants, mostly gorging on seafood buffets. To our family, buffets, with their limitless servings and copious amounts of raw salad greens, seafood, roasted meats and dainty pastel desserts, were an indulgence, the antithesis of the food we ate at home. I remember my siblings and I wondering about this sudden burst of "eating out" instigated by my father. We may have joked that it felt like our last supper; we didn't know that it was almost his. When we were young, my parents put a lot of trust in "tomorrow" or "another day"—it was their typical answer to big questions like *When are we going to go on a family vacation? When are we getting a new car? When can I have a genuine Cabbage Patch Kid?* Looking back, I assume these indulgent lunches were a sign that my father had stopped living for tomorrow.

My father's work ethic, his generosity, his openness and his kindness, are attributes that inform the way I navigate the world as a mother, as a writer, as a cook, as a human. His influence is not as overt or as present as my mother's, but it is still there, a flame that flickers with constancy and devotion. And nowhere do I feel his presence more than when I fill my kitchen and dining table with fresh vegetables and fruit.

Everyday Heroes

This is a book about my favorite vegetables, though some of them are technically fruit. But for the purposes of this book, I will be treating them and referring to them as vegetables.

Vegetables are foundational to my everyday cooking and at the very heart of every dish I create. Preparing them daily, with respect and care, is a ritual that I observed in my parents' kitchen growing up and is now crucial to my days, too. At the end of the day, no matter how tired I am, the act of washing, peeling, chopping and preparing vegetables for dinner helps me stay grounded, a way to bring order to my day.

My approach to vegetables is unapologetic. I've long believed that almost any dish—even dishes that are meaty in origin—can be created with vegetables at the helm. Vegetables are inherently more flexible and adaptable than people think, and the more you cook with them, the more you experiment and explore, the more multifaceted they become. Having grown up around big-flavored vegetable meals, and as a vegetarian for almost three decades, I have always seen plants as the most exciting couriers of flavor. Often, vegetables are treated with excessive delicacy, or simply overlooked on the plate. But vegetables are robust, they are hardy, and they are ready to be challenged.

While vegetables have been central to my cooking for many years, my relationship with them continues to evolve. Our year plus–long quarantine in New York changed my appreciation of vegetables and made me think about them in a different way. I reveled in experimenting with them, scheming on all the ways I could fashion several diverse meals from just one cabbage or a single butternut squash. With access to food, and particularly fresh vegetables, uncertain, I would stock up on carrots, potatoes, broccoli, cauliflower, squash and the like, always seeing how far I could push them. Frozen vegetables, such as peas and corn, became indispensable—they could be used to make curries, stews, pasta and salads. Choosing vegetables that were easily accessible and versatile became my lockdown priority. I found myself seeking solace in the everyday vegetables I grew up eating and cooking them in ways that I normally may not have considered. To me, these vegetables were my everyday heroes.

When I set out to choose the vegetables I would include in this book, it wasn't hard. In short, these are my favorites, the hardworking, dependable vegetables that I turn to most in my daily cooking. They were also chosen for their accessibility, versatility, adaptability and practicality—with our busy lives, these qualities are always paramount to me. I've also included a few of the lesser-known vegetables that I grew up eating; vegetables like taro, daikon or seaweed may not be household names to some but, in many parts of the world and in homes like mine, they are staples. I felt it important to share my love of these vegetables, too, and perhaps inspire more people to cook creatively with them.

Many will be surprised by the vegetables that don't get their own chapter—for example, there is no onion or garlic chapter, yet they feature in almost every savory recipe. This is because I rarely conceive a recipe based upon these two ingredients; it is automatic that they will be used. There are also many "notable" everyday vegetables that I have not afforded their own chapter—corn, asparagus, leeks, cucumber, avocado, bell peppers, etc.—but they do appear in recipes throughout this book.

The Luxury of Seasonality

For the first 15 years of my life, I only ate the most seasonal of fresh produce. Working at the markets meant that my father was right on the pulse of all the latest harvests. But after he passed, we had to rely on our local greengrocer and nearby supermarkets for our fruits and vegetables. My mother often commented that this was the first time, since moving to Australia some 20 years earlier, that she had to buy her own produce. This marked a real change in our appreciation for the seasonal vegetables that we had always lived among. My mother was a dedicated shopper and, being a nondriver, would catch buses or trains to purchase her weekly groceries. We still ate as seasonally as we could, but often, due to practicality and lack of access, it wasn't always possible.

It is impossible to separate vegetables from seasonality, but this book does not strictly prescribe cooking with the seasons. This is because I largely consider seasonality to be a luxury. While eating with the seasons may be easy and practical for some people, for others it is not. My intention with this book is to liberate home cooks from the anxiety of sourcing produce at specific times of the year. My manifesto is this: eat seasonally if you can, but don't stress if you can't. If you are craving a tomato in winter, and you can nab one from the supermarket knowing it has been sitting for a while in cold storage, then that is completely okay. If you eat broccoli all year round like me, that works, too. There are enough causes of angst in the world; sourcing vegetables should not be one of them.

The Tenderheart Pantry

In recent years, "umami" has become a hackneyed term in food. But for vegetarians like me, the presence of umami, or "deliciousness" as it roughly translates to from the Japanese, is paramount. It is the flavor high that I am always chasing in my food. That note of savoriness is what keeps us coming back for the next bite; it is ultimately the difference between a dish that is good and one that is delicious. As my mother would always ask when tasting her food, "hou hou mei?," meaning "good flavor?" There are many ingredients that offer umami and many of them feature repeatedly in this book—well-known umami agents such as seaweed, kimchi, soy sauce, garlic and, of course, mushrooms and tomatoes, but I also look to fermented pastes and condiments like doubanjiang, miso paste, doenjang and dou si (Chinese fermented black soybeans) for that flavor x-factor.

While the recipes in this book are rooted in vegetables, I also call them "pantry-led." Many of the dishes came about through the real-life predicament of needing to cook dinner—the sum of whatever vegetables I unearthed in the fridge, and a few select, hard-hitting pantry items. What I loved about this way of cooking—and developing recipes for this book—is that it required me to trust my pantry, while also establishing a sense of freedom in the kitchen.

Independence and courage in the kitchen are what I'm always encouraging in my readers. Don't be afraid to break the rules, and substitute whenever you need to. Being free when cooking is made much easier when you have a robust pantry. No matter the cooking method, the recipes in *Tenderheart* reflect how I cook during the week, which embraces my global pantry and digs deep into staples. A typical *Tenderheart* meal may look like this: a vegetable or two combined with a workhorse carb, such as rice, grains, pasta or noodles, perhaps a protein like tofu or eggs, amplified with spices, sauces, vinegars, condiments, nuts and seeds.

Along with your dry pantry and your fridge, use your freezer. Keep bags of frozen peas, corn, edamame, spinach and mixed vegetables (carrot, peas, corn) on hand. The freezer is also a great place to keep leftover soup broths, curry pastes, dumplings (homemade or store-bought), noodles, filled pasta, gnocchi, pastry (filo or puff) and noodles. I also follow in my mum's footsteps by freezing ginger (peel it and cut it into handy ¾–1¼-inch/2–3 cm chunks), sliced green onions, chiles, makrut lime leaves and curry leaves.

The Power of Chili Oil

Chili oils add multidimensional power to a dish—flavor, depth and spice. Here are two oils that will complement the meals in this book. As always, the amount of chile I prescribe is according to how I like it (pretty hot!), so I encourage you to vary the amount of red pepper flakes and/or peppercorns according to your spice tolerance.

Umami Crisp

Umami crisp offers a fiery wallop of flavor. Part chili oil, part chili crisp, this rich condiment is packed with natural flavor enhancers that impart a deep, dark, "meaty" intensity. Dried porcini mushroom (or substitute with dried shiitake) is the standout star of this oil, turning slightly jammy as it simmers in the oil, while the garlic, almonds, red pepper flakes and sesame seeds become crisp. For those who fell irrevocably in love with my gutsy Everything Oil in *To Asia, With Love*, think of umami crisp as Everything Oil 2.0—fiercely delicious, undeniably craveworthy. Serve on top of noodles, rice dishes, salads or fried or jammy eggs.

MAKES ABOUT 2 CUPS

½ cup (20 g) dried porcini mushrooms, roughly chopped

1 shallot, roughly diced

4 garlic cloves, finely chopped

½ cup sliced almonds

½ cup toasted white sesame seeds

1 cinnamon stick

1–2 tablespoons red pepper flakes

1 tablespoon gochugaru

1⅓ cups (320 ml) neutral oil

1 tablespoon soy sauce or tamari

2 tablespoons toasted sesame oil

2–3 teaspoons sea salt flakes (to your taste)

Place the mushrooms, shallot, garlic, almonds, sesame seeds, cinnamon stick, red pepper flakes, gochugaru and neutral oil in a saucepan and heat over medium-high heat for 1–3 minutes, until the oil starts to bubble around the edge. Reduce the heat to medium-low and cook for 15–20 minutes, stirring occasionally, until the shallot, garlic, almonds and sesame seeds are golden and crispy. (Be watchful—the time this takes will depend upon your stovetop heat and the size of your pan, so I recommend staying close by to monitor progress. I also recommend tasting along the way.) Strain the oil through a fine-mesh sieve set over a bowl and let the mixture cool—this will allow it to crisp up further. Set the oil aside.

When the mushroom mixture is completely cool, stir it back into the oil (including the cinnamon stick as this will continue to flavor the oil once stored) and add the soy sauce or tamari, sesame oil and sea salt flakes (I recommend starting with 2 teaspoons of salt and increasing to 3 if you want it saltier). Store the umami crisp in a sterilized jar in the fridge for up to 3 months.

Gluten-free

Vegan

Garlicky Chili Oil

This is inspired by my favorite commercial chili oil: Chiu Chow Chili Oil by Lee Kum Kee, a recipe said to originate from Chiu Chow (also spelled Chaozhou or Teochew) in Guangdong Province, China. Garlicky, salty and heavy on the heat, this is a real flavor bomb, and is spicier than the Umami Crisp on page 27. Toss with noodles with black vinegar for a simple meal or add to stir-fries for a pungent kick. You can use the oil and the "sediment" (garlicky chiles) together, the oil on its own, or the sediment can be used as a spicy topping for roasted veggies, salads, noodles, rice or eggs. Bird's eye chiles are one of the hottest varieties and will give you the right amount of heat, but you can use other fresh chiles, too, adding more or less dried red pepper flakes to achieve the level of spice that is right for you.

MAKES 1 CUP

10–12 bird's eye chiles (about ¾ oz/20 g), very finely chopped

1 teaspoon sea salt

¾ cup (180 ml) neutral oil

8–10 garlic cloves, finely chopped

2 tablespoons toasted sesame oil

1–1½ tablespoons red pepper flakes

½–1 tablespoon Sichuan peppercorns (optional but recommended), pounded until flaky

¼ teaspoon sugar

2 tablespoons soy sauce or tamari

Combine the chopped chiles and salt and let sit for 30 minutes while you prepare the other ingredients.

Heat ½ cup (120 ml) of the oil, along with the garlic, in a small saucepan over low heat. Cook, stirring often, for 10–12 minutes, until the garlic is dehydrated and a light golden color. You don't want the garlic to fry or turn golden, so watch it closely to ensure it doesn't burn. Add the salted chiles and cook for 5–7 minutes; again watch it closely to prevent burning.

Add the remaining ¼ cup (60 ml) of oil, the sesame oil, red pepper flakes and Sichuan peppercorns (if using) and stir. Finally, add the sugar and soy sauce or tamari and stir until well combined.

Transfer to a sterilized jar and allow to cool completely. Store in the fridge for up to 3 months.

Gluten-free

Vegan

Cook's Notes

- **Cheese**—it is worth noting that certain cheeses, such as parmesan, pecorino, Manchego, Gruyère and Gorgonzola (just to name a few), are made with rennet (an animal enzyme) so are not technically vegetarian. While I haven't cut these cheeses from my diet (though I tend to eat less of them nowadays), this is something for those following a meat-free diet to be aware of. There are many vegetarian cheeses on the market that are made without animal rennet, so keep an eye out for those.

   While the exact amount of grated cheese used in a recipe should be fluid and not too prescribed, if you are looking for accuracy, my grated cheese weights are based upon cheese grated using a fine Microplane for hard cheeses such as pecorino or Parmigiano-Reggiano, while grated cheddar is based upon the amounts and weights of store-bought shredded cheese.

- **Digital scales**—I highly recommend measuring ingredients with digital scales, rather than cups, particularly when it comes to baking. In fact, in baking, and for any instances where you are using flours or starches, such as flatbread, noodle or dumpling wrapper recipes, dry-to-wet ratios matter, so a scale is essential to give you the right results. Digital scales are not a big investment—I purchased one years ago for about $10 and it is one of the most-used items in my kitchen.

- **Eggs**—large eggs were used in testing these recipes.

- **(Faux) deep-frying**—I am not a huge fan of deep-frying or large quantities of scary hot oil, but in recent years I have developed a method that works for me. I use a small, deep cast-iron pan (mine is the small cocotte from Staub), and I fill this with 1–1¼ inches (2.5–3 cm) of oil. This allows me to have more control because I'm frying only a few items at a time. This method takes longer but I find it less intimidating. If you are a confident deep-fryer, proceed as you always do!

- **Flax eggs**—these are an excellent vegan substitute for eggs in baking (but not in general cooking—don't try scrambled flax eggs!). To substitute 1 large egg, combine 1 tablespoon ground flaxseed with 3 tablespoons of water and rest for 5 minutes. It will become thick and gluey.

- **Garlic powder**—I had never used garlic powder until the pandemic. Such is my reliance on garlic as a base for cooking, that I added garlic powder to my pantry while in lockdown, spurred by the irrational fear that I would not have access to fresh garlic. I learned that garlic powder is not a direct replacement for the pungent aroma of fresh garlic; it is its own ingredient altogether—it performs well in salad dressings (particularly if you don't like the raw garlic taste) and marinades, or sprinkled on veggies before roasting. If used with restraint, it adds a nice umami flavor that doesn't overpower. If you do find yourself needing to substitute fresh garlic with garlic powder, 1 regular-sized garlic clove can be subbed with about ¼–½ teaspoon garlic powder, but it's always best to add it slowly until you get your desired pungency.

- **Leeks**—people often ask me what to do with the green parts of the leek. In the past, I would have advised to use them to make stock. But now I use the entire leek, green and white parts, discarding just the straggly tip from the upper part of the leaves. The greens are a little tougher, slightly stronger in flavor, but they can absolutely be used along with the whites. Leeks can be very dirty—to clean, slice them first, then rinse in cold water.

- **Neutral oil**—I use many types of neutral oils in my kitchen. Most often, it will be grapeseed or sunflower oil, but rice bran, vegetable, canola or avocado oil are great, too.

- **Oven temperatures**—all recipes were tested using a conventional gas oven and stovetop. If using a fan-forced oven, reduce the temperature by 10–20°C (check your oven manual for guidance).

- **Salt**—I always use sea salt in my recipes. I have two types—a fine sea salt that I use for flavoring cooking water, for baking and most general cooking. And then I have sea salt flakes, which I use for seasoning before eating (I use Maldon brand). However, I am not arbitrary when it comes to salt. Everyone has a different palate, so I encourage you to use your discretion and season to your liking. The most important thing about salt is that it is vital to bringing out flavor, so some is better than none!

- **Veganize**—most of the recipes in this book—apart from egg-based dishes—can be veganized. There are excellent vegan cheeses on the market now and these will work in any of the recipes that require melty cheese. When topping a dish, in place of parmesan or grated hard cheese, use nutritional yeast. I use flax eggs (see opposite) to great success in baking. I usually use nondairy milk (oat is my favorite) in everyday cooking.

- **Vegetable swaps**—in many of the recipes, I have provided a "vegetable swap." This is to encourage you to consider a recipe, even if you don't have the exact vegetable in your fridge or pantry. There is never only one way to cook a dish. If you do swap veggies, please adjust the cooking times according to the vegetable you are using.

- **Vegetarian stir-fry sauce**—this is a commercial sauce that I use as a replacement for oyster sauce. It is sometimes sold as "mushroom-flavored stir-fry sauce." If you are not vegetarian, substitute with oyster sauce.

asian greens

"Gleefully economical and incomparably fresh"

Every day, my father arrived home from work with another box of greens: bok choy, gai lan, choy sum, ong choy, gai choy, amaranth. My mother tells me that the sheer volume of greens often intimidated her. But she persisted. Filling the sink with water, she diligently soaked them first, then rubbed them to remove grit, finally rinsing them again until they glistened. She was obsessive about washing Asian greens, usually repeating this whole process again. Over the years, I endured many lectures about the best and optimum way to wash greens.

"Asian greens" is the way I categorize the abundant green leafy vegetables that I grew up eating. Namely, gai lan (Chinese broccoli), choy sum, yu choy, ong choy, tatsoi, bok choy and baby bok choy (sometimes called pak choy). There are many types of Asian greens but, for the purposes of this chapter, these are the ones I focus on. Bok choy is more peppery, while choy sum and tatsoi offer mustard vibes, but the three varieties can be used interchangeably. Gai lan is more robust and has a more pronounced flavor that hints of kale. There's one dish in this chapter that I tried to leave out, but I simply could not in all good conscience do so. Even though lettuce is not seen as Asian in origin, we ate cooked lettuce a lot growing up, either braised or stir-fried, and it felt important for me to share this dish. So, there you have it.

I've long dreamed of writing this collection of recipes to show how Asian greens can do more. While stir-frying at high heat gives us reliable vibrance and crisp-tenderness, I've broken Asian greens out of their box and afforded them the freedom to be whoever they want to be. I've discovered they can be happy in a galette and become joyously smoky when grilled or charred. They can and should be used as you would kale or spinach, in pastas, noodles and salads. Mostly, they are gleefully economical and incomparably fresh from Asian grocery stores—a huge bunch (or bag) will cost just a few dollars and will last you several meals.

Choy Sum and Feta Galette

This recipe illustrates the versatility of choy sum's mustardy stems. In a dish where we would normally turn to a more common green, such as spinach or kale, choy sum brings a tapestry of more considered, bitter-earth flavors, along with a robust sturdiness. The golden turmeric dough is a good foundational galette dough to have up your sleeve, simple to put together, yet delicate and flaky. To ensure an airy crust, make sure you use ice-cold water, always keep the dough cold and work it as little as possible. The choy sum releases a little liquid as it cooks and when it comes out of the oven it may look too wet but, once it rests for 10–15 minutes, the moisture settles back into the filling. This galette is transportable and can be eaten both hot and at room temperature.

SERVES 4

1¾ cups plus 2 tablespoons (225 g) all-purpose flour, plus more for dusting

1 teaspoon sea salt

½ teaspoon ground turmeric

black pepper

8 tablespoons (112 g) cold unsalted butter, cut into ⅜-inch (1 cm) pieces

⅓–½ cup (80–120 ml) ice-cold water

Choy sum and feta filling

5 ounces (150 g) choy sum (or yu choy, tatsoi), washed and patted dry, stems trimmed

1 cup (220 g) mascarpone

2 green onions, finely sliced

1 garlic clove, grated

sea salt and black pepper

extra-virgin olive oil, for drizzling

1 large egg, beaten

3½ ounces (100 g) feta, crumbled

handful of toasted sesame seeds (white, black or both)

For gluten-free • use gluten-free all-purpose flour

Substitute • feta: Halloumi, goat cheese, brie • mascarpone: cream cheese, sour cream, crème fraîche

Vegetable swap • choy sum: gai lan, spinach, kale, asparagus

Place the flour, salt, turmeric and a few turns of black pepper in a mixing bowl and whisk to combine. Add the butter and toss it to coat then, using your fingertips, squeeze the butter to flatten the pieces (the butter does not have to be uniform; some pieces will be bigger while others will break down into smaller chunks), then toss it thoroughly through the flour mixture. Add about ⅓ cup (80 ml) of iced water to start and, using your hands, toss well to hydrate the flour. If the mixture is still dry, slowly add another tablespoon of water and toss well again. Continue to hydrate the dough with a tiny amount of water at a time, until it just comes together (don't add too much water—you want the dough to come together but not be at all sticky). When the dough is ready, shape it into a flat disc, wrap in plastic wrap and refrigerate until chilled, about 30 minutes, or up to overnight (if chilling overnight, remove from the fridge about 20 minutes before rolling).

When you're ready to make the galette, preheat the oven to 400°F (200°C). Line a large sheet pan with parchment paper.

To make the filling, prepare the choy sum by separating the stems from the leaves. Finely slice the stems and leave the leaves whole.

Place the mascarpone, green onion and garlic in a bowl and whisk to combine and loosen up the mixture. Season generously with sea salt and black pepper.

Transfer the parchment paper to a work surface and place the dough in the center. Dust a small amount of flour on top and roll the dough into a round roughly 12 inches (30 cm) in diameter. Spread the mascarpone mix over the dough, leaving a 1-inch (2.5 cm) border around the edge. Lay the choy sum stems and leaves on top to fully cover the mascarpone (it will look like a mountain of greens but it will cook down). Season the choy sum with sea salt and black pepper and drizzle with olive oil. Using the parchment paper as a guide, fold the edges of the dough inward over the filling, pinching together any tears in the dough. Brush the beaten egg over the exposed crust and scatter the feta over the whole galette. Carefully transfer the parchment paper and galette to the sheet pan.

Bake for 30–35 minutes, until the crust is golden. Rest for 10–15 minutes, then scatter with the sesame seeds and eat warm or at room temperature.

Charred Gai Lan and Farro with Soy Tahini

Gai lan is one of the most robust Asian greens, with a solid stem and strong leaves that are evocative of broccoli or kale, with slightly more bitterness. It has less water content than other Asian greens, so is well suited to more rugged cooking methods. Chargrilling gai lan in a pan or on the outdoor grill is a wonderful way to build flavors—it's expected that it will become smoky, but it's the sweetness that disarms and charms. I adore the perfectly balanced layers of this salad—the chewy farro brings so much heart, while the soy-infused tahini is divinely nutty and intensely savory, an exceptional foil to gai lan's natural bitterness.

SERVES 4

1⅓ cups (250 g) farro

2 bunches of gai lan (about 14 oz/400 g), washed and patted dry, stems trimmed

extra-virgin olive oil

sea salt and black pepper

handful of cilantro leaves

2 tablespoons toasted sesame seeds (black, white or both)

Soy tahini

¼ cup (60 g) tahini

1 tablespoon soy sauce

1 teaspoon chili oil

1 garlic clove, grated

Bring a saucepan of salted water to a boil. Add the farro, reduce the heat to medium, then cover and cook for 20–25 minutes, until the farro is tender to the bite. Drain and set aside.

Slice each gai lan stem in half lengthwise. Heat a large skillet over medium-high heat (or heat a griddle on the grill on high). Working in batches, drizzle oil into the pan (or brush the griddle surface) and add the gai lan in a single layer. Char on each side for 1–2 minutes, until there are crispy, golden bits. Immediately remove from the heat and slide the greens onto a plate. Season with sea salt and black pepper, then repeat with the remaining gai lan.

To make the soy tahini, whisk the tahini, soy sauce, chili oil and garlic in a bowl until combined. Add 2–3 tablespoons of water until you have a smooth, pourable dressing.

To serve, spoon the farro onto a platter or into a bowl and top with the gai lan. Drizzle with the soy tahini and season with sea salt and a few turns of black pepper. Top with the cilantro leaves and sesame seeds and serve.

For gluten-free • use quinoa or brown rice, and use tamari in place of soy sauce

Vegan

Vegetable swap • gai lan: broccoli, cauliflower, kale

Curry Gai Lan Chow Fun

Sar hor fun (fresh thick rice noodles) are the star of many of our most beloved Southeast Asian noodle dishes—char kway teow, pad mee kao and pad see ew. Chow hor fun (fried rice noodles) is a Cantonese dish, one that can be served as dry-fried noodles with meat and vegetables, or a saucier dish, topped with a gravy. My mother's chow hor fun, glistening with soy sauce and lao chou (dark soy sauce), is suitably wok-charred and served with bean sprouts and an abundance of green vegetables. Devouring unreasonably large mouthfuls of these bouncy, slippery noodles is a vivid childhood memory. These noodles are best bought fresh and eaten on the same day, as they become hard in the fridge overnight (if you do store them in the fridge, refresh by dunking them in a saucepan of boiling water until they become soft again). This recipe is inspired by my mum's Singapore noodles, re-creating the same flavors of her dish, but replacing the rice vermicelli with these fresh rice noodles.

SERVES 4

neutral oil

1 yellow onion, finely sliced

2 tablespoons curry powder

½ teaspoon sugar

sea salt and white pepper

1¾ pounds (800 g) fresh rice noodles, rinsed in water to separate

4 teaspoons soy sauce or tamari

2 garlic cloves, finely chopped

9 ounces (250 g) gai lan, washed and patted dry, trimmed and thick stems halved lengthwise

2 cups (230 g) bean sprouts

2 green onions, finely sliced

2 tablespoons toasted sesame seeds (black, white or both)

Maggi seasoning sauce, to serve (optional)

Place a wok or large skillet over high heat. Add approximately 2 tablespoons of oil and, when it shimmers, add the onion and stir-fry for 2 minutes, until softened. Add the curry powder and sugar, then season with about 1 teaspoon of salt and toss well for about 1 minute. Add the noodles and soy sauce or tamari, toss and leave to cook undisturbed for 45–60 seconds, until the bottom is a little charred. Then, using a spatula, lift the noodles from the surface, including any browned bits, and toss for 1–2 minutes. Add the garlic and gai lan and cook for 2 minutes, until the greens are just wilted but still crisp-tender. Add the bean sprouts and half the green onion, season with white pepper and toss until the sprouts soften slightly, about 30 seconds. Turn off the heat and transfer to a serving plate.

To serve, top with the remaining green onion and the sesame seeds. A few sprinkles of Maggi are nice, but optional.

Note: For added protein, scramble 2–3 eggs and add to the noodles with the bean sprouts.

Gluten-free and vegan

Substitute • fresh rice noodles: 10½ ounces (300 g) dried wide rice noodles or rice vermicelli

Vegetable swap • gai lan: other Asian greens, broccoli

Grilled Baby Bok Choy
with Miso-Gochujang Butter and Crispy Chickpeas

This dish has it all—bold spices, profound smokiness, unmatched crispiness. The miso-gochujang butter is something special, a unique sweet, salty and creamy marinade for the baby bok choy. Make sure you don't waste any of the leftover marinade—add the charred greens back into the bowl to lick up any precious remnants of flavor. The chickpeas are no ordinary crispy chickpeas—I've made a lot of crispy legumes in my life, but these are by far the crunchiest and most flavorful, thanks to a light coating of chickpea flour. Don't think twice about making a double batch for future meals or snacking.

SERVES 4

3 cups (500 g) cooked chickpeas (about two 15 oz/425 g cans, drained)

⅓ cup (35 g) chickpea flour (besan)

1 tablespoon gochugaru or ½–1 teaspoon red pepper flakes

sea salt and black pepper

extra-virgin olive oil

1 pound 10 ounces (750 g) baby bok choy (or choy sum, tatsoi), washed and patted dry, stems trimmed

½ cup (125 g) Greek or vegan coconut yogurt

handful of cilantro leaves, to serve

handful of toasted white sesame seeds, for topping

rice, to serve (optional)

Miso-gochujang butter

4 tablespoons (56 g) regular or vegan butter

2½ tablespoons gochujang paste

2½ tablespoons white (shiro) miso

1 garlic clove, grated

½-inch (1.5 cm) piece of ginger, peeled and grated

Preheat the oven to 425°F (220°C).

In a bowl, combine the chickpeas, chickpea flour, gochugaru or red pepper flakes, ½ teaspoon of sea salt and a few turns of black pepper. Drizzle generously with olive oil and stir to combine. Transfer to a sheet pan, place on the lowest rack in the oven and roast for 18–20 minutes, until crispy and golden.

Cut the baby bok choy in half lengthwise through the stem. If you have larger ones, quarter them.

To make the miso-gochujang butter, place all the ingredients in a small saucepan over medium-low heat and whisk until the butter is melted and everything is well combined. Transfer to a large bowl, add the baby bok choy and toss to coat.

Heat a grill pan or large skillet over high heat or a griddle on an outdoor grill on high until you can see wisps of smoke rising from the surface. Drizzle the pan with olive oil (or brush the griddle surface) and, working in batches, place the marinated baby bok choy, cut-side down, onto the hot surface and cook for 3–4 minutes, until charred. Turn and repeat on the other side. Transfer to a plate and cook the rest of the baby bok choy. When all the greens are cooked, return them to the bowl that the marinade was in to reabsorb any of the sauce that may be left in the bowl, then toss. If there are any larger pieces of baby bok choy, slice them in half through the stem to make them more manageable.

To serve, place the baby bok choy on a plate and dollop with the yogurt. Top with the crispy chickpeas, cilantro and sesame seeds. Eat as is, or with rice.

Gluten-free and vegan

Vegetable swap • baby bok choy: broccoli, cauliflower

Soy-Butter Bok Choy Pasta

This soy-butter sauce is typical of Japan's innovative wafu cuisine. "Wafu" refers to something that has been cooked in the "Japanese style" and, specifically, wafu pasta refers to spaghetti dishes interwoven with umami-loaded soy sauce and butter emulsions. Wafu is a true hybrid cuisine, emerging not from immigration, but as the result of war. While Italian pasta was introduced to Japan during the Edo period (1603–1868), it didn't become part of the mainstream cuisine until the American occupation of Japan following World War II, when spaghetti featured heavily in military food rations. This recipe is inspired by these innovative, resilient Japanese-influenced pasta recipes, with an extremely simple sauce made of butter and soy, and a hefty amount of bok choy, which becomes melty and heavy with umami notes.

SERVES 4

1 pound (450 g) spaghetti or other long pasta

1 tablespoon extra-virgin olive oil

2 garlic cloves, finely chopped

1 pound (450 g) bok choy (or tatsoi), washed and patted dry, stems trimmed, finely chopped

6 tablespoons (84 g) unsalted regular or vegan butter

½ cup (120 ml) soy sauce or tamari

2 green onions, finely sliced

1 tablespoon toasted white sesame seeds

Bring a large saucepan of salted water to a boil and add the pasta. Cook according to the package directions, but about 2 minutes less than the time specified. Drain and reserve 1 cup (240 ml) of the pasta cooking water.

Heat a large skillet over medium-high heat. Add the olive oil, garlic and bok choy and sauté for 4–5 minutes, until the greens are wilted and have released their liquid. Push the greens to the side and add the butter to the pan, along with the soy sauce or tamari. Allow the butter to melt and stir to combine with the soy sauce. Add the pasta to the pan, along with about ½ cup (120 ml) of the reserved pasta cooking water (or more, if the pasta looks dry) and toss for 2–3 minutes, until the buttery soy sauce has thickened and coats the pasta.

Serve the spaghetti topped with the green onion and sesame seeds.

Serving suggestion: Top with Fish-Free Furikake (see page 359) or torn nori sheets.

For gluten-free • use gluten-free pasta

Vegan

Substitute • spaghetti: ramen, egg or udon noodles

Vegetable swap • bok choy: spinach, kale, Swiss chard

The Reinvention of Mother

During my first year or two of university, I remember a lot of weekday lunches at home, just my mother and me. These were the early years after my father passed and, with my light study load, which included many night classes, I was able to spend most of my days at home, keeping my mum company. I used to wonder whether I would have been such a homebody if my father hadn't died, whether I felt some sort of duty to stay with my mum, to watch over her, to let her watch over me. But I now realize that there was no sacrifice on my part. I gained; time is such a luxury.

After my father passed away, my mother went through a period of huge change. Her trajectory in life perhaps did not anticipate such upheaval. As a girl born in China toward the end of World War II, her path was typical for girls of her generation—with minimal schooling, her teenage years were dedicated to finding a way out of pre–Cultural Revolution China, to get to the West, get married, have children, and to make a new home in a foreign land. But behind her facade as a quiet-spoken Chinese woman, there was a fire, a resilience and a dogged determination, which never showed until she lost her husband prematurely. My mother worked hard not to show her devastation after my dad passed. But in the quiet moments, I saw it. What I also witnessed was a woman who lifted herself every day for her children. Up until that point, her opportunities had been limited—she never had the chance to work, didn't speak English, didn't drive, had never gone to a bank on her own, had never taken herself to buy groceries. In her forties, she found herself a widow, and so she had to learn to live again. An enforced reinvention. Life forces our hand sometimes. The woman that my mother became, that she still is today, is the pillar to which I hold myself, that I hold my children to. Simply, she is strength.

Those quiet days my mother and I spent at home after my father died are so vivid to me. Our mornings were spent on opposite ends of our sprawling L-shaped sofa—she would be reading a Chinese newspaper while I devoured the novels of Jane Austen. We were together, but in solitude. We didn't talk much; maybe she would mutter a headline, or would tell me about the latest domestic tragedy in Hong Kong or the sudden demise of a Chinese celebrity whom I'd never heard of. But I was really lost in my own world, hanging on to the fortunes of the impoverished Dashwood sisters, Elinor and Marianne. Come midday, she would rise and wander into the kitchen to make lunch. Often it was macaroni soup, or ma ma mian (instant noodles), but a lot of the time it was mei fun tong (rice vermicelli soup). It was a quick meal, a stock made of chicken bouillon cubes and some greens thrown in. A simple lunch, to satiate our hunger after a morning awash with stories.

Baby Bok Choy and Rice Vermicelli Soup

This is a clean broth with hints of anise, inspired by the quick noodle soups my mother made for lunch during my university days. Mei fun, or rice vermicelli, is quick to cook, with signature thin strands that allow a satisfying mouthful. I love the simplicity of noodles with baby bok choy, it feels cleansing and restorative. If you're looking for a hint of protein, add some cubes of firm tofu.

SERVES 4

1 tablespoon toasted sesame oil

1-inch (2.5 cm) piece of ginger, peeled and grated

1 garlic clove, grated

2 star anise

5¼ cups (1.25 liters) vegetable stock

2 teaspoons soy sauce or tamari

sea salt

9 ounces (250 g) rice vermicelli, soaked in warm water for 10–15 minutes

14 ounces (400 g) baby bok choy (or tatsoi), washed and patted dry, stems trimmed and halved lengthwise

Spicy green onion oil

4 green onions, finely sliced

1 jalapeño or Thai green chile, finely chopped

1 teaspoon sea salt

½ cup (120 ml) neutral oil

Place a large saucepan over medium heat. Add the sesame oil, along with the ginger, garlic and star anise, and sizzle for 15 seconds, until aromatic. Add the stock, cover and bring to a boil. Add the soy sauce or tamari and season with sea salt until you achieve your preferred level of saltiness.

Meanwhile, to make the spicy green onion oil, place the green onion, jalapeño, and sea salt in a heatproof bowl. Place the oil in a small saucepan over medium heat. To test the readiness of the oil, place a wooden chopstick or spoon into the oil and, if it sizzles, the oil is hot enough. Very, very carefully, pour the oil over the green onion and chile, standing back as it will sizzle and splutter. Set aside to cool.

Drain the vermicelli and add it to the broth, along with the baby bok choy. Cook for just 1-2 minutes, until the bok choy is bright green and the noodles are tender. Using tongs, fish the noodles and greens out of the broth and divide among four bowls. Ladle the soup over the top and finish with the spicy green onion oil.

Gluten-free and vegan

Substitute • rice vermicelli: thick rice noodles, mung bean vermicelli

Vegetable swap • baby bok choy: other Asian greens, broccoli, snow peas

Ong Choy, Five-Spice Tofu and Noodle Stir-Fry

This recipe is an homage to one of my favorite Chinese vegetable dishes—stir-fried ong choy with garlic, chile and fermented bean curd (there's a recipe in *To Asia, With Love*)—but steps outside of tradition with the addition of noodles and tofu. This dish comes together quickly, but is bursting with flavor and texture—the fermented bean curd or miso paste adds a salty, spicy kick, while the unique hollow ong choy stems offer a pleasing chew alongside the smooth noodles. Prior to cooking, the volume of greens will feel immense, but it cooks down considerably and releases water, which combines with the aromatics and seasonings to form a silky sauce.

SERVES 4

9 ounces (250 g) dried wheat noodles or rice noodles

neutral oil

2 garlic cloves, finely sliced

1 bird's eye or Thai red chile, finely chopped (remove the seeds if you prefer less heat)

1 pound (450 g) ong choy, cut into 3-inch (7.5 cm) pieces

2½ tablespoons soy sauce or tamari

2½ tablespoons toasted sesame oil

sea salt

4 ounces (115 g) five-spice, marinated or extra-firm tofu, cut into thin 2-inch (5 cm) strips

1 heaping tablespoon fermented bean curd or white (shiro) miso

1 tablespoon toasted white sesame seeds

Bring a large saucepan of salted water to a boil. Add the noodles and cook according to the package directions until just tender. Drain.

Meanwhile, heat a drizzle of oil in a wok or large skillet over medium-high heat. When the oil is hot, add the garlic and chile and cook for 10 seconds. Add the ong choy, soy sauce or tamari, 4 teaspoons of the sesame oil, 1–2 tablespoons of water and a big pinch of sea salt. Stir-fry for 2–3 minutes, until the greens are wilted. Add the tofu and toss well.

Reduce the heat to medium-low and stir in the fermented bean curd or miso until it is melted through the greens. Add the noodles and toss gently until combined. Allow to cook for 30–60 seconds, until everything is heated through. Immediately transfer to a serving plate or individual bowls and top with the remaining sesame oil and the sesame seeds.

Gluten-free and vegan

Substitute • fermented bean curd or miso: salted black beans, doenjang, black bean sauce, doubanjiang

Vegetable swap • ong choy: other Asian greens, amaranth leaves, sweet potato leaves, iceberg lettuce

Stir-Fried Lettuce

Lettuce is not technically an Asian green, but in Chinese cuisine this dish of stir-fried lettuce is a classic. Considered a "lucky" food, it is served during the Lunar New Year to symbolize wealth and prosperity (the Cantonese word for lettuce is sang choy, or shēngcài in Mandarin, which is a homonym for "abundance and wealth"). Lettuce is almost always served cooked in Chinese cuisine (apart from dishes like sang choy bao), often served as a cradle for braised mushrooms or abalone. When lettuce is quickly stir-fried it wilts, but retains texture and crunch. Serve as part of a Chinese banquet or enjoy simply with a bowl of rice. Add a fried egg, and dinner is done.

SERVES 4

1 head iceberg or romaine lettuce (1–1½ lb/450–675 g)

1 tablespoon soy sauce or tamari

2 teaspoons vegetarian stir-fry sauce or dark soy sauce

1 tablespoon toasted sesame oil

sea salt and white pepper

1 tablespoon neutral oil

1-inch (2.5 cm) piece of ginger, peeled and finely chopped

1 garlic clove, finely chopped

toasted sesame seeds (white, black or both), to serve

rice, to serve

Run a sharp paring knife around the core of the lettuce, then gently pull it out and discard. If the outer layers of the lettuce are loose and discolored, remove and discard. Tear the lettuce into large chunks. Wash the leaves and allow them to dry in a colander.

In a small bowl, whisk together the soy sauce or tamari, vegetarian stir-fry sauce or dark soy sauce, sesame oil and a pinch of sea salt and white pepper.

Heat a wok or large skillet over medium-high heat, add the oil, along with the ginger and garlic, and cook for 30 seconds. Add the lettuce and stir-fry for 1–2 minutes, until the leaves are wilted. Pour the sauce over the lettuce and stir-fry for 1 minute longer. Take care not to overcook the lettuce, as you want it to retain some crunch.

Season with a little more salt and white pepper, scatter with sesame seeds and serve with rice.

For gluten-free • use gluten-free hoisin or stir-fry sauce

Vegan

Substitute • vegetarian stir-fry sauce or dark soy sauce: oyster sauce for nonvegetarians, hoisin sauce, kecap manis

Vegetable swap • lettuce: bok choy, choy sum, napa cabbage

Broccoli

"My heart belongs to broccoli."

Those who know me well know that my heart belongs to broccoli. It is the vegetable that showed me the potential of greens to excite, to delight. The first chargrilled broccoli salad I made—one with chickpeas, capers, mint and lemon—dared me to dream of new possibilities, with flavors so pure, and so precise, that it inspired me to imagine sharing salads, and vegetables, with the world. Years later, many will agree with me that this is perhaps the perfect salad. If you don't already know it, you will find the recipe in my book *Community*, and there is a soup version of this dish further into this chapter on page 76.

Broccoli has its origins in Southern Italy, where it was popular with the Etruscans and ancient Romans. The first variety was cultivated from cabbage and was called *broccolo calabrese* (Calabrian broccoli) in Italian, which derived from the Latin word *brachium*, meaning "arm," "branch" or "sprout." It is said that Romans ate raw broccoli before banquets so the body could better absorb the large quantities of alcohol consumed. When broccoli was introduced to England in the 1700s, it was referred to as "Italian asparagus."

Today, it is one of the most popular modern vegetables, at once simple yet elegant. A true stem-to-flower vegetable, there is no need to waste any of it; I cook the stalks, and any sprouting leaves, right alongside the florets. Though it is seasonal during autumn and winter, broccoli endures as our most loved year-round vegetable in my house.

Broccoli Forest Loaf

My vision for this recipe was simple: broccoli trees growing out of a loaf. The image itself was inspired by an iconic photograph in the book *Breakfast, Lunch, Tea* by Rose Carrarini, showing a cross section of a cake where broccoli spears are seemingly suspended within batter. I've actually never made Rose's broccoli cake, but I knew I wanted to re-create this whimsical broccoli forest. Savory cakes deserve more love, in my opinion. I prefer them to savory muffins or scones, as they stay moister in loaf form. They are also a wonderful treat for brunch or a light lunch, great in lunchboxes and are transportable, too, so consider them for picnics or gatherings.

SERVES 6–8

1 small head of broccoli (about 9 oz/250 g), cut into large florets

1½ cups (185 g) all-purpose flour

1 teaspoon baking powder

½ teaspoon baking soda

½ teaspoon ground turmeric

½ teaspoon chile powder

1 tablespoon sugar

1½ cups (170 g) grated cheddar

1 bunch of chives (about 1 oz/25 g), finely chopped

⅓ cup (65 g) black or green olives, pitted and roughly chopped

½ cup (120 ml) extra-virgin olive oil

¾ cup (150 g) sour cream

1 large egg

Preheat the oven to 350°F (180°C).

Bring a saucepan of salted water to a boil. Add the broccoli and cook for 2 minutes, then drain immediately and run under cold water until completely cool to stop it from cooking further.

Grease and line an 8 × 4-inch (20 cm × 10 cm) loaf pan with parchment paper.

Place the flour, baking powder, baking soda, turmeric, chile powder and sugar in a large bowl and whisk well to combine. Fold in the cheddar, chives and olives.

In another large bowl, whisk together the olive oil, sour cream and egg until smooth.

Fold the dry ingredients into the wet ingredients and mix until just combined. Pour the batter into the prepared pan.

Press the broccoli into the batter so the florets are standing up like trees (you may have a few pieces left over—snack on those!). Bake for 1–1¼ hours until the top is golden and an inserted skewer comes out clean. Let cool in the pan for 10 minutes, then turn out onto a wire rack to cool completely before slicing.

Storage: Place any leftovers in an airtight container or wrap tightly in plastic wrap and store in the fridge for up to 2 days. To reheat, slice and warm in the oven or toaster.

For gluten-free • use gluten-free plain flour

Veganize • use vegan sour cream and cheese; replace the egg with flax egg (see Cook's Notes, page 30)

Vegetable swap • broccoli: cauliflower, sweet potato

Charred Broccoli Reuben Salad

The Reuben is an American classic of corned beef, Swiss cheese, sauerkraut and Russian dressing, grilled between slices of rye bread. The New York gourmet grocer Court Street Grocers reinvented this iconic dish as a thrilling vegetarian grilled sandwich, replete with broccoli, sauerkraut and their secret sauce named "comeback sauce." Inspired by this sandwich, here is my broccoli Reuben salad, with charred broccoli bringing lovely smoky flavors, crunchy croutons made of rye bread and my very own special sauce—a creamy, briny dressing that is loosely based upon Thousand Island dressing.

SERVES 4

5–6 thick slices of rye bread (about 7 oz/200 g total)

2 tablespoons chopped dill, plus more for topping

extra-virgin olive oil

sea salt and black pepper

1 large head of broccoli (about 1 lb/450 g), cut into small florets, stalks trimmed

2 big handfuls of baby spinach or salad leaves (about 2 oz/50 g)

⅓ cup (70 g) sauerkraut, drained

Special sauce

generous ½ cup (125 g) good-quality regular or vegan mayonnaise

1 small gherkin (about 1 oz/25 g), finely chopped

1 small garlic clove or ½ teaspoon garlic powder

2 tablespoons ketchup

2 green onions, finely chopped

sea salt and black pepper

Preheat the oven to 375°F (190°C).

Tear the rye bread into small chunks and place on a small baking sheet. Add the dill, drizzle with about 2 tablespoons of olive oil, season with sea salt and black pepper and toss to combine. Bake for 10 minutes, then remove the baking sheet from the oven and toss the bread. Return to the oven for 5 minutes, until the croutons are golden. Set aside to cool.

Heat a large skillet over medium-high heat, drizzle with olive oil and add the broccoli florets (work in batches if your pan isn't big enough). Season with sea salt and black pepper and let fry, undisturbed, for 2–3 minutes, until charred; turn the broccoli over and cook the other side until charred and crisp-tender. Remove from the pan and allow to cool.

To make the special sauce, place the mayonnaise, gherkin, garlic or garlic powder, ketchup and green onion in a small bowl and whisk to combine. Season with sea salt and black pepper.

Combine the broccoli, baby spinach or salad leaves, sauerkraut and croutons in a bowl. Add the sauce and toss to combine. Top with dill and serve immediately.

Do ahead: The broccoli and the special sauce can be prepared 1 day earlier and stored in an airtight container in the fridge. The croutons can be prepared and kept in an airtight container at room temperature for up to 3 days.

For gluten-free • use gluten-free rye bread

Vegan

Substitute • rye bread: seeded bread, pumpernickel, sourdough • dill: parsley

Vegetable swap • broccoli: broccolini, cauliflower

Sesame Broccoli with Crumbled Tofu

There are not many recipes in life where I'd call for boiled broccoli. But for this dish, I'm making an exception. The salted boiling water is the unlikely hero here, first seasoning the tofu, and then the broccoli, extracting just enough sweetness, imparting just enough salinity. The texture of the broccoli should be tender yet crisp, while a brief soak gives us tofu that is bouncy and supple. This is a refined dish, with delicate flavors that illustrate how boundless vegetables can be when we exercise restraint. I've added creamy butter beans here to make this a hearty one-bowl meal, though you could leave out the beans and serve the tofu and broccoli with a side of brown rice. Though the flavors are chiefly clean, you can lend a heavy hand with the sesame seeds, which add a breath of intensity to the dish.

SERVES 4

1-pound (450 g) block of medium–firm tofu

1 large head of broccoli (about 1 lb/450 g), cut into florets, stem peeled and cut into discs a scant ¼ inch (5 mm) thick

1 garlic clove, grated

1 cup (250 g) cooked butter beans (about one 15 oz/425 g can, drained)

2 teaspoons sea salt

¼ teaspoon white pepper

1 teaspoon rayu (Japanese sesame chili oil) or ¼–½ teaspoon red pepper flakes

1 tablespoon toasted sesame oil

2–3 tablespoons toasted white sesame seeds

2 green onions, finely chopped

Bring a large saucepan of water to a boil and season well with salt (taste it—it should taste salty, but not as salty as sea water). Add the whole block of tofu and let it simmer over medium heat for 3–4 minutes, until softened. Remove the tofu with a large slotted spoon (I like to use a traditional Chinese spider ladle) and drain in a colander.

To the same pan of water, add the broccoli and simmer for 3–4 minutes, until the broccoli is just tender, but still a little crisp and bright green. Drain immediately and run under cold water until completely cool to stop it from cooking further (alternatively, you could plunge the drained broccoli into an ice bath). Drain again.

Place the block of tofu in a large bowl and gently squeeze with your hands to break it up into rough chunks (it doesn't have to be uniform at all). Squeeze out any excess liquid from the broccoli florets and stem and add these to the bowl as well. Add the garlic, butter beans, sea salt, white pepper, rayu oil or red pepper flakes, sesame oil, sesame seeds and green onion and, using a large spoon (or your hands), toss well to ensure that everything is combined. Serve immediately.

Leftovers: Use any leftovers for fried rice. Leftovers can be kept in the fridge for up to 3 days.

Gluten-free and vegan

Substitute • butter beans: chickpeas, cannellini beans, black-eyed peas

Vegetable swap • broccoli: cauliflower

Roasted Broccoli and Crispy Chickpeas
with Sichuan Dukkah

It's no secret that I find the pairing of broccoli and chickpeas a love match, and here they come together again, blanketed with a nutty, piquant, perky topping that I call Sichuan dukkah. Dukkah is one of my favorite, most-used salad toppers—when a salad is on the precipice of achieving transcendency, a scatter of this beloved Middle Eastern and Egyptian blend of nuts, herbs and spices will allow it to soar. There are many different recipes for dukkah, often featuring pistachios or hazelnuts, but this is my Asian spin, with the heavy use of sesame seeds and cashew nuts, and Sichuan peppercorns to provide a sharp, peppery bite.

SERVES 4

3 cups (500 g) cooked chickpeas (about two 15 oz/425 g cans, drained)

extra-virgin olive oil

2 teaspoons ground coriander

sea salt and black pepper

2 large heads of broccoli (about 2 lb/900 g total), cut into florets, stalks peeled and cut into discs a scant ¼ inch (5 mm) thick

1–2 tablespoons toasted sesame oil

1–2 tablespoons black vinegar (optional)

2 green onions, sliced

**Sichuan dukkah
(makes about 1 cup)**

2 tablespoons coriander seeds

1 tablespoon Sichuan peppercorns

½ cup toasted cashews

2 tablespoons toasted white sesame seeds

1 tablespoon black sesame seeds

1 teaspoon sea salt flakes

Preheat the oven to 400°F (200°C).

Place the chickpeas on a sheet pan, drizzle with 2–3 tablespoons of olive oil, add the ground coriander and season well with sea salt and black pepper. Roast for 30–35 minutes, until the chickpeas are crispy.

Place the broccoli on another sheet pan, drizzle with some olive oil and season with sea salt and black pepper. Roast for 15–20 minutes, until the broccoli is browned and just tender.

To make the Sichuan dukkah, place a small skillet over medium heat, add the coriander seeds and Sichuan peppercorns and dry-fry, shaking the pan every now and then, for 2 minutes or until they are fragrant. Add to a mortar and grind to a coarse powder with the pestle. Add the cashews and pound again. Stir in the sesame seeds and sea salt.

Combine the chickpeas and broccoli in a bowl and drizzle with the sesame oil and black vinegar (if using). Add 1–2 tablespoons of the Sichuan dukkah and toss. Taste and, if needed, season with salt. To serve, sprinkle with more dukkah and scatter on the green onion.

Leftovers: Store leftover Sichuan dukkah in an airtight jar in your pantry for up to 2 months.

Gluten-free and vegan

Substitute • chickpeas: cannellini beans, lentils • cashews: hazelnuts, pistachios, peanuts

Vegetable swap • broccoli: sweet potato, cauliflower, Brussels sprouts

Food Court Omelet

This omelet is full of sweet nostalgia, inspired by a dish my husband and I often enjoyed for dinner while we were still university students and part-time theatre ushers. We met at the Capitol Theatre in Sydney's Chinatown, a site opposite a building where my dad lived during his early days in Sydney. The significance of this was lost on me back then, as I busily reveled in my newfound independence and the diverse group of friends we had made on the job. We spent a lot of time in Chinatown and we enjoyed many inexpensive meals at nearby food courts. One of our favorite dishes was a generous plate of rice, topped with a mound of stir-fried veggies, blanketed with a fluffy omelet and finished with a thick, umami gravy. I'd never really eaten a meal like this at home, but it did remind me of my mother's egg and rice dishes. When we relocated to America and started to explore the distinct dishes of Chinese-American cuisine, we discovered that our food court omelet was very close to a fried egg dish known as egg foo young.

MAKES FOUR TO FIVE 6-INCH (15 CM) OMELETS

6 large eggs

1 teaspoon sea salt

⅛ teaspoon white pepper

1 head of broccoli (about 12 oz/350 g), cut into small florets, stem peeled and cut into discs a scant ¼ inch (5 mm) thick

1 yellow onion, finely diced

4 green onions, sliced

1 garlic clove, finely chopped

2–3 tablespoons neutral oil

white or brown rice, to serve

Gravy

1 tablespoon cornstarch

2 tablespoons soy sauce or tamari

1 tablespoon vegetarian stir-fry sauce or oyster sauce

1 tablespoon Shaoxing rice wine

2 teaspoons toasted sesame oil

1 cup (240 ml) vegetable stock or water

pinch of white pepper

To make the gravy, place all the ingredients in a saucepan. Bring to a boil over medium heat, whisking constantly, for 4–5 minutes, until the gravy thickens. Set aside.

Place the eggs, salt and white pepper in a mixing bowl and whisk until smooth. Add the broccoli, onion, three-quarters of the green onion and the garlic and mix well.

Place a small skillet over high heat. When hot (you should see wisps of smoke rising from the surface), add 1 tablespoon of the oil to the pan, then ladle about ½ cup of the batter straight into the hot oil. Fry for 1–1½ minutes, until golden and puffy. Using a large wide spatula, confidently flip the omelet over and cook for about 1 minute on the other side, until golden. Remove from the pan and continue cooking the remaining batter.

To serve, place some rice in a bowl, top with an omelet and pour over some of the gravy. Top with the remaining green onion.

Tips: If you have any extra broccoli stalks saved up, cut them into discs a scant ¼ inch (5 mm) thick and use in this recipe.

I like to fry one omelet at a time, which gives me more control over the cooking process. If you have a small skillet, use that as it will keep the egg from running all over the pan.

For gluten-free • use mirin in place of Shaoxing rice wine

Substitute • Shaoxing rice wine: mirin, dry white wine or dry sherry

Vegetable swap • broccoli: broccoli stalks, cauliflower, baby bok choy, gai lan

Huck's Broccoli and Lettuce Salad with an Accidental Ranch

Ranch is an iconic American salad dressing, which the *New York Times* once declared "the one true American dressing." Invented in the 1950s, ranch is a salty, creamy emulsion made with buttermilk, garlic and other possible additions, such as onion, black pepper, mustard, herbs and spices. What began as a salad dressing is now its own food group—ranch is served with chicken wings, as a dip for vegetable crudités, drizzled over French fries, mozzarella sticks or pizza (somewhat controversial, yes). My recipe is an accidental ranch, of sorts; it came about from the half-used bottle of buttermilk that always seems to adorn my fridge door. To the buttermilk, I added a few big scoops of mayonnaise and scattered in some garlic powder. I drizzled it on top of roasted broccoli and crunchy romaine lettuce. When I served it to the family, my son Huck's eyes lit up and he declared that he loved the "ranch" dressing. As a ranch novice, I hadn't realized that this creation was basically America's most popular dressing. This is a wonderfully light salad to enjoy on its own, or with heavier dishes, such as pasta or pastries.

**SERVES 2 AS A MAIN
OR 4 AS A SIDE**

1 large head of broccoli (about 1 lb/450 g), cut into florets, stem peeled and cut into discs a scant ¼ inch (5 mm) thick

extra-virgin olive oil

sea salt and black pepper

1 baby romaine lettuce (about 9 oz/250 g), finely sliced

½ lemon

2 tablespoons toasted pine nuts

2 green onions, finely sliced

Accidental ranch dressing

½ cup (125 g) regular or vegan mayonnaise

¼ cup (60 ml) buttermilk

½ teaspoon garlic powder or 1 garlic clove, grated

1 green onion, finely sliced

Preheat the oven to 375°F (190°C).

Place the broccoli on a sheet pan and drizzle with olive oil. Season with sea salt and black pepper and roast for 15 minutes, until the broccoli is just tender and browned. Allow to cool for a few minutes.

Meanwhile, make the dressing by whisking together the mayonnaise, buttermilk and garlic powder or garlic in a small bowl. Add the green onion and stir to combine.

Place the lettuce on a large serving plate or in a bowl and top with the broccoli. Squeeze over the lemon half and top with the pine nuts, green onion and ranch dressing (as much or as little as you like). Serve immediately.

Notes: This salad is also endlessly adaptable—bulk it up by topping with chickpeas, grains, avocado, peas, feta or roasted vegetables.

I used garlic powder the first time I made this dressing (for convenience), but a small clove of grated garlic works just fine as well.

Gluten-free

Veganize • substitute the buttermilk with vegan yogurt, such as coconut, and add a little lemon juice to loosen it up

Substitute • romaine lettuce: salad greens, iceberg lettuce, shredded cabbage

Turmeric-Yogurt Roasted Broccoli

It is very special to see a vegetable, in the untamed form that nature prescribed, on a plate. This is one of the things I love most about this dish—it's visually definitive, striking to the senses. Broccoli is roasted in a golden, spiced yogurt marinade and roasted at high heat; the trees get crispy at the tips and caramelized on the bottom, bringing a host of immutable flavors and textures. Exact roasting time will depend upon the size of your broccoli, so start testing for doneness with a fork at the 20-minute mark. Enjoy the broccoli on its own, with a side of greens, or as a hearty meal with rice, lentils or quinoa.

SERVES 4

1½ cups (375 g) plain or vegan coconut yogurt

1½ teaspoons ground coriander

1 teaspoon ground turmeric

½ teaspoon chile powder

2 garlic cloves, grated

sea salt and black pepper

3 tablespoons extra-virgin olive oil, plus more for drizzling

4 small heads of broccoli (about 2¼ lb/1 kg total), preferably with stalks attached

handful of cilantro leaves

½ cup toasted almonds, roughly chopped

green salad, white/brown rice, quinoa or lentils, to serve

Preheat the oven to 425°F (220°C).

Add the yogurt, ground coriander, turmeric, chile powder, garlic, ½ teaspoon of sea salt, a few turns of black pepper and the olive oil to a baking dish or large bowl and stir to combine. Taste and add more salt, if needed.

Using a vegetable peeler, remove the woody exterior from the broccoli stalks. Cut each broccoli in half lengthwise through the center of the flower head and stem.

Place the broccoli halves in the yogurt marinade and coat them all over. It's easiest to do this with your hands.

Drizzle olive oil onto a sheet pan and add the broccoli, cut-side down, reserving any yogurt marinade left behind in the baking dish or bowl. Place in the oven and roast for 20–25 minutes, until the broccoli is browned and just tender (test by inserting a fork into the stalks, if it goes in and comes out easily, the broccoli is ready). Remove from the oven and brush the broccoli with the reserved yogurt marinade.

Top with the cilantro leaves and almonds and serve alongside a green salad or rice, quinoa or lentils.

Notes: The broccoli can also be cooked on the grill, which gives it an extra smoky flavor.

The marinade can be used to baste and roast other vegetables too— it's lovely with cauliflower.

Gluten-free and vegan

Broccoli and Mint Soup
with Spicy Fried Chickpeas

Many years ago, I made a chargrilled broccoli salad that would change the trajectory of my life. In many ways, it was the salad that inspired me to start a business. It was a simple dish, really—broccoli florets charred on the grill, served with chickpeas, mint and spinach, dressed in a caper, garlic and chile oil, finished with lemon juice, shards of parmesan and flaked almonds. Smoky, zesty, spicy. In this dish, there was a realization that a vegetable could emphatically command the plate, without adornment, fancy techniques or ingredients. This salad changed the way I regarded and cooked vegetables. It was my most popular recipe during my weekly salad deliveries in Sydney and is now a worldwide favorite from my first book, *Community*. I adore this recipe so much that I have taken it as inspiration and transformed it into a soup. Devotees of the original salad will find these flavors very familiar but will be surprised by how effortlessly this dish morphs into liquid form. The base is broccoli, chickpeas and mint, and the topping is an irresistible mix of crispy fried chickpeas, capers, chile, parsley and almonds (it's good enough to eat as a snack).

SERVES 4

extra-virgin olive oil

1 shallot or small yellow onion, finely diced

4 garlic cloves, finely chopped

1 large head of broccoli (about 1 lb/450 g), cut into florets, stem peeled and sliced

3 cups (500 g) cooked chickpeas (about two 15 oz/425 g cans, drained)

5¼ cups (1.25 liters) vegetable stock

2 cups baby spinach leaves

½ cup mint leaves, plus more to serve

sea salt and black pepper

2 tablespoons capers, rinsed and drained

¼ cup sliced almonds

1 fresh Thai red chile, finely sliced

½ cup parsley leaves

1 lemon, halved

Heat a large saucepan over medium heat. Add 1 tablespoon of olive oil, the shallot or onion and half the garlic. Sauté for 2–3 minutes, until softened. Add the broccoli, half the chickpeas and the vegetable stock. Increase the heat to medium-high and cover with a lid, leaving it slightly ajar to let steam escape. Cook for 8–10 minutes, until the broccoli is softened. Turn off the heat, add the spinach leaves and mint leaves and stir until the spinach is wilted. Using a stick blender (or regular blender/food processor), blend the mixture until smooth. Add 1 teaspoon of sea salt and some freshly ground black pepper.

Meanwhile, heat a skillet over medium-high heat. When hot, add ¼ cup (60 ml) of olive oil along with the remaining chickpeas. Reduce the heat to medium or medium-low and fry, shaking the pan every now and then, until the chickpeas are crisp. The chickpeas may burst and splatter out of the pan and if they do, reduce the heat to low, increasing the heat again once the bursting stops. Continue to cook for 10–12 minutes, until the chickpeas are crispy all over. Add the remaining garlic, the capers, almonds and chile, increase the heat to medium-high and cook until the almonds are golden, 4–5 minutes. Add the parsley and cook for another 1–2 minutes, until everything looks toasted and crispy. Season with ½–1 teaspoon of sea salt.

Ladle the soup into bowls and top with the spicy fried chickpea mixture, some mint leaves and a squeeze of lemon juice.

Serving suggestion: Finish with shaved parmesan.

Gluten-free and vegan

Substitute • chickpeas: cannellini beans • sliced almonds: chopped whole almonds, slivered almonds

Broccoli Wontons with Umami Crisp

Like dumplings, making wontons is a mindful ritual, an exercise of patience. Folding wontons would take up an entire afternoon for my mother, as she always made them in bulk, ready for freezing. With some planning, wontons are a wonderful last-minute meal. Broccoli once again flexes its versatility, providing bright-green notes, which make every mouthful a delight. The potato performs two vital functions: it provides body to the filling, while also binding the ingredients together. Here, I have served the wontons simply, blanketed in my Umami Crisp, but you could also serve them in a broth—the Mushroom and Ginger Broth on page 282 would be a great base.

MAKES 45–50 WONTONS

1 large potato (about 9 oz/250 g), peeled and diced

1 tablespoon toasted sesame oil

1 yellow onion, finely diced

1 small head of broccoli (about 9 oz/250 g), florets and stem roughly chopped

1 garlic clove, finely chopped

sea salt and white pepper

2 teaspoons white (shiro) miso

2 green onions, finely sliced

45–50 square wonton wrappers

handful of cilantro leaves

3–4 tablespoons Umami Crisp (see page 27), chili oil or chili crisp

toasted white sesame seeds, to serve

Bring a saucepan of salted water to a boil. Add the potato and cook for 8–10 minutes, until very tender. Drain and place in a bowl, then roughly mash with a fork.

Heat a skillet over medium heat. Add the sesame oil and onion and cook for 2–3 minutes, until softened. Add the broccoli and garlic and season with about ½ teaspoon of sea salt and ¼ teaspoon of white pepper. Cook for 5–7 minutes, until the broccoli is very tender. Remove from the heat and allow to cool. Transfer the mixture to a cutting board and finely chop until the broccoli is almost minced. Add the broccoli mixture to the potato, then add the miso and green onion. Mix well, then taste and season with more sea salt and white pepper, if needed.

Fill a small bowl with water for wetting the edges of the wonton wrappers. Keep the wrappers covered with a damp tea towel or in their original packaging while you work, as they dry out quickly. Holding a wrapper in the palm of your hand, place a heaped teaspoon of the filling in the center of the wrapper (don't overfill). Moisten the wrapper around the filling with a dab of water, then carefully fold one corner to the next to form a triangle, making sure you enclose the filling tightly to avoid any air pockets, which can make the wontons burst. Bring the two opposite corners together, dab one corner with water, then overlap them and press to seal. Repeat with the remaining wrappers and filling. At this point, you can freeze the wontons, or cook immediately.

Bring a large saucepan of salted water to a boil. Add the wontons, a few at a time, and cook for 1–2 minutes. When the wontons float to the top, cook for another 20 seconds, until the skins are translucent. Remove immediately with a slotted spoon.

To serve, scatter with cilantro leaves, top with the umami crisp, chili oil or chili crisp and finish with sesame seeds.

For gluten-free • use gluten-free wonton wrappers

Veganize • use vegan wonton wrappers

Substitute • potato: drained firm tofu

Vegetable swap • broccoli: spinach, kale

Storage: To prepare wontons for storage, line a tray with parchment paper and line the wontons up in a single layer. Place them in the freezer and, when they are hard, remove them from the tray, place in an airtight container and return to the freezer, where they will keep for up to 3 months.

Longtime Broccoli

If you're looking for a broccoli change of pace, this dish introduces you to a very different side of this beloved brassica. This is a confit, of sorts—the broccoli is cooked in an oil bath, over very low heat, for longer than you'd expect is wise when it comes to vegetables. The result feels unspeakably luxurious, collapsing florets so tender they melt upon contact, intensely rich, and imbued with the savory, piquant notes of the olive oil and aromatics. The creamy broccoli can be smeared onto crusty bread, served with salad greens or polenta, or alongside eggs. My favorite way to enjoy this dish is to toss the entire thing—broccoli *and* the oil—with pasta, grains or couscous. The oil is like gold, infused with the earthy sweetness of the broccoli, and can be used to make salad dressings, drizzled on fried eggs or tossed with noodles.

SERVES 4, WITH BREAD OR PASTA

1 large head of broccoli (about 1 lb/450 g), cut into florets, stem trimmed and sliced into thick discs

1 cup (240 ml) extra-virgin olive oil

3 garlic cloves, finely sliced

1 tablespoon capers, rinsed and drained

½–1 teaspoon red pepper flakes

½ teaspoon sea salt

black pepper

Place a large Dutch oven or saucepan over medium heat. Add the broccoli, olive oil, garlic, capers, red pepper flakes and sea salt, season with a few turns of black pepper and heat for 5–7 minutes, until the oil starts to gently bubble. Cover and cook over the very lowest heat for 1½ hours, until the broccoli is very soft and on the verge of falling apart.

Serve smeared on bread, or stirred into pasta or pearl couscous, or on top of polenta.

Do ahead: The broccoli can be prepared up to 24 hours in advance and kept covered at room temperature. No need to reheat, it is great eaten at room temperature.

Gluten-free and vegan

Vegetable swap • broccoli: eggplant, cauliflower, carrots, green beans

Brussels sprouts

"My mother calls Brussels sprouts
'little cabbage.'"

I am one of the lucky ones. I have nothing but good memories of Brussels sprouts. We never ate them at home growing up, so I was a fully fledged, vegetable-toting adult before I tried these cruciferous gems. I first fell in love with Brussels sprouts when my husband and I were living in London. Our top-floor flat overlooked the produce stalls at Portobello Road Market. For me, this was meant to be; markets smell and sound like home to me, the bustling atmosphere a balm for my soul. Vendors hawking their daily specials, enmeshed bodies jostling for the best produce, stray fruit crushed on the road underfoot. Every week, we stopped by to see boisterous Barry, a beloved vendor who loved to banter with my husband Ross (whom he called "Skip") about the rugby or cricket. I adored living with the energy of the market below and the pure magic of peering out of our window during the winter and seeing the stalls lit up by fairy lights.

At the markets, they sold Brussels sprouts on the stalk. During the cooler months, but especially at Christmas, Brussels sprouts became a staple. In the early years, I did nothing fancy with them. Butter, salt and pepper was all it took. But when we moved back to Australia, I started cooking them on the grill and this was when my world opened up. Brussels sprouts, like many hardy vegetables, come to life atop flaming heat. The smoke is an antidote to its mustardy notes.

My mother calls Brussels sprouts "little cabbage," and that is an apt description. Brussels sprouts are brassicas, the same species as cabbage, along with cauliflower, kale, broccoli, kohlrabi and more. And if, like me, you have always wondered, *Are Brussels sprouts actually from Belgium?* The answer is yes. While early cultivars first appeared in the Mediterranean around the 5th century, Brussels sprouts as we know them today were first cultivated in Belgium during the 16th century, and are so named after the capital city.

Red-Braised Brussels Sprouts and Tofu

This flavorful braise is inspired by the deeply complex flavors of hong shao rou, the classic Chinese pork belly dish from Hunan Province that is nowadays traditionally associated with Shanghai. *Hong shao* translates to "red cooking" and is used to describe the meat that takes on a reddish tone after a long braise. My vegan take comes together quickly—Brussels sprouts are not an obvious vegetable to give the "hong shao" treatment, but they seamlessly embrace the rich sauce, the texture becoming creamy and smooth. There are many ways to adapt this dish—traditional recipes often add hard-boiled eggs or tofu knots, but you could also add puffed tofu, mushrooms or root vegetables, such as potato, taro or carrot, or water chestnuts.

SERVES 4

14 ounces (400 g) extra-firm tofu, cut into slices ⅜-inch (1 cm) thick

⅓ cup (80 ml) neutral oil

sea salt

¼ cup (50 g) sugar

1 pound (450 g) Brussels sprouts, trimmed and halved

2½ tablespoons dark soy sauce

4 teaspoons soy sauce or tamari

¼ cup (60 ml) Shaoxing rice wine

2 star anise

1-inch (2.5 cm) piece of ginger, peeled and finely sliced

4 green onions, 3 cut into 1-inch (2.5 cm) segments and 1 finely sliced

1 whole dried red chile or ½ teaspoon red pepper flakes (optional)

rice, to serve

Cut the tofu slices into triangles—I do this by cutting each slice in half to form squares, then cutting each square in half diagonally to form two triangles.

Heat a large skillet over medium-high heat until you can see wisps of smoke rising from the surface. Add about 2½ tablespoons of oil, then lay the tofu flat in the pan (depending on the size of your pan, you may need to work in batches) and sprinkle the top with sea salt. Cook for 2–3 minutes, until the bottom of the tofu is golden, then flip the triangles over and repeat on the other side. Remove from the pan and set aside.

In the same skillet over medium-high heat, heat another 2½ tablespoons of oil until it shimmers. Add the sugar and very carefully swirl the oil for about 30 seconds to encourage the sugar to melt (the sugar won't completely melt in this time but some of it may start to caramelize or burn; if it does, moving ahead quickly to the next step should stop the burning). Add the Brussels sprouts and fry for 2–3 minutes, until they are covered in the sugar and golden in parts. Add the dark soy sauce and cook for 1 minute.

Reduce the heat to medium and add 1 cup (240 ml) of water, the soy sauce or tamari, Shaoxing rice wine, star anise, ginger, green onion segments, dried chile or red pepper flakes (if using) and cooked tofu. Bring to a boil, then cover and simmer for 10–12 minutes, until the sprouts are completely tender.

Top with the finely sliced green onion and serve with rice.

For gluten-free • replace the Shaoxing rice wine with dry white wine or sherry

Vegan

Substitute • Shaoxing rice wine: dry white wine, sherry

Vegetable swap • Brussels sprouts: cabbage, cauliflower

Brussels Sprouts Two Ways
with Pear and Mustard Chutney

The natural bitterness of Brussels sprouts pairs well with this piquant sweet-and-spicy condiment. This pear chutney is basically a cheat's version of mostarda di frutta, the traditional Italian condiment that combines sweet fruit with the slight heat of mustard seeds and is prepared over several days. My recipe comes together much quicker. This chutney recipe is flexible—you could use other fruits, such as apple or quince, as a base, adding figs, cherries, Asian pears, candied citrus peel and more. It also improves with time, so keep a jar in the fridge to serve with cheese or roasted veggies. Here, I use the chutney as a wonderful sorta-salad-dressing, tangling roasted and raw shaved Brussels sprouts, chickpeas and a sharp, salty hard cheese—a combination that evokes distinct cheese board vibes.

SERVES 4

1 pound 5 ounces (600 g) Brussels sprouts

extra-virgin olive oil

sea salt and black pepper

3 cups (500 g) cooked chickpeas (about two 15 oz/425 g cans, drained)

handful of parsley leaves

1¾ ounces (50 g) sharp cheese, such as ricotta salata or cheddar, shaved

Pear and mustard chutney

2 pounds (900 g) Bosc pears, peeled, cored and cut into ½ inch (1.5 cm) pieces

generous ½ cup (115 g) sugar

2½ tablespoons mustard seeds, toasted

1 lemon, finely sliced and seeded

2 teaspoons sea salt

2 bay leaves

2½ tablespoons Dijon mustard

¼ teaspoon chile powder or cayenne pepper

1 tablespoon apple cider vinegar

Gluten-free

Veganize • omit the cheese

Substitute • chickpeas: lentils, quinoa, farro

Vegetable swap • Brussels sprouts: cauliflower

To make the pear and mustard chutney, place the pear, sugar, mustard seeds, lemon slices, sea salt, bay leaves, Dijon mustard and chile powder or cayenne pepper in a saucepan and bring to a boil over medium-high heat. Reduce the heat to medium-low and cook, stirring frequently, until the pear has broken down and the liquid is reduced and thickened, 1½–2 hours. Turn off the heat, add the vinegar and stir to combine. Set aside to cool.

Preheat the oven to 400°F (200°C).

Trim and halve about 14 ounces (400 g) of the Brussels sprouts and set the other 7 ounces (200 g) aside. Place the halved Brussels sprouts on a sheet pan, drizzle with olive oil and season with sea salt and black pepper. Roast for 20–25 minutes, until golden and tender. Remove from the oven and set aside.

Using a sharp knife or mandoline, finely slice or shave the remaining Brussels sprouts.

Combine the roasted sprouts and raw sprouts, along with the chickpeas and parsley, in a large bowl. Add a few tablespoons of the pear and mustard chutney, drizzle with olive oil and season with sea salt and black pepper. Taste and add more chutney if you prefer it sweeter and more tangy. Top with the cheese and serve.

Storage: To store the leftover chutney, cool it to room temperature, then transfer to a sterilized, airtight jar and store in the fridge for up to 1 month.

Alternative: If you prefer your chickpeas crispy in this recipe, roast them alongside the Brussels sprouts.

Brussels Sprout Tempura Salad

In Japan, tempura is a treasured craft, with chefs spending years learning the art form of frying the perfect crisp and light batter. For the crispiest batter, it's important to minimize the gluten formation, so I've opted for a combination of rice flour and cornstarch for a feather-light crust. An ice-cold batter is also crucial, helping the batter cling to the surface of the ingredients. Brussels sprouts are a wonderful vegetable for tempura, perfect for this unexpectedly light salad. The dressing mirrors tentsuyu, a sweet-savory dipping sauce that is traditionally served with tempura.

SERVES 4

neutral oil

1 pound (450 g) Brussels sprouts, trimmed and halved if large or left whole if small

5 ounces (150 g) salad greens

2 avocados, sliced into wedges

9 ounces (250 g) cherry tomatoes, halved

1 tablespoon toasted sesame seeds (white or black)

handful of cilantro leaves

toasted sesame oil, to serve

sea salt and black pepper

Tempura batter

1 large egg

⅔ cup (160 ml) ice-cold water

8½ tablespoons (85 g) rice flour

7½ tablespoons (60 g) cornstarch

½ teaspoon sea salt

Dressing

¼ cup (60 ml) mirin

½ cup (120 ml) Vegan Dashi (see page 360) or vegetable stock

4 teaspoons soy sauce or tamari

4 teaspoons sugar

Gluten-free

Veganize • replace the egg with ½ teaspoon baking powder and use sparkling water (instead of water) to provide a lighter texture

Substitute • rice flour and cornstarch: equal amount of all-purpose flour (avoid overmixing the batter)

Vegetable swap • Brussels sprouts: asparagus or sliced sweet potato, butternut squash, potato, eggplant

To make the tempura batter, whisk the egg and water together in a bowl. Add the rice flour, cornstarch and salt and whisk until smooth. Place in the fridge to chill while you prepare the vegetables.

Line a plate with paper towel. Pour enough oil into a small, deep saucepan to come about 1 inch (2.5 cm) up the side, then set over high heat. Test if the oil is ready by inserting a wooden skewer or spoon into the oil; if it sizzles, the oil is ready.

Whisk the batter every now and then to ensure it remains well mixed (the rice flour has a tendency to settle at the bottom). Dunk the Brussels sprouts into the batter and lift them out, letting any excess batter drip off. Carefully add the sprouts to the oil, taking care not to overcrowd the pan, and cook for 2–3 minutes, turning once or twice, until crispy and turning golden. Continually watch the heat of the oil, turning it down if the sprouts brown too quickly—I find it best cooked over medium heat. Using a slotted spoon or spider ladle, fish the sprouts out of the oil, including any crispy bits, and place them on the paper towel to drain.

To make the dressing, heat a small saucepan over medium-high heat, add the mirin and let it come to a boil and bubble for 30 seconds (this allows the alcohol to evaporate). Add the dashi or stock, soy sauce or tamari and sugar and stir until the sugar is dissolved. Turn off the heat and set aside to cool.

To serve, place the salad greens on a platter or plate. Top with the tempura Brussels sprouts, avocado and tomato, and scatter with the sesame seeds and cilantro leaves. Spoon the dressing over the top and finish with a drizzle of toasted sesame oil and some sea salt and black pepper.

Notes: Tempura is always best eaten immediately. Don't add the dressing until ready to serve. Leftover tempura can be kept in an airtight container in the fridge for 1–2 days and reheated in the oven.

Caramelized Brussels Sprouts and Kimchi with Rice Cakes

In this rice noodle stir-fry, kimchi is caramelized to darken its tangy, salty and spicy flavor, perfectly complementing the smoky charred Brussels sprouts. Rice cakes are traditionally eaten during the Lunar New Year as their name *nian gao* translates to "higher year," and, as such, symbolize good luck, fortune and an elevated status for the new year. They are also a wonderful weeknight ingredient—sold either in shelf-stable, vacuum-sealed packs or frozen at Chinese, Korean and Asian supermarkets, they can be stored for many months. There are two types of rice cakes—the Chinese version is sliced in an oval shape, while the Korean rice sticks, which are used in the beloved dish tteokbokki, are longer and thicker (see page 250 for my Cheesy Kale and Rice Cake Bake). They can both be used in this recipe.

SERVES 4

1 pound 10 ounces (750 g) sliced rice cakes or sticks

1 pound (450 g) Brussels sprouts, trimmed

extra-virgin olive oil

sea salt and black pepper

2 garlic cloves, finely chopped

1-inch (2.5 cm) piece of ginger, peeled and finely chopped

1 cup (200 g) regular or vegan kimchi, roughly chopped

4 teaspoons soy sauce or tamari

1 tablespoon toasted sesame oil

1 tablespoon toasted white sesame seeds

2 green onions, finely sliced

Bring a large saucepan of salted water to a boil and add the rice cakes. Cook according to the package directions—most brands only need about 2 minutes. Drain and refresh under cold water, then drain again.

Prepare the Brussels sprouts by cutting larger ones into quarters; smaller ones can be halved. Heat a large skillet over medium-high heat, drizzle generously with olive oil and add the sprouts to the pan, seasoning generously with sea salt. Allow the sprouts to cook, undisturbed, for 1–2 minutes, until you can see them charring on the underside. Toss the sprouts and leave to cook, undisturbed again, for 1–2 minutes. Continue doing this until your sprouts are tender and charred in parts—in total, this should take 7–8 minutes. Transfer the sprouts to a bowl and set aside. Place the pan back on the heat.

Add another 1–2 tablespoons of olive oil to the pan, then add the garlic, ginger and kimchi. Using a spatula, press the kimchi into the pan and leave to cook, undisturbed, for 2–3 minutes, until the kimchi is charred in parts.

Meanwhile, run some water over the rice cakes to loosen them up. Add the rice cakes to the pan, along with the Brussels sprouts, and toss everything to combine. Add the soy sauce or tamari and sesame oil, and season with two or three big pinches of sea salt and a good grind of black pepper. Toss well to combine and, when everything is glistening and heated through, turn off the heat.

To serve, top with the sesame seeds and green onion.

Gluten-free and vegan

Substitute • rice cakes: gnocchi, short pasta

Vegetable swap • Brussels sprouts: broccoli, asparagus

Sticky Gochujang Brussels Sprouts

This sticky, hot gochujang marinade brings swagger to these Brussels sprouts. Spicy, sweet and very savory, it turns each morsel into a party of flavors, simultaneously bolstering the earthiness of the sprouts while also highlighting their natural sweetness. This marinade is a versatile one—use it to marinate veggies for the grill, slather it on firm tofu before and after roasting, or thin it out with some olive oil and use it as a salad dressing. Plain or coconut yogurt helps to ameliorate the heat of the gochujang, providing a refreshing tang to the meal. The sticky sprouts can also be served on their own, as a vegetable side.

SERVES 4

1¾ pounds (800 g) Brussels sprouts, trimmed and halved

extra-virgin olive oil

sea salt and black pepper

1 tablespoon toasted white sesame seeds, plus more to serve

white or brown rice, to serve

1 cup (250 g) Greek or vegan coconut yogurt

handful of cilantro leaves

Gochujang marinade

2½ tablespoons gochujang

4 teaspoons soy sauce or tamari

4 teaspoons toasted sesame oil

2 tablespoons maple syrup

1 teaspoon rice vinegar

1 garlic clove, finely chopped, or ¼ teaspoon garlic powder

Preheat the oven to 400°F (200°C).

Place the Brussels sprouts on a sheet pan and drizzle with olive oil. Season with sea salt and black pepper and roast for 15 minutes.

Meanwhile, whisk together all the ingredients for the gochujang marinade until well combined.

Remove the Brussels sprouts from the oven and pour the gochujang marinade over them. Using a rubber spatula, toss until they are well coated. Return to the oven and roast for another 8–10 minutes, until the sprouts are tender and golden. Scatter with the sesame seeds and toss to combine.

To serve, spoon some rice into a bowl, add a dollop of yogurt and top with the Brussels sprouts. Scatter with cilantro leaves and more sesame seeds, if you like.

Gluten-free and vegan

Substitute • gochujang: sriracha sauce • maple syrup: honey

Vegetable swap • Brussels sprouts: broccoli, cauliflower

Brussels Sprouts and Green Onion Oil Noodles

Green onion oil noodles, or cong you ban mian, is a treasured dish from Shanghai, one that requires only simple ingredients and a little patience to produce spectacular results. For this recipe, I've used the principles of cong you bian mian, and added Brussels sprouts to the mix, cooking them low and slow with the green onion, drawing out not only the deeply savory and oniony flavors, but also the earthiness of the sprouts. The green onion and sprouts are left to gently bubble away until they become golden and crispy, flavoring the oil while also transforming into a perfect crunchy topper for the noodles. The key to achieving the crispiness is to slice the green onions and Brussels sprouts finely. I suggest using all the Brussels sprouts and green onion to top the noodles, but only half the soy-onion oil—I reserve the rest in a jar, which I use for topping white rice, a favorite quick "meal" from my childhood.

SERVES 4

¾ cup (180 ml) neutral oil

8 green onions (about 3½ oz/100 g), finely julienned

9 ounces (250 g) Brussels sprouts, trimmed and very finely sliced

1 pound (450 g) dried noodles (any variety)

2½ tablespoons dark soy sauce

2½ tablespoons soy sauce or tamari

1 tablespoon sugar

1 teaspoon black vinegar (optional)

Add the oil to a large, wide skillet or saucepan along with the green onion and Brussels sprouts. Place over medium heat and simmer, stirring occasionally, for 30–35 minutes, until the green onion and sprouts are golden and crispy.

Meanwhile, bring a large saucepan of salted water to a boil. Add the noodles and cook according to the package directions, until al dente. Drain.

Place a sieve on top of a bowl and pour the green onion and Brussels sprout mixture through it to separate it from the oil. Let the green onion and sprouts sit over the bowl for a few minutes, to allow the oil to drain out of the vegetables (this also allows the veggies to stay crispy).

Combine the flavored oil, soy sauces, sugar and vinegar (if using) in a bowl. Place the noodles in a bowl or serving dish and add ¼–⅓ cup (60–80 ml) of the soy-onion oil to the noodles, tossing to coat well. Taste and if you would like more flavor, add more of the oil. When you are happy with the seasonings, top with the crispy green onion and Brussels sprouts and serve.

Notes: This recipe makes about ½ cup (120 ml) of soy-onion oil, which is more than you will need for the noodles. The leftover oil can be kept in an airtight container at room temperature for many weeks, and can be used to top rice, vegetables, blanched Asian greens, eggs, etc.

For gluten-free • use rice noodles and gluten-free soy sauces

Vegan

Substitute • green onions: leeks • dark soy sauce: regular soy sauce or tamari

Vegetable swap • Brussels sprouts: green cabbage

Brussels-Sprouts-Instead-of-Egg Salad

The elements that we love most about egg salad—the creamy dressing, the herbs, the tangy pickled mix-ins—are all here, but there's no egg. Instead, I have found a new, peppy canvas for these flavors—roasted Brussels sprouts. Best of all, this is a very customizable recipe—add spinach leaves to amplify the salad vibes, maximize umami by adding shards of salty hard cheese or cubes of soft brie, and, of course, you could even add boiled eggs. To bring a bright tang, replace the mayonnaise with Greek or coconut yogurt. The "pickle-ly" additions bring acidity, which cuts through the richness of the mayonnaise. You could really add as many pickled ingredients as you wish—perhaps some chopped marinated artichokes would work here, too, along with salty olives or sharp sun-dried tomatoes. Cutting the sprouts into quarters provides more surface area for roasting, and also means they cook quicker.

SERVES 4

1 pound 10 ounces (750 g) Brussels sprouts, trimmed and quartered

extra-virgin olive oil

sea salt and black pepper

4 small gherkins (about 3 oz/80 g), finely chopped

2 teaspoons capers, rinsed and drained, roughly chopped

¼ cup (50 g) sauerkraut

2 green onions, finely sliced

handful of dill, leaves picked and roughly chopped

2½ tablespoons gherkin pickle juice

2 teaspoons Dijon mustard

¾ cup (180 g) regular or vegan mayonnaise

bread, to serve (optional)

Preheat the oven to 400°F (200°C).

Place the Brussels sprouts on a sheet pan and drizzle generously with olive oil. Season with sea salt and black pepper and roast for 10–15 minutes, until the sprouts are golden and tender. Remove from the oven and allow to cool.

Meanwhile, in a large bowl, combine the gherkins, capers, sauerkraut, green onion, dill, pickle juice, mustard and mayonnaise. Season with black pepper and, if needed, sea salt. When the sprouts are cool, add them to the mayonnaise mixture and fold in to coat.

Eat the sprouts as they are or pile onto bread.

Gluten-free and vegan

Substitute • gherkins: cornichons • capers: olives • green onions: chives • mayonnaise: Greek or coconut yogurt • sauerkraut: kimchi

Vegetable swap • Brussels sprouts: broccoli, cauliflower, asparagus

Cabbage

"In good times and bad,
cabbage will save us."

I have always loved cabbage, but it was during the depths of our 2020 quarantine that I came to understand how vital it had become in my daily cooking. During those first few months, fresh food deliveries were not assured, so I began to consider, perhaps slightly irrationally, cabbage as my lifeline. I schemed on ways to make multiple hearty meals from one cabbage. Half a green or red cabbage could be sliced into thick wedges and braised in turmeric-spiced coconut milk—a perfect dinner served with rice. The other half could then be split in two to make two more meals: okonomiyaki and stir-fried glass noodles. All three iterations of these quarantine meals are in this chapter. My cabbage rationing soon bled over to other vegetables, too—how many meals could I make from a bunch of carrots, a large butternut squash, a head of cauliflower, a bag of green beans? And as the lockdown dragged, on I went. As the Welsh writer Ken Follett wrote, "Pray for miracles, but plant cabbages." In good times and bad, cabbage will save us.

Cabbage is supremely versatile, with a more complex personality than its humble status may suggest. Green cabbage is our everyday workhorse, accessible, inexpensive and delicious—its tightly bound leaves are slightly peppery but become mellow and sweet when cooked. Red (or purple) cabbage offers a crunch that makes it an excellent option for salads. Savoy cabbages bring some welcome drama to the vegetable plot, their sweeping, crinkly leaves pliable, tender and sweet. Napa cabbage, known in some parts of the world as Chinese cabbage, Chinese leaf or wombok, has a mild flavor and crisp stems and, when cooked, it becomes a sponge, ravenously soaking up sauces and seasonings. I really enjoy cabbage with bold flavors—lots of garlic, onion, lashings of butter, sweet vinegars such as balsamic, tart dried fruits like raisins or cranberries, and punchy sauces and dressings.

Roasted Napa Cabbage with Sesame Sauce

While napa cabbage (also known as wombok or Chinese cabbage) is most often considered for stir-fries or braises, roasting or cooking at high heat further unlocks its unique flavor. The high oven temperature chars the ruffled outer leaves, leaving them smoky yet crisp, while the internal flesh remains mildly sweet. If you're cooking outdoors, you could also chargrill the napa cabbage, cut-side down, on a grill, until char marks appear and the leaves have softened slightly. The rich dressing is reminiscent of Japanese goma dare (sesame sauce)—earthy, sweet and deeply nutty. For ease and versatility, I've used tahini in this recipe, but you could use toasted white sesame seeds, ground using a mortar and pestle or spice grinder, especially if you would prefer a sauce with more texture. This dish can be eaten on its own or with rice.

SERVES 4

1 napa cabbage (about 2¼ lb/1 kg)

extra-virgin olive oil

sea salt and black pepper

1 tablespoon toasted sesame seeds
(white, black or both)

handful of cilantro leaves

Sesame sauce

2½ tablespoons tahini

1 small garlic clove, grated

4 teaspoons rice vinegar

4 teaspoons mirin

4 teaspoons soy sauce or tamari

4 teaspoons white (shiro) miso

2 teaspoons sugar

1 tablespoon toasted white
sesame seeds

Preheat the oven to 450°F (230°C).

Remove any loose outer leaves from the napa cabbage, then slice it in half lengthwise. Place the two halves, cut-side up, on a sheet pan, drizzle with olive oil and season with sea salt and black pepper. Transfer to the oven and roast for 25 minutes or until the cabbage is golden on the outside.

Meanwhile, place all the ingredients for the sesame sauce in a bowl, add 1 teaspoon of water and whisk until combined and smooth.

Place the golden cabbage halves, cut-side up, on a plate and spoon on the sesame sauce. Season with sea salt and black pepper, drizzle with some olive oil, scatter with the sesame seeds and top with cilantro leaves.

Do ahead: The sesame sauce can be made a day in advance and kept in the fridge. It will thicken up the longer it rests, so just add a teaspoon or so of water to loosen it up.

Gluten-free and vegan

Substitute • tahini: black sesame paste or ¼ cup toasted white sesame seeds, ground

Vegetable swap • napa cabbage: green or savoy cabbage wedges, cauliflower wedges

Cabbage and Kimchi Okonomiyaki

Okonomiyaki is a beloved savory pancake from Japan, where the dish differs from region to region—Hiroshima-style is a layered pancake, while in Osaka it is made by mixing all the ingredients together before being fried. This recipe is akin to an Osaka-style okonomiyaki, which is traditionally made primarily with cabbage, flour and eggs. The dish is ultimately adaptable—in Japanese, *okonomi* means "how you want it" or "what you like" and *yaki* means "grill." Cabbage is a common filling, but while kimchi is not, it imparts a salty tang and welcome spice. I've used rice flour in this version, which makes it a bit lighter, but regular flour works, too. Kewpie, the Japanese brand of mayonnaise, is essential for topping okonomiyaki, but good-quality whole-egg mayonnaise also works fine.

MAKES FOUR 6-INCH (15 CM) PANCAKES

1 cup minus 1 tablespoon (150 g) rice flour or 1¼ cups (150 g) all-purpose flour

½ teaspoon baking powder

sea salt and white pepper

½ teaspoon sugar

3 large eggs, lightly beaten

¾ cup (180 ml) Vegan Dashi (see page 360) or vegetable stock

1 tablespoon white (shiro) miso

1 cup (200 g) regular or vegan kimchi, drained and chopped

½ small head green or savoy cabbage (about 14 oz/400 g), finely chopped

2 green onions, finely sliced, plus extra to serve

neutral oil

Kewpie mayonnaise or regular good-quality mayonnaise, to serve

handful of toasted white sesame seeds, to serve

Gochujang ketchup

¼ cup (60 ml) ketchup

4 teaspoons soy sauce or tamari

1 teaspoon toasted sesame oil

4 teaspoons gluten-free gochujang

Gluten-free

Veganize • replace the eggs with flax eggs (see Cook's Notes, page 30)

Vegetable swap • cabbage: carrots, Brussels sprouts

To make the gochujang ketchup, whisk together all the ingredients with 2½ tablespoons of water in a bowl. Set aside.

In a large bowl, whisk together the flour, baking powder, ½ teaspoon of sea salt and the sugar to combine. Add the egg, dashi or vegetable stock and miso and stir to form a batter. Add the kimchi, cabbage and green onion and fold everything together until well combined.

Heat a medium skillet over medium heat. Add a drizzle of oil and spoon one-quarter of the batter into the pan, using a spatula to shape the pancake into a neat round. Reduce the heat to medium low, then cover and cook for 4–5 minutes, until the underside is golden, lowering the heat as necessary if the okonomiyaki threatens to burn. Lift the lid and flip the pancake with a wide spatula. If parts of the pancake fall off during the flip, simply tuck them back in to reassemble the round. If the pan is dry, add a little more oil and swirl it under the pancake. Cover and cook for another 4–5 minutes, until both sides are golden. Repeat with the rest of the batter.

Place a pancake on a serving plate and season with sea salt and white pepper. Drizzle with some of the gochujang ketchup, squeeze or spoon over some mayonnaise, sprinkle with the sesame seeds and scatter with green onion.

Napa Cabbage and Pomelo Salad
with Coconut-Peanut Crunch

Pomelos are a sacred fruit grown in Southeast Asia and have been cultivated in China for centuries. In Chinese culture, pomelos are a symbol of good luck and family unity and are often displayed and eaten during the Lunar New Year. A pomelo is the centerpiece of the Taoist altar at my mother's house, a corner where she fulfills her daily ritual of lighting incense and paying respects to our ancestors and our family, past and present. Pomelos taste like a sweeter, more floral grapefruit. The flesh is firm and perfect for salads. The skin is thick, but it peels away easily; tearing away the chunky white pith to reveal the meaty flesh inside, which can range from yellow to ruby pink, is immensely satisfying. This salad feels like a palate cleanser, packed with sweet, sour and salty flavors that are refreshing and light. The coconut-peanut crunch amplifies the tropical vibes and can be used as a topper for all sorts of salads. Make sure you taste and tweak the seasonings as you go, until you find that perfect balance.

SERVES 4

1 large pomelo (about 1 lb 7 oz/ 650 g) or 2 ruby red grapefruit

1 napa cabbage (about 2¼ lb/1 kg), finely sliced

10 shiso or perilla leaves, finely sliced

handful of cilantro leaves

2 green onions, finely sliced

sea salt

Chile-lime dressing

zest and juice of 1 large lime (about 3 tablespoons juice)

½ fresh Thai red chile, finely chopped

1 garlic clove, grated

4 teaspoons soy sauce or tamari

3 tablespoons brown sugar

½ teaspoon sea salt

1 teaspoon toasted sesame oil

Coconut-peanut crunch

6 tablespoons unsweetened shredded coconut

⅓ cup roasted peanuts, chopped

¼–½ teaspoon red pepper flakes

2 tablespoons brown sugar

1 teaspoon sea salt

Gluten-free and vegan

Substitute • pomelo or ruby red grapefruit: sweet orange variety • shiso or perilla leaves: mint leaves

Vegetable swap • napa cabbage: kale (finely shredded), green or red cabbage

To make the chile-lime dressing, whisk together all the ingredients, along with 1–2 tablespoons of water, until well mixed and the sugar is dissolved. Taste and adjust the salt, sugar and lime to your liking.

To make the coconut-peanut crunch, heat a small skillet over low heat. Add the coconut, peanuts and red pepper flakes and toast, stirring constantly, for 4–5 minutes, until golden. Transfer to a small bowl and add the sugar and salt.

Cut the top and bottom off the pomelo and, using a sharp knife or your hands, remove the peel and the thick layer of white pith. Tear open the segments and extract the flesh, reserving any juice. Place the pomelo and any juice in a bowl, along with the napa cabbage, shiso or perilla, cilantro leaves and green onion. Add the dressing and about half of the coconut-peanut crunch. Season with a touch of sea salt and toss to combine. To serve, sprinkle with more of the coconut-peanut crunch.

Tangy Stir-Fried Cabbage
and Glass Noodles

This dish is very loosely inspired by the Chinese dish "ants climbing a tree," where glass noodles are stir-fried with minced pork, green onions and vegetables. The curious name refers to the bits of minced meat, which resemble "ants" climbing up glass noodles—the tree branches. Here, the "ants" are more like centipedes, with finely sliced strands of cabbage tangling joyfully with springy, chewy glass noodles. This is another of the cabbage-centric dishes I started cooking during lockdown—a lesson in how humble ingredients and pantry staples can merge in a memorable, soulful dish. Any type of cabbage will work in this dish, including napa cabbage. Glass noodles is the general category to describe noodles made of starches—mung bean vermicelli or sweet potato starch noodles (like the ones used for the Korean dish japchae) are the most accessible.

SERVES 4

neutral oil

1 shallot, finely sliced

3 garlic cloves, finely chopped

½ small head red or green cabbage (about 14 oz/400 g), finely sliced

sea salt and white pepper

7 ounces (200 g) mung bean vermicelli or sweet potato starch glass noodles, soaked in warm water for 10–15 minutes

1 tablespoon toasted white sesame seeds

2 green onions, finely sliced

chili oil, to serve

Seasoning sauce

¼ cup (60 ml) soy sauce or tamari

2½ tablespoons maple syrup or sugar

¼ cup (60 ml) ketchup

2½ tablespoons toasted sesame oil

2½ tablespoons toasted white sesame seeds

¼ cup (60 ml) black or rice vinegar

Gluten-free and vegan

Substitute • glass noodles: rice vermicelli

Vegetable swap • cabbage: Brussels sprouts

Heat a wok or large skillet over medium-high heat. When hot, add 2 tablespoons of oil and the shallot, then reduce the heat to medium and cook for 2 minutes until soft. Add the garlic and cabbage, season well with sea salt and white pepper and cook for 5–6 minutes, until the cabbage is tender.

Meanwhile, place all the ingredients for the seasoning sauce in a small bowl and whisk together.

Drain the noodles, then add them to the pan along with the seasoning sauce and, using chopsticks or tongs, toss well to combine. If it looks dry, add another drizzle of oil. Toss for 2–3 minutes, until the noodles are cooked and everything is well combined.

Serve, topped with the sesame seeds, green onion and chili oil.

Cabbage and Kimchi Rolls

Cabbage rolls are a cozy dish with broad international roots, traversing continents, countries and cultures, with diverse interpretations. From Ukrainian holubtsi to Polish golabki, Romanian sarmale, Jewish holishkes and Scandinavian kaalikaarryle, cabbage rolls can also be found in Chinese, Japanese and Vietnamese cuisines.

My version is a global rollick—it is created using the principles of Ukrainian holubtsi (a dish introduced to me by my friend Kris Warman), with a twist, substituting kimchi for the more traditional sauerkraut. You could also use leftover rice—combine about 3 cups of cooked rice with 1 cup of cooked lentils (canned work, too). Serve alone or with roasted or mashed potatoes, blistered green beans or a green salad.

SERVES 4

1 cup (200 g) medium-grain, long-grain or Arborio rice, rinsed three times

½ cup (100 g) black lentils, rinsed

1 large head green or savoy cabbage (about 2 lb 10 oz/1.2 kg)

handful of ice cubes

sea salt and black pepper

extra-virgin olive oil

1 yellow onion, finely diced

1 cup (200 g) regular or vegan kimchi or sauerkraut, chopped

¼ cup (60 ml) apple cider vinegar or white vinegar

handful of chopped dill

Tomato sauce

extra-virgin olive oil

2 tablespoons plus 2 teaspoons (38 g) salted regular or vegan butter

4 garlic cloves, finely chopped

one 28-ounce (800 g) can diced tomatoes

1 teaspoon sugar

sea salt and black pepper

Place the rinsed rice and lentils in a saucepan and top with 3 cups (720 ml) of water. Cover with a lid and place over medium-high heat. When it comes to a boil, reduce the heat to medium low and simmer for 18–20 minutes, until the rice and lentils are tender. If the lentils still have some bite, that is okay, as long as the rice is cooked. Remove the lid (don't stir), take it off the heat and set aside to cool.

Find a deep saucepan that will fit your entire cabbage, with some room to spare. Fill this pan with water until it's three-quarters full. Bring to a boil.

Fill a large bowl with cold water and add a few ice cubes. Turn the cabbage upside-down and run a sharp knife around the core, then carefully shimmy it out and discard. When the water is boiling, add 2–3 teaspoons of sea salt and place the entire cabbage in the water, root-side up. Using tongs, push the cabbage into the water and hold it there to keep it submerged. After 30–60 seconds, the outer leaves will begin to fall away. Remove them and place them in the ice bath. Continue cooking until you have 12 leaves. Remove the remaining inner cabbage heart from the pan and chop it up finely, then set aside. Drain the cabbage leaves and let dry out.

Prepare the filling. Heat a large saucepan over medium-high heat. Add 2 tablespoons of olive oil, along with the onion, and cook for 2 minutes until softened. Add the kimchi or sauerkraut (along with any juices) and the chopped cabbage and stir for 8–10 minutes, until the cabbage is completely wilted and sweet. Turn off the heat and add the rice and lentils, vinegar, 1–2 teaspoons of sea salt (to your taste) and season well with black pepper. Fold everything together and taste again, adjusting the seasonings as needed. Set aside.

To make the the tomato sauce, heat a large Dutch oven over medium-high heat. When hot, add 2 tablespoons of olive oil, along with the butter. When the butter has melted, add the garlic and stir to soften, about 1 minute. Add the tomatoes, along with 1 cup (240 ml) of water, the sugar and about 1 teaspoon of sea salt. Season with black pepper and stir to combine. Reduce the heat to medium low, cover with a lid and allow to simmer gently while you make the cabbage rolls.

Preheat the oven to 400°F (200°C).

Remove the tough middle vein from each cabbage leaf by laying them on a flat surface and cutting a V-shaped notch to remove the thick part of the cabbage rib (but don't cut more than a third of the way into the leaf).

Working with one leaf at a time, with the uncut side closest to you, place ¼–⅓ cup of the filling in the center of the leaf. Fold the sides of the leaf tightly over the filling, then roll it up. Place it, seam-side down, on a large plate and repeat with the remaining leaves and filling.

Nestle the stuffed cabbage rolls, seam-side down, in a single layer in the tomato sauce. Sprinkle with sea salt and drizzle with oil. Cover with a lid (or foil), then place in the oven and cook for 15 minutes. After this time, remove the lid and increase the temperature to 450°F (230°C). Cook for another 8–10 minutes, until the tops of the cabbage rolls have some golden color.

Remove from the oven and allow to cool for a few minutes, before topping with dill and serving.

Shortcut: If you're short on time, use a store-bought tomato-based pasta sauce.

Do ahead: These cabbage rolls can be fully prepped the day before: assemble the rolls, top with sauce and cover tightly. Store in the fridge until ready to bake; remove from the fridge 30 minutes before baking.

Pictured overleaf ›

Gluten-free and vegan

Substitute • lentils: chickpeas, black-eyed peas

Vegetable swap • green or savoy cabbage: napa cabbage

Cabbage and Kimchi Rolls

Tomato and Coconut-Braised Cabbage and Lentils

This style of one-pot braised cabbage is something I started cooking with zeal during quarantine, inspired by the need to create a flavorful, multilayered meal from minimal ingredients and using pantry staples. I have made several versions of this dish over the past few years, but this one is particularly hearty—a spiced tomato and coconut braising liquid in which the lentils are cooked, along with the cabbage. The initial searing of the cabbage over high heat is important, as it creates a slight smoky flavor. This is a versatile dish—you can use canned chickpeas or butter beans in place of the lentils (this also reduces the cooking time) or mix up the spices (ground coriander and paprika would work well, along with a Thai curry paste). You can use any type of cabbage for this recipe.

SERVES 4

extra-virgin olive oil

½ cabbage (about 1 lb/450 g), cut into 4 wedges

1 red onion, finely diced

3 garlic cloves, finely chopped

1 teaspoon ground cumin

1 teaspoon ground turmeric

one 14.5-ounce (411 g) can pureed or diced tomatoes

2 teaspoons sea salt, or more to taste

1 teaspoon sugar

1 cup (200 g) Puy (French) or brown lentils

2 cups (480 ml) vegetable stock

one 13.5-ounce (400 ml) can coconut milk

1 lime, halved

handful of cilantro leaves

rice, flatbread or crusty bread, to serve (optional)

Heat a wide deep saucepan over high heat and, when hot, add 2 tablespoons of olive oil. When the oil shimmers, add the cabbage wedges, one cut side down, and cook for 4–5 minutes, until charred. Flip and repeat on the other cut side. Transfer to a plate along with any stray leaves.

Using the now-empty pan, reduce the heat to medium high and add 1–2 tablespoons of olive oil, along with the onion, and cook for 2 minutes until softened. Add the garlic, cumin and turmeric and stir for 30 seconds, until fragrant. Add the tomatoes, salt and sugar and stir for 1 minute, until combined. Add the lentils and vegetable stock, then reduce the heat to medium and cook for 15 minutes (the lentils should be soft on the outside, with a center that is still uncooked). Add the coconut milk and taste, seasoning with more salt, if needed.

Place the seared cabbage wedges (and stray leaves) into the pan, cover with a lid and cook for 10–15 minutes, until the lentils and cabbage are both completely tender.

Remove from the heat and squeeze on the lime juice, drizzle with olive oil and top with the cilantro leaves. Eat as is, or enjoy with rice, flatbread or crusty bread.

Serving suggestion: Serve with a dollop of Greek yogurt or coconut yogurt.

Gluten-free and vegan

Substitute • lentils: canned chickpeas, butter beans or white beans (reduce the cooking time) • red onion: yellow or white onion, shallot

Vegetable swap • cabbage: cauliflower

Cabbage Carbonara-ish

Carbonara is a classic Roman pasta dish, with an indulgent, creamy sauce of eggs, cheese and cured pork (guanciale is traditional, but bacon or pancetta may be more widely used at home), which are coaxed together with the help of a little starchy pasta cooking water. It is also a dish that tends to intimidate home cooks, who fear the shame of scrambling the egg mix (don't worry, we have all done it!). Don't let the curdle-hurdle hold you back—for me, the trick is committing to the vigorous stirring of the pasta once you have added the eggs. Stirring slowly actually gives more time for the eggs to scramble, but if you keep your movements swift and decisive, you should be okay.

Clearly this is not your classic carbonara—there's no pork, but there is sweet, earthy cabbage, which cooks down and becomes jammy and unctuous. I add a little pasta cooking water to my eggy mix to loosen it up—this also tempers the egg so it doesn't scramble when it is applied to the hot pasta.

SERVES 4

5 large eggs (see Notes)
2½ tablespoons white (shiro) miso
1¾ ounces (50 g) parmesan, pecorino or cheddar, grated, plus more to serve
sea salt and black pepper
¼ cup (60 ml) extra-virgin olive oil
½ large head cabbage (about 1 lb 5 oz/600 g), finely sliced (discard the core)
1 yellow onion, finely sliced
4 garlic cloves, finely chopped
1 pound (450 g) spaghetti or other long pasta
1 bunch of parsley leaves (about 2½ oz/70 g), finely chopped

Bring a large pot of salted water to a boil.

In a bowl, whisk together 3 egg yolks (see Notes), 2 whole eggs and the miso until smooth. Stir in the cheese and a generous grind of black pepper.

Heat a large wide Dutch oven or deep skillet over medium-high heat until very hot. Add the oil, cabbage and onion, along with ½ teaspoon of sea salt, and cook for 8–10 minutes, mainly undisturbed (stirring every 3–4 minutes), until the cabbage is tender, wilted and starting to turn golden in parts. Reduce the heat to low, add the garlic and 1 teaspoon of sea salt and stir to combine. Keep over low heat while your pasta cooks.

Meanwhile, add the pasta to the boiling water and set your timer for 2 minutes less than the recommended cooking time on the package. For example, if the recommended al dente cooking time is 10 minutes, set the timer for 8 minutes. When the pasta is ready, using tongs, drag the pasta straight into the pan with the cabbage—don't drain, leave the pasta cooking water in the pot—and add 1 cup (120 ml) of pasta water. Increase the heat to medium high and cook for 2 minutes to finish cooking the pasta. Remove the pan from the heat and allow it to cool for 30–60 seconds.

Very gradually add ¼ cup (60 ml) of pasta water to the egg mixture to loosen it up. Slowly pour the egg mixture into the hot pasta, stirring vigorously and continuously with a wooden spoon, until the eggy mix gently cooks and turns into a creamy sauce. To serve, top with the parsley, more cheese and black pepper.

Notes: You can use more or fewer eggs in this dish. The number of eggs you use will impact how creamy it gets. If you wanted an even richer dish, you could add another yolk or whole egg. Experiment until you find your creamy sweet spot.

Place the leftover egg whites in a zip-seal bag and freeze for up to 3 months. I use thawed egg whites for pavlova or other meringues.

Tea Leaf and Cabbage Salad

A few years ago, during a family vacation to Palm Springs, California, we dined at a restaurant called Rooster and the Pig, where we were mistakenly served a fermented jasmine leaf salad. The error was lucky as I completely fell in love with the fresh, funky flavors. This recipe includes elements of that salad, with a nod to the classic Burmese dish, laphet thoke. Laphet, or pickled tea leaf, is a treasured ingredient in Burmese culture—it is made from the finest freshly harvested tea crops, which are fermented for 3–4 months—and during ancient times, it was used as a peace offering between kingdoms at war. This recipe uses freshly brewed green tea leaves (such as sencha), which, despite a short fermentation, still become deeply savory (perhaps it would be worthwhile to mention that this salad is caffeinated!). Traditional laphet thoke may be topped with fish sauce, but I've substituted Maggi seasoning sauce for that extra shout of umami.

SERVES 4

½ large head green cabbage or napa cabbage (about 1 lb 5 oz/600 g), finely sliced

2 tomatoes (about 14 oz/400 g), chopped

1 cup roasted peanuts, chopped

½ cup toasted sunflower seeds

½ cup toasted white sesame seeds

¼ cup crispy fried garlic (see Notes) or crispy fried shallots

1 fresh red or green Thai chile, finely sliced

Maggi seasoning sauce

1 lime or lemon, quartered

Tea leaf dressing

2½ tablespoons loose green tea

2 cups (480 ml) just-boiled water

1 garlic clove, grated

1-inch (2.5 cm) piece of ginger, peeled and grated

2½ tablespoons lemon juice (from 1 small lemon)

1 teaspoon white vinegar

¼ cup (60 ml) extra-virgin olive oil or garlic oil (see Notes)

sea salt and black pepper

For gluten-free • omit Maggi or substitute with tamari

Vegan

Substitute • peanuts: cashews
• green tea: jasmine tea

Vegetable swap • cabbage: romaine lettuce, arugula, baby spinach, kale

To make the tea leaf dressing, steep the green tea leaves in the just-boiled water for 5 minutes.

While the tea is steeping, get started on the rest of the dressing. In a small bowl, add the garlic, ginger, lemon juice and vinegar and allow to sit for a few minutes. When your tea is ready, drain it (save the tea to drink, but you may need to add more water as it will be strong!), squeeze out any excess water from the leaves and finely chop. Add the leaves to the garlic and ginger mixture, along with the olive oil or garlic oil. Add about ¾ teaspoon of sea salt (or more to taste) and a few turns of freshly ground black pepper.

Assemble the salad on a large platter or four individual plates. Spread the cabbage on the platter or plates, then spoon the tea leaf dressing into the center. Arrange piles of the tomato, peanuts, seeds, crispy fried garlic or shallots and red or green chile around the dressing. Shake a few drops of Maggi over the top and, when ready to eat, toss everything together. Serve with lime or lemon wedges on the side.

Notes: The dressing can be prepared ahead and stored in the fridge for 2–3 days. It improves in flavor after a few days.

To make your own crispy fried garlic and garlic oil, add 10–12 cloves of finely sliced garlic to a small saucepan and place over medium heat. Add enough olive oil or neutral oil to just cover the garlic. Cook until the garlic just starts to turn a light golden brown, then immediately transfer to paper towel to absorb any excess oil and allow it to crisp up as it cools. Some slices may turn golden before others so you may have to remove them at different stages. The garlic oil can be used to make the dressing.

Carrot

"Enduringly dependable and
delightfully affable"

I'm always rooting for carrots. Enduringly dependable and delightfully affable, carrot is the vegetable friend that has never let me down. If you dangle the carrot, I'll be the donkey that bites.

Carrots smell of the earth, of pine, grass and the woods. Its robust bucolic character stems from a complex genealogy that belies its "humble veg" status. The plump carrot that we know today is highly engineered—over time, botanists have used science to improve the appearance, flavor and size of ancient carrots. Originating in what is now modern-day Iran and Afghanistan, they were originally believed to be purple, with mutated crops offering yellow and white cultivars. During the 17th century, Dutch growers used mutant strains of the purple carrot to develop the orange variety that we devour today.

My mother believes passionately in the power of hong lo bak tong (carrot soup) to heal everyday ailments. Her tonic for coughs—but "not for itchy throats"—is a clear soup of carrot, often with potato or daikon, that is said to moisturize and release what Chinese medicine calls "dry heat" from the body. Carrot soup also nourishes the lungs. In cooking, carrots are equally compelling, pairing well with warm spices, such as ginger, cinnamon, cumin and coriander, woodsy herbs, such as thyme and parsley, and bold citrus, such as lemon, orange or blood orange.

Carrot Top Gremolata Breadcrumbs

Carrot tops sing with an earthy flavor that is somewhere between parsley and carrots. They can be used for herbaceous oils and sauces, such as pesto or chimichurri, added to smoothies, or used as an herb to finish a meal. Here, they add a fresh grassy element to gremolata. Use to top salads, soups, pasta or roasted veggies.

MAKES 1½ CUPS

4 teaspoons extra-virgin olive oil

⅔ cup (40 g) panko breadcrumbs

zest of 1 lemon

1 small garlic clove, grated

1 cup washed and finely chopped carrot tops

1 teaspoon sea salt

Heat a skillet over medium heat. When hot, add the oil and breadcrumbs and stir constantly until golden, about 2 minutes. Add the lemon zest and garlic and stir for 30 seconds until fragrant. Remove from the heat, add the carrot tops and sea salt and stir to combine.

Storage: If not using straight away, let the gremolata breadcrumbs cool, then place in an airtight container. Store in the fridge for 1 month or the freezer for up to 3 months. Reheat in a pan until crispy again. For gluten-free • use gluten-free breadcrumbs

Vegan

Substitute • panko breadcrumbs: fresh breadcrumbs

Vegetable swap • carrot tops: turnip or radish greens, parsley

Roasted Carrots with
Black-Eyed Peas and Basil Green Goddess

Carrots and black-eyed peas are two ingredients that evoke strong memories of my mother's cooking. Her daily tong (soup), a fortifying, often medicinal broth, kicked off our evening meals, and carrots and black-eyed peas both had their part to play in these soups. Carrot and potato soup was served to nourish the lungs and to treat dry coughs. Black-eyed peas were used to help clear "dampness," aiding digestion and nurturing the spleen and kidneys. These foods were both nourishment and medicine in our daily diets. This recipe brings together these two healing ingredients in a vibrant salad. The earthy roasted carrots and nutty black-eyed peas are balanced with an herbaceous, time-honored Green Goddess dressing. While the original dressing, which was reportedly created at the Palace Hotel in San Francisco in 1923, was believed to feature mayonnaise, sour cream, chives and parsley, my take is basil-centric, and a bit lighter with the use of Greek (or coconut) yogurt.

SERVES 4

2 pounds (900 g) carrots, trimmed and peeled

extra-virgin olive oil

sea salt and black pepper

1½ cups (275 g) cooked black-eyed peas (about one 15 oz/425 g can, drained)

handful of basil or parsley leaves, to serve

2–3 tablespoons Carrot Top Gremolata Breadcrumbs (see page 127) or chopped pistachios

Basil green goddess

1 cup basil leaves

2 green onions, finely sliced

½ cup parsley leaves

1 tablespoon capers, rinsed

2 garlic cloves, roughly chopped

1 cup (250 g) Greek or vegan coconut yogurt

1 teaspoon sea salt

1 teaspoon sugar

2½ tablespoons extra-virgin olive oil

2 teaspoons lemon juice (from about ½ small lemon)

black pepper

Gluten-free and vegan

Substitute • black-eyed peas: cannellini beans, chickpeas, borlotti beans

Vegetable swap • carrots: potatoes, sweet potatoes

Preheat the oven to 400°F (200°C).

Cut the carrots into equal-sized pieces, about 4 inches (10 cm) long and ¾ inch (2 cm) thick. If you have baby carrots, just scrub them and don't bother peeling, then roast them whole. Place the carrot on a sheet pan and drizzle with olive oil. Season well with sea salt and black pepper and roast for 20–25 minutes, until tender and slightly caramelized. Remove from the oven and set aside to cool.

Meanwhile, to make the basil Green Goddess, place the basil, green onion, parsley, capers, garlic and yogurt in a blender or food processor and blend until smooth. Add the salt, sugar, olive oil and lemon juice, season with black pepper and pulse once or twice, just to combine. Taste to make sure it has enough sea salt and black pepper, and adjust to your liking.

In a large bowl, combine the carrots, black-eyed peas, basil or parsley, and about half of the dressing. Toss and season with sea salt and black pepper. To serve, spoon over some more dressing (if you like), drizzle with a little olive oil and top with the Carrot Top Gremolata Breadcrumbs or pistachios.

Leftovers: Extra Green Goddess dressing can be used to make potato salad, drizzled on eggs, or as a pasta sauce. It can be stored in an airtight container in the fridge for up to 3 days.

Carrot Peanut Satay Ramen

The smell of satay takes me right back to childhood barbecues, when my mother would make satay chicken skewers, and the aroma of them cooking would waft over the entire neighborhood, filling the streets with the rich, heady perfume of Southeast Asia. My father loved to grill—it is an Australian tradition, after all. With a can of Tab (sugar-free cola that was popular in the 1970s) in his hand, he would command the grill while the rest of us waited inside for the food to be cooked (we always ate the barbecued meats inside, around the dining table). Here, I've used satay as the inspiration for this carrot-laden ramen. Peanut butter is the base of this broth, which is combined with grated carrots to provide heft and flavor, both thickening it up and adding a natural sweetness. You can blitz it up if you prefer a smooth broth, but I enjoy the occasional specks of carrot while I'm slurping the noodles.

SERVES 4

1–2 tablespoons neutral oil

2 garlic cloves, finely chopped

1½-inch (4 cm) piece of ginger, peeled and finely chopped

3 carrots (about 9 oz/250 g), scrubbed and coarsely grated

1 teaspoon sea salt

½ teaspoon sugar

¾ cup (200 g) creamy peanut butter

32 ounces (1 liter) Vegan Dashi (see page 360) or vegetable stock

12 ounces (340 g) instant or ramen noodles

handful of Asian greens, such as baby bok boy, tatsoi or choy sum, washed and patted dry, leaves picked

handful of cilantro leaves

2 green onions, sliced

¼ cup roasted peanuts, chopped

4 soft-boiled eggs, halved (optional)

Seasonings

4 teaspoons sugar

8 teaspoons soy sauce or tamari

4 teaspoons rice vinegar

4 teaspoons toasted sesame oil

4 teaspoons doubanjiang or chili oil

Gluten-free and vegan

Substitute • eggs: sliced tofu
• Asian greens: broccoli florets, kale

Heat a saucepan over medium-high heat. Drizzle with the oil and add the garlic and ginger. Cook for 1 minute until fragrant, then add the carrot, salt and sugar and cook for 3–5 minutes, until the carrot is softened and starting to caramelize. Add the peanut butter and dashi or vegetable stock and stir. Bring to a boil, then reduce the heat to low, cover and simmer for 5 minutes. This is a textured soup base—if you prefer it smooth, use a stick blender to puree.

Meanwhile, bring a large saucepan of salted water to a boil. Add the noodles and cook according to the package directions. Drain.

Lay out four bowls. In each bowl, add the following seasonings: 1 teaspoon of sugar, 2 teaspoons of soy sauce or tamari, 1 teaspoon of rice vinegar, 1 teaspoon of sesame oil and 1 teaspoon of doubanjiang or chili oil. Whisk to combine.

Add your greens to the broth, cook for 30 seconds, then immediately pour the broth and greens into the four bowls, on top of the seasonings, dividing it equally. Stir to combine. Divide the noodles among the bowls, top with the cilantro leaves, green onion, peanuts and soft-boiled egg, if desired. Serve immediately.

Carrot and Vermicelli Buns

I think of these juicy carrot- and vermicelli-filled buns as oversized dumplings. Similar to the Shanghai street food sheng jian bao, which are yeasted buns, this dough is made just from all-purpose flour and water (the same hot water dough that I use for dumpling wrappers) and is fried, then steamed, the same process that is used for potstickers. This cooking method gives us a crispy exterior and a bun that stays moist.

MAKES 12

2½ cups (300 g) all-purpose flour, plus more for dusting

¾ cup (180 ml) boiling water, cooled for 1–2 minutes

2 oz (55 g) mung bean vermicelli, soaked in water for 10 minutes

neutral oil

2 large carrots (about 9 oz/250 g), scrubbed and coarsely grated

2 garlic cloves, grated

2 teaspoons soy sauce or tamari

¼ teaspoon white pepper

¼ teaspoon sea salt

6 green onions, finely sliced

2 tablespoons toasted sesame seeds (white, black or both)

Soy–black vinegar dipping sauce

1 tablespoon soy sauce or tamari

1 tablespoon black vinegar

1 green onion, finely sliced

Vegan

Vegetable swap • carrot: sweet potato, potato, spinach

Place the flour in a bowl. Add the boiling water and stir with chopsticks or a wooden spoon, hydrating as much of the flour as possible. Using your hands (be careful as it will still be hot), knead the dough in the bowl until it all comes together in a ball. Turn it out onto a lightly floured surface and knead for 2–3 minutes, until soft and only slightly sticky (it will still look a little lumpy). Wrap the dough tightly in plastic wrap or place in a zip-seal bag and rest at room temperature for at least 30 minutes and up to 2 hours. You can also rest the dough in the fridge overnight (see Do Ahead below).

Drain the mung bean vermicelli and, using kitchen scissors, randomly snip the noodles to create shorter strands.

Heat a skillet over medium-high heat. Drizzle with 1–2 tablespoons of oil and add the carrot. Cook for 2 minutes to soften, then add the mung bean vermicelli, garlic, soy sauce or tamari, white pepper and sea salt. Toss and cook for 2–3 minutes, until softened. Remove from the heat and add the green onion, tossing to combine. Taste and add more sea salt if needed. Cool completely.

Cut the dough in half, then divide each half into 6 pieces, to make 12 pieces in total. Roll each piece into a ball. Take one ball and flatten it slightly, then roll it out into a 4¾–5-inch (12–13 cm) disc. Holding it in the palm of your nondominant hand, add 1½–2 tablespoons of the filling to the middle of the dough. Pleat by overlapping the dough edge, all the way around, then rotate and pinch the top of the pleats to fully seal the bun. Place the sesame seeds on a plate and dip the bottom of the bun in the sesame seeds and flatten. Repeat until you have used all the dough and filling.

You may need to cook the buns in two batches. Heat a nonstick skillet over medium-high heat. Add 1 tablespoon of oil and place the buns, seam-side down, into the oil, spaced apart, in one layer. Cook for 1–2 minutes, until the bottom of the buns is golden, then flip them over and add ½ cup (120 ml) of water. Cover immediately and reduce the heat to medium. Cook for 5–8 minutes, until the water has mostly evaporated. Remove the lid and continue to cook until the water is all gone and the bottom is golden.

Combine all the ingredients for the dipping sauce with 1 tablespoon of water in a small bowl. Serve the buns with the dipping sauce.

Do ahead: Make the dough up to 24 hours ahead and store, tightly wrapped, in the fridge. This hot water dough can be used cold, straight from the fridge.

Carrot and Cannellini Bean Sheet-Pan Dinner with Yuzu Vinaigrette

Carrot has a natural affinity with citrus, its woodiness calling out for some sweetness and acidity. While it is often orange that I team with carrots, here I've interplayed them with lemon and yuzu. Yuzu tastes as though it is the lovechild of grapefruit and lemon—not as bitter as grapefruit, nor as sour as lemon. It falls somewhere in between sharp and acidic, with a floral note. Used widely in Japanese cooking, bottles of yuzu juice can be found in Japanese and Asian supermarkets. This sheet-pan dish is a wonderful weeknight meal, quick to throw together and full of nutrition. Top with feta or goat cheese if you'd like to add a creamy, salty finish.

SERVES 4

1 pound (450 g) baby carrots, scrubbed and trimmed

extra-virgin olive oil

sea salt and black pepper

3 cups (500 g) cooked cannellini beans (about two 15 oz/425 g cans, drained)

2 small (or 1 large) leek, white and green parts finely sliced and washed well

1 lemon, sliced

handful of cilantro leaves

handful of toasted sliced almonds

Yuzu vinaigrette

4 teaspoons yuzu juice

2½ tablespoons extra-virgin olive oil

2 teaspoons maple syrup

1 garlic clove, grated

sea salt and black pepper

Preheat the oven to 400°F (200°C).

Make sure your carrots are approximately the same size—if you have some larger ones, halve them lengthwise. If you are using regular carrots, peel them and cut them to size. Place the carrots on a sheet pan, drizzle with oil, season with sea salt and roast for 15 minutes.

Place the cannellini beans, leek and lemon in a bowl, drizzle with olive oil and season well with sea salt and black pepper.

After the carrots have been in the oven for 15 minutes, add the beans, leek and lemon to the pan, arranging them around the carrots. Return to the oven for another 15–18 minutes, until the carrots are tender and golden.

Meanwhile, to make the yuzu vinaigrette, combine the yuzu juice, olive oil, maple syrup and garlic in a bowl and whisk to combine. Season with sea salt and black pepper.

Remove the carrot pan from the oven. While still warm, drizzle everything with the yuzu vinaigrette. Season the whole pan with sea salt and black pepper and scatter on the cilantro leaves and almonds.

Gluten-free and vegan

Substitute • cannellini beans: chickpeas • leeks: onions, shallots • sliced almonds: hazelnuts

Vegetable swap • carrot: parsnip, sweet potato

Olive Oil–Braised Carrots and Chickpeas

This one-pan dish of olive oil–braised carrots is rich, earthy and sweet. Unexpectedly indulgent, the carrots and chickpeas are bathed in olive oil, with sticky dates and warming spices building a jackpot of flavor. There are many ways to enjoy this dish—make a pan of couscous or quinoa and stir it into the carrots (or simply serve alongside), top with toasted almonds or feta (recommended), break a few eggs into the braise during the final moments of cooking for a shakshuka-esque finish, dollop with Greek yogurt, or serve with bread to mop up the scented oil. If your carrots come with tops, use them to make the gremolata breadcrumbs on page 127, which reinforces the carrot-ness of this dish and adds a fresh grassy finish.

SERVES 4

extra-virgin olive oil

1 yellow onion, finely diced

6 garlic cloves, finely chopped

1 fresh red or green Thai chile, roughly chopped (or ¼–½ teaspoon red pepper flakes)

¼ cup (65 g) tomato paste

6 dates, pitted and torn into small pieces

3 cups (500 g) cooked chickpeas (about two 15 oz/425 g cans, drained)

2 teaspoons ground coriander

handful of dill, roughly chopped

1 teaspoon sugar

sea salt and black pepper

2 bunches of baby carrots (about 1½ pounds/700 g, scrubbed, green tops trimmed and reserved (see recipe introduction)

1 small lemon, finely sliced and seeded

Carrot Top Gremolata Breadcrumbs (see page 127), to top (optional)

bread, rice or couscous, to serve

Heat a wide, deep saucepan or a large Dutch oven over medium heat. Drizzle in about 1 tablespoon of olive oil, then add the onion and cook for 2–3 minutes, until softened. Add the garlic and chile and stir for 1 minute, until aromatic. Next, add the tomato paste, dates, chickpeas, ground coriander, dill, sugar, 1 teaspoon of sea salt and a few turns of black pepper and stir for 1 minute to ensure the chickpeas are well coated. Lay the baby carrots on top of the chickpeas and pour in 1 cup (240 ml) of olive oil. Top with the lemon slices, cover with a lid, then reduce the heat to low and cook for 45–50 minutes, until the chickpeas and carrots are meltingly soft.

Taste and season generously with sea salt and black pepper. Serve topped with carrot top gremolata breadcrumbs (if using), alongside bread, rice or couscous.

Gluten-free and vegan

Substitute • chickpeas: cannellini beans or butter beans • dates: dried figs • dill: parsley

Vegetable swap • carrot: eggplant, fennel

Carrot-Almond Polenta Cake
with Lemon Drizzle

Carrot cake crosses over with polenta cake in this moist and textural sweet treat. The polenta cake is infused with rich flavors—nutty almond meal, velvety olive oil and warm spices—with the added texture and sweetness from grated carrots. The lemony drizzle is optional, but will make the cake even fudgier. Mix things up by substituting the lemon zest and juice with orange or lime, or you could even try yuzu juice in the syrup for a sharper citrusy tone.

SERVES 8

1 cup plus 2 tablespoons (160 g) polenta

1½ cups (175 g) almond meal

2 teaspoons baking powder

½ teaspoon baking soda

1 teaspoon sea salt

1 teaspoon ground cinnamon

½ teaspoon ground ginger

¼ teaspoon ground cardamom

7 tablespoons (100 ml) olive oil

zest of 1 lemon

1 cup (250 g) vegan yogurt, such as cashew or coconut yogurt

1 cup plus 2 tablespoons (220 g) granulated sugar

1 teaspoon vanilla extract

10 ounces (300 g) carrots, scrubbed and grated

Lemon drizzle

½ cup (65 g) powdered sugar

juice of 1 lemon (about ¼ cup)

Preheat the oven to 350°F (180°C). Line the bottom and grease the side of an 8-inch (20 cm) springform pan.

Place the polenta, almond meal, baking powder, baking soda, sea salt and spices in a bowl and whisk to combine.

In another bowl, combine the olive oil, lemon zest, yogurt, granulated sugar and vanilla and whisk until smooth. Fold in the grated carrot.

Add the wet ingredients to the dry ingredients and fold together until well combined. Pour the batter into the springform pan and bake for 50–55 minutes, until an inserted skewer comes out clean.

Meanwhile, to make the lemon drizzle, combine the powdered sugar and lemon juice in a small saucepan over medium-low heat, whisking constantly, until the syrup is completely smooth and there are no more lumps. Set aside to cool.

When the cake is ready, place the springform pan on a wire rack and carefully unclip the sides to release the cake (take care as it will be very hot, but doing this now will prevent any sticking from the syrup). Using a bamboo skewer or cake tester, prick the cake all over, going almost to the bottom of the cake (but not the whole way). Slowly spoon the cooled lemon drizzle over the cake while it is still hot, adding a little at a time to allow the liquid to soak into the cake (if you add it too quickly, the syrup may pool on the top).

Let the cake cool before slicing.

Gluten-free and vegan

Vegetable swap • carrot: sweet potato, parsnip

Cauliflower

"Frothy, curdlike flowers
that are sweet and musky"

In 2017, *Time* magazine declared cauliflower the "It" vegetable. Its "sudden" surge in popularity stemmed from the carb-loathing circles who looked to the cauliflower to replace rice or traditional pizza crust. Let's get this straight: nothing replaces rice, not even the mighty cauliflower.

But neither does cauliflower need to masquerade as rice, or pizza crust, breadcrumbs or hashbrowns. The joy in cauliflower is not its ability to replicate another food, but in its pure physical form—frothy, curdlike flowers that are sweet and musky. Cauliflowers featured prominently on our Cantonese table, stir-fried with a punchy seasoning like dou si (fermented black beans) or fermented soybean. For high-heat stir-frying, ensure that the cauliflower florets are not too small as we don't want them to soften too quickly; a firm, crisp texture is what we covet.

The market cauliflowers that my father brought home were larger than our heads, plump and firm, with compact flowers and a smooth, creamy complexion. Of course, there are many varieties of cauliflower on the market today—there are orange, purple and yellow ones, while Romanesco cauliflower (also called Romanesco broccoli, Roman cauliflower or broccoflower) is a vivid lime-green cauliflower-broccoli hybrid, with mini spiky pine trees in a unique fractal pattern on its head. Taishan cauliflower (also known as Chinese cauliflower, fioretto cauliflower, flowering cauliflower and many more names) looks like a brassica wild child: slithering, angular, bifurcate stems, finished with tiny white buds. Taishan cauliflower is much like other varieties, but is sweeter and more vegetal, with a firmer stem and a less intense cauli flavor. These varieties can all be cooked in the same manner as the white cauliflower.

Cauliflower Manchurian

Cauliflower (or gobi in Hindi) Manchurian is a classic Indo-Chinese dish. One of the greatest blended cuisines in the world, Indo-Chinese originated in India at the end of the 19th century, when Hakka-speaking Chinese immigrated to Kolkata (formerly known as Calcutta), settling in an area called Tangra, where many set up leather tanneries. Soon, restaurants were established in the area, gradually incorporating techniques and flavor adjustments, like the addition of more chile, to make food more appealing to Indian customers. Quintessential Indo-Chinese dishes feature spicy gravies, saucy noodles and fried ingredients that are reminiscent of classic Indian fried delicacies, such as pakora. This cauliflower manchurian dish features the "holy trinity" of this hybrid cuisine: tomatoes, soy sauce and chile. Manchurian dishes can be either saucy or a dry-fry—this recipe is the latter, and is best served with fried rice, noodles or roti.

SERVES 4

1 large head of cauliflower (about 2¼ lb/1 kg), cut into florets

neutral oil

2-inch (5 cm) piece of ginger, peeled and finely chopped

3 garlic cloves, finely chopped

1 fresh Thai green chile, finely chopped

1 celery stalk, finely chopped

½ red or green bell pepper, finely chopped

4 green onions, white and green parts separated and finely chopped

4 teaspoons soy sauce or tamari

4 teaspoons ketchup

1 teaspoon apple cider vinegar or rice vinegar

⅛ teaspoon ground white pepper

sea salt

rice, noodles or roti, to serve

Batter

scant 1 cup (150 g) rice flour or all-purpose flour

½ cup (60 g) cornstarch

½ teaspoon chile powder

black pepper

1 cup (240 ml) vegetable stock or water

1 teaspoon soy sauce or tamari

Gluten-free and vegan

Vegetable swap • cauliflower: tofu, eggplant

To make the batter, combine all the ingredients in a large mixing bowl and whisk until completely smooth. The batter should be free flowing and loose, so if it looks thick, add a bit more water. If you are using rice flour, you will need to whisk the mixture every now and then as the rice flour settles at the bottom of the bowl. Add the cauliflower florets to the batter and toss to coat.

You will need to cook the cauliflower in several batches. Heat a deep skillet over medium-high heat. Add a generous amount of oil, until it covers the bottom of the pan and comes a scant ¼ inch (5 mm) up the sides. When the oil is hot (test by inserting a wooden chopstick or spoon and if it sizzles, it's ready), pick up a cauliflower floret, holding it upside-down above the bowl to allow any excess batter to run off, and place it straight into the hot oil. Continue adding the cauliflower until the pan is full. If the oil starts to get too hot and smoky, reduce the heat slightly to medium, but a higher heat will give you a crispier result. Fry the cauliflower for 2–3 minutes on each side, until golden and crispy all over. Place the cauliflower on a plate lined with paper towel and continue cooking the remaining florets.

When all the cauliflower has been cooked, use the same pan to prepare the aromatic sauce. If there is still some oil in your pan, there is no need to add any more—you need the equivalent of 1–2 tablespoons of oil, so drain off any excess; if your pan is dry, add another drizzle of oil. Reduce the heat to medium, add the ginger, garlic and chile and stir for 1 minute until aromatic. Add the celery, bell pepper, and white part of the green onion and sauté for 2 minutes until soft. Add the soy sauce or tamari, ketchup, vinegar and white pepper and season with sea salt. Stir to combine, then turn off the heat, add the cauliflower to the pan and toss to coat the florets in the aromatics.

Top with the remaining green onion and serve with rice, noodles or roti.

Cauliflower Adobo

Adobo is the most beloved dish of the Philippines, a savory and acidic chicken stew for which every Filipino family will have its own and best recipe. These heirloom recipes, most often passed orally from one generation to another, are imbued with the flavors of memory and nostalgia and, hence, are often the most difficult to replicate. Therefore, this adobo recipe, made with cauliflower, is not traditional by any means, but it celebrates the lively spirit and punchy attitude of the original dish. This is a wonderful prep-ahead dish as it benefits from a day's rest, which allows the vinegar to mellow out and become more rounded.

SERVES 4

2 tablespoons extra-virgin olive oil, plus more if needed

1 head of cauliflower (about 2 lb/900 g), stem trimmed and cut into 8 wedges

5 garlic cloves, finely sliced

2 bay leaves

1 teaspoon whole black peppercorns

½ cup (120 ml) soy sauce or tamari

½ cup (120 ml) rice vinegar

2½ tablespoons brown sugar

2 green onions, finely sliced

white or brown rice, or farro, to serve

Place a wide Dutch oven or heavy-bottomed saucepan over medium-high heat and add the oil. When it starts to shimmer, add the cauliflower wedges in a single layer and cook on one side, undisturbed, for 6–8 minutes, until well browned, then flip over and repeat on the other side. If all your cauliflower doesn't fit at once, you can cook it in batches, adding more oil as needed. Transfer the cauliflower, along with any bits that have separated, to a plate and set aside.

To the same pan, add the garlic, bay leaves and peppercorns and cook over medium heat, stirring, for 30–60 seconds, until it is very fragrant and the garlic turns a light golden color. Add 1 cup (240 ml) of water and stir, scraping up any browned bits on the bottom of the pan. Add the soy sauce or tamari, rice vinegar and sugar and return the cauliflower to the pan. Increase the heat to high and bring the liquid to a boil. Reduce the heat to low, cover and simmer for 15–20 minutes, until the cauliflower is tender all the way through.

This cauliflower adobo can be enjoyed immediately or the next day (the flavors really develop overnight). Serve topped with the green onion, with rice or farro alongside.

Storage: Keep the cauliflower adobo in an airtight container in the fridge for up to 1 week.

Gluten-free and vegan

Substitute • rice vinegar: white vinegar

Vegetable swap • cauliflower: potato, broccoli, Brussels sprouts

Stir-Fried Cauliflower with Capers, Chile and Parsley

During my early twenties, as a young university student living at home, I introduced my mother to a few of the dishes I had learned from my favorite cooking shows or from the recipe pages in magazines. My spaghetti with parsley, chile and capers is one she instantly loved. She adored the fiery heat, the briny saltiness of the capers (a new ingredient to her) and the surprising grassiness of the parsley. She often requested that I cook this dish, and later, once I moved out, she would make this dish for herself and my brother. This recipe employs this formidable triptych of parsley, chile and capers in a different way, as the seasoning for stir-fried cauliflower. If you can find it, use Taishan cauliflower, which is sweet and vegetal and remains delightfully crisp. I love stumbling across these wild-looking stems at roadside stalls in Chinatown in the spring (although I often see them during the autumn, too). This stir-fry is a blank canvas—toss it with pasta, add some feta and chickpeas to turn it into a salad, or serve with a fried egg on top. Or, of course, eat with rice.

SERVES 4

extra-virgin olive oil

1 small red onion, finely sliced

1 pound (450 g) Taishan (Chinese flowering) or regular cauliflower, cut into thin uniform stems

3 garlic cloves, finely chopped

1–2 bird's eye chiles, finely sliced (remove the seeds if you prefer less spice)

3 tablespoons capers, rinsed and roughly chopped

½ bunch of parsley, stems and leaves finely chopped

sea salt

½ lemon

rice or pasta, to serve

Heat a wok or large skillet over medium-high heat. When hot, add 2 tablespoons of olive oil, along with the onion. Stir-fry for 2 minutes, until softened and turning golden. Add the cauliflower, garlic, chile, capers and parsley, along with another 2 tablespoons of olive oil and about ½ teaspoon of sea salt, and toss for 1 minute until the cauliflower is well coated in the seasoning. Add 2–3 tablespoons of water and cover with a lid (if you don't have a lid, use a large heatproof plate) and leave for 2 minutes. Remove the lid and stir-fry for another 2–3 minutes, until the cauliflower is crisp-tender and charred in some places. The cooking time will depend upon how large your stems are so don't be afraid to taste to check for doneness. If you are using Taishan cauliflower, the stems will stay quite crisp. Finish with a squeeze of lemon.

Serve with rice, toss with pasta or try one of the serving suggestions in the recipe introduction.

Gluten-free and vegan

Substitute • bird's eye chiles: 1–2 Thai red chiles or ½–1 teaspoon red pepper flakes

Vegetable swap • cauliflower: broccoli, Brussels sprouts, green or savoy cabbage

Hoisin-Glazed Cauliflower with Mixed Grains and Peanuts

This hoisin-glazed cauliflower is simple enough for weeknight cooking, but it is also an impressive dish to pull out at dinner parties—it has deep flavors and a lovely earthy sweetness that will please the crowd. Hoisin sauce is often used as a sweet and savory glaze for meat or as a stir-fry seasoning in Chinese cooking. There are many regional versions of hoisin, but this homemade one is very close to the Cantonese version that I grew up eating (Lee Kum Kee brand). The key ingredient of hoisin is fermented soybeans, which gives it a deep umami flavor—doubanjiang is traditional but other fermented soybean pastes, such as miso, would work, too. This hoisin sauce keeps in the fridge for about a month so consider doubling the quantity.

The "mixed grains" is how I often cook rice—mixing white and brown rice, with a quick-cooking grain like quinoa tossed in for extra heartiness. Many have questioned the cooking of brown and white rice together because they are believed to have different cooking times, but this recipe works every time, and gives me a wonderful textured accompaniment for any meals that I might eat with white rice.

SERVES 4

1 head of cauliflower (about 2 lb/900 g)

extra-virgin olive oil

sea salt and black pepper

⅓ cup roasted peanuts, chopped

handful of cilantro leaves, to serve

Homemade hoisin (makes ½ cup)

¼ cup (60 ml) soy sauce or tamari

2½ tablespoons tahini

1 garlic clove, grated

2½ tablespoons brown sugar

2 teaspoons toasted sesame oil

1 teaspoon rice vinegar

⅛–¼ teaspoon black pepper

1–2 teaspoons doubanjiang or miso

Mixed grains

1 cup (185 g) brown rice

½ cup (95 g) white rice

¼ cup (45 g) white, red or mixed quinoa

1 teaspoon sea salt

1 tablespoon extra-virgin olive oil (optional)

Gluten-free and vegan

Substitute • tahini: creamy peanut butter • brown sugar: maple syrup

Vegetable swap • cauliflower: cabbage, broccoli

Preheat the oven to 400°F (200°C).

To make the homemade hoisin, place all the ingredients in a bowl and whisk to combine.

Cut the cauliflower in half, then slice it into wedges 1 inch (2.5 cm) thick. Arrange on a sheet pan and spoon over 3–4 tablespoons of the hoisin sauce, drizzle with 2–3 tablespoons of olive oil and season with sea salt and black pepper. Using a spatula or your hands, toss the cauliflower in the mixture to coat. Roast for 25–30 minutes, until golden and tender.

Meanwhile, for the mixed grains, place the brown rice, white rice and quinoa in a saucepan. Rinse the grains well—add some tap water to the pan, squeeze and rub the grains in the water, then drain; repeat two more times or until the water runs clear-ish. Top with 2⅓ cups (560 ml) of water and stir in the sea salt and olive oil (if using). Place over medium-high heat, cover with a lid and bring to a gentle simmer (this should take 8–10 minutes), then reduce the heat to medium and cook for 30–35 minutes, until the water has been absorbed and the grains are tender. Watch the rice and check it from time to time as different brands can cook at different speeds. When it is ready, turn the heat off, leave the lid on and allow the rice to steam for 10 minutes (or longer)—do not stir.

To serve, place the mixed grains on a plate, top with the cauliflower wedges, drizzle with some hoisin sauce and finish with the peanuts, cilantro leaves and a drizzle of olive oil.

Cauliflower and Kale Pesto Pasta Salad with Burrata

Pasta salad is a go-to family meal—it ticks a lot of boxes for my teens (carbs) while also giving me the opportunity to load up on veggies. Here, cauliflower and kale combine to make a sweet and earthy "pesto" that is not at all like the traditional version, but possesses a redolent nutty, vegetal vibe. The pesto sauce is lemony and zesty, a vegetable-packed dressing for the pasta salad. This is an adaptable dish, too: add seasonal additions, such as charred corn, sweet cherry tomatoes or slices of raw zucchini; add chickpeas or lentils for more heft; use a hearty grain, such as farro or freekeh, instead of the pasta; and, if burrata is scarce, replace with fresh mozzarella or dollops of ricotta (vegans can leave out the dairy altogether).

SERVES 4–6

1 head of cauliflower (about 2 lb/900 g)

extra-virgin olive oil

sea salt and black pepper

1 pound (450 g) farfalle or other short pasta

9 ounces (250 g) kale leaves (from about ½ bunch), torn

1 cup toasted walnuts

2 garlic cloves, roughly chopped

zest and juice of 1 lemon

1–2 balls of burrata or fresh mozzarella

Preheat the oven to 400°F (200°C).

Cut the cauliflower into florets, including any sturdy leaves and tender stems; discard anything woody or browned. Lay the cauliflower florets, stems, and leaves on a sheet pan, drizzle with olive oil and season with sea salt and black pepper. Roast in the oven for 10 minutes.

Bring a large saucepan of salted water to a boil and add the pasta. Cook according to the package directions, until al dente. Drain and run under cold water; drain again.

Remove the pan with the cauliflower from the oven, push the cauliflower to one side and add the kale leaves to the other side of the pan. Drizzle the kale with olive oil, season with sea salt and place the pan back in the oven. Roast for 10 minutes, until the kale is tender and starting to get crispy; the cauliflower should be completely soft and slightly golden by now.

For the pesto, add about 1 cup (100 g) of the roasted cauliflower, 1 tightly packed cup (30 g) of the roasted kale, half the walnuts and the garlic to a blender or the bowl of a food processor. Pulse a few times to break everything up. Add half the lemon zest and juice, ½ cup (120 ml) of olive oil, ½ teaspoon of sea salt and a few turns of freshly ground black pepper. Pulse again until you have a chunky paste (this pesto should not be smooth).

Place the pasta in a large bowl and add the remaining roasted cauliflower and kale, along with the pesto. Toss to combine. Add the remaining lemon zest and juice, season with sea salt and black pepper and toss again. To serve, add a ball or balls of burrata to the pasta and scatter with the remaining walnuts.

For gluten-free • use gluten-free pasta

Veganize: omit the burrata

Substitute • burrata: fresh mozzarella (such as bocconcini), ricotta • walnuts: pine nuts, pistachios

Vegetable swap • cauliflower: broccoli

Ras el Hanout Cauliflower Wedges with Mashed Chickpeas

If a whole roasted cauliflower brings drama and ceremony to the table, serving cauliflower by the wedge is grounded in pragmatism. The smaller-yet-still-substantial segments cook in less time and offer more surface area to be burnished by the oven's rabid heat. The cauliflower is showered with ras el hanout, the heady North African spice blend made of coriander seeds, cumin, ginger, clove, turmeric and more (some blends can have up to 50 spices). Traditionally made using the best ingredients the spice vendor has to offer (*ras el hanout* literally means "head of the shop"), here it brings warmth and richness to the cauliflower. The spiced wedge is served with chunky chickpeas mashed with tahini, garlic, cumin, lemon and herbs—the mixture has strong hummus vibes but is simpler because you don't need to blend it. The texture should be rough and tumble, some chickpeas broken up, others left whole. Importantly, this chickpea mash is akin to msabbcha (also with alternative spellings including masabacha, musabbaha, musbacha), a dish that pioneering cookbook author Paula Wolfert dubbed "deconstructed hummus."

SERVES 4

1 head of cauliflower (about 2 lb/900 g), stem end trimmed

extra-virgin olive oil

4 teaspoons ras el hanout

sea salt and black pepper

4 teaspoons red wine vinegar

handful of parsley or dill, to serve

Mashed chickpeas

½ cup (130 g) tahini

juice of 1 lemon (2–3 tablespoons)

2 garlic cloves, grated

½ teaspoon ground cumin

3 cups (500 g) cooked chickpeas (about two 15 oz/425 g cans, drained)

sea salt and black pepper

¼ cup chopped parsley or dill

1 tablespoon extra-virgin olive oil

Preheat the oven to 450°F (230°C).

Place the cauliflower, stem-side down, on a cutting board and cut it into four equal-sized wedges. Arrange the cauliflower wedges on a sheet pan, drizzle with a generous amount of olive oil, add the ras el hanout and season well with sea salt and black pepper. Massage the oil and seasonings into the cauliflower so the wedges are well coated. Place in the oven and roast for 30–35 minutes, until golden and tender (test for doneness by inserting a skewer or small paring knife into the cauliflower).

Meanwhile, to make the mashed chickpeas, place the tahini, lemon juice, garlic and cumin in a bowl and add ½ cup (120 ml) of water. Whisk until smooth. Mash half the chickpeas—I do this simply by squeezing the chickpeas with my hands, but you can also use a potato masher or fork—then add them to the tahini mixture. Stir to combine, then add the remaining whole chickpeas, along with about 1 teaspoon of sea salt, the parsley or dill and olive oil and season well with black pepper. Taste and adjust the lemon, salt and pepper as needed.

When the cauliflower is ready, remove the pan from the oven and drizzle with the red wine vinegar.

Serve the cauliflower alongside the mashed chickpeas, drizzle everything with a little olive oil and scatter with more parsley or dill.

Gluten-free and vegan

Substitute • ras el hanout: ground cumin, baharat spice • red wine vinegar: lemon juice

Vegetable swap • cauliflower: cabbage

Charred Cauliflower and Crispy Tofu
with Sweet Peanut Sauce

I adore the community of self-assembly meals—the adaptability and the informality in both the process and the result. This salad is one of those, a recipe of separate elements that are anchored on the plate by a sweet, slightly spicy peanut sauce. This dish is most definitely inspired by one of the world's ultimate self-assembly dishes, Indonesia's beloved gado-gado, a name that translates to "mix-mix." There are elements here that are common to gado-gado—cucumber, boiled eggs, bean sprouts and crispy fried onions—but there is also distinction with the inclusion of charred cauliflower and crispy golden tofu, which deliver a mix of crisp textures and overall heartiness. The peanut sauce is one of the easiest you'll make, a truncated satay sauce made simpler with the use of peanut butter.

SERVES 4

extra-virgin olive oil

1 head of cauliflower (about 2 lb/900 g), stem trimmed, and cut into florets

sea salt and black pepper

⅔ cup (75 g) chickpea flour (besan)

½ teaspoon garlic powder or 1 small garlic clove, grated

14 ounces (400 g) extra-firm tofu, sliced into ¼-inch (5–6 mm) thick slices

2 Persian (mini) cucumbers, cut into ¾-inch (2 cm) chunks

4 jammy or medium-boiled large eggs, halved

handful of bean sprouts

handful of crispy fried shallots/onion

1 lime, quartered

Sweet peanut sauce

½ cup (135 g) creamy peanut butter

2 garlic cloves, finely chopped

½ teaspoon red pepper flakes

2½ tablespoons kecap manis

½ teaspoon sea salt

Gluten-free

Veganize: omit the eggs

Substitute • chickpea flour: rice flour, all-purpose flour • extra-firm tofu: marinated five-spice tofu, tofu puffs (both are precooked, so no need to cook)

Vegetable swap • cauliflower: broccoli, Brussels sprouts, potato

Heat a large saucepan over medium-high heat. Add 2 tablespoons of olive oil to the pan and heat for 15 seconds. Working in batches, add the cauliflower florets, making sure not to overcrowd the pan, and fry for 8–10 minutes, turning every few minutes, until charred and tender. Remove from the pan and season with sea salt and black pepper.

Scatter the chickpea flour onto a large plate and add the garlic powder or garlic, ½ teaspoon of sea salt and season with black pepper. Stir to combine. Place each tofu slice in the chickpea flour mixture and toss to coat on both sides.

Wipe out the pan and place again over medium-high heat. Drizzle with 1–2 tablespoons of olive oil and, working in batches, add the tofu slices and fry for 2–3 minutes on each side, until golden and crispy. Remove from the pan and set aside. When cool, cut each tofu slice into triangles.

To make the sweet peanut sauce, place a small saucepan over medium heat and add all the ingredients. Add ¾ cup (180 ml) of water and whisk until smooth and combined. The sauce should be the consistency of thickened cream; if the sauce is still too thick, add another ¼ cup (60 ml) of water and keep whisking until smooth. Remove from the heat. The sauce will thicken over time, so if you aren't using it straight away, add a tablespoon or so of water to loosen it up again.

To serve, place the cauliflower, tofu, cucumber, egg, bean sprouts, crispy fried shallots/onions and lime quarters on a plate. Serve with the peanut sauce on the side or drizzle over the top.

Celery

"Match celery with fellow
big flavors to create delicious
anarchy on the plate."

I think about celery more than I probably should. It's a vegetable that doesn't get the love it deserves and that makes me feel defensive. As I type this now, I have rummaged through the drawer of my fridge and am defiantly munching on a raw celery stick—unadorned, crunchy, perfect.

What I adore about celery is likely what others find divisive. It has a big, complex flavor—salinity, a hint of anise, a slight bitter bite—and leaves a curious tingling sensation on the tongue, like you have just sucked on a breath mint. Celery is unapologetic and gutsy, and therefore it is an essential part of mirepoix, the aromatic vegetable base that begins many soups, sauces, stews and braises. Match celery with fellow big flavors—chile, vinegar, rich sauces—to create delicious anarchy on the plate.

The outer ribs (or stalks) are watery, crisp and stronger in flavor—some people like to peel the fibrous exterior, but I enjoy the sensation of chomping through the stringy facade. Cooking celery will soften the aggressive flavor. The inner ribs are less fibrous and more tender, with a subtle crunch and delicate flavor. Don't forget the leaves—they can be used to make soup or utilized in moderation as a salad leaf or as a garnish.

As F. Scott Fitzgerald said, "Never miss a party . . . good for the nerves—like celery."

Cashew Celery

This uncomplicated-yet-elegant cashew and celery stir-fry offers lovely textures and just enough sauce to make it a perfect with-rice dish. Celery is an ingredient that my mother used often in stir-fries as it perfumes the entire dish and delivers a gratifying crisp-tender crunch. You can use any leafy greens in this dish, but if they have thick stems (like gai lan), make sure you cut them in half, so they cook evenly. Cashews add a creamy nuttiness, but their use in Chinese cooking has health benefits, too (an angle that my mother constantly subscribed to in her everyday cooking)—cashews are said to moisturize the lungs, and are good for treating dry coughs and general colds. Growing up, I didn't pay much heed to my mother's food-as-medicine evangelism, but nowadays I do find myself reaching for cashews whenever my throat feels it's a little dusty.

SERVES 4

2 teaspoons cornstarch

¼ cup (60 ml) vegetable stock or water

4 teaspoons soy sauce or tamari

2½ tablespoons Shaoxing rice wine

neutral oil

4 celery stalks (about 8 oz/225 g), trimmed and sliced diagonally

1-inch (2.5 cm) piece of ginger, peeled and finely chopped

2 garlic cloves, finely chopped

3 green onions, sliced

6 ounces (180 g) greens (gai lan, choy sum, kale, spinach), cut into 2-inch (5 cm) lengths

5 ounces (150 g) five-spice, store-bought marinated or extra-firm tofu, sliced into strips a scant ¼ inch (5 mm) thick

1 cup roasted cashews

toasted white sesame seeds, to serve

white or brown rice, to serve

Combine the cornstarch, stock or water, soy sauce or tamari and Shaoxing rice wine in a bowl and whisk until smooth. Set aside.

Heat a wok or large skillet over medium-high heat. When hot, add 1–2 tablespoons of oil, along with the celery. Toss for 2–3 minutes, until the celery is slightly softened. Push it to the side and add the ginger, garlic and three-quarters of the green onion, then toss for 30 seconds until fragrant. Add the greens, tofu and cashews and toss for 1 minute, until the greens are wilted. Re-stir the cornstarch mixture and swirl it into the wok or pan and toss until the sauce thickens and coats everything.

Top with the remaining green onion, sprinkle with sesame seeds and serve with rice.

For gluten-free • replace the Shaoxing rice wine with dry sherry or white wine

Vegan

Substitute • tofu: shiitake mushrooms

Vegetable swap • celery: kohlrabi

Black Bean, Chinese Celery and Noodle Stir-Fry

Chinese celery, also known as leaf celery, is thought to have originated from a wild form of celery. The stems are thinner, hollow, extremely crunchy and are more strongly perfumed than regular celery. I describe it as "celery, untamed." The stems range from white, to green, to pink and are believed to aid digestion. In Chinese cooking, it can be used as an herb to add flavor to soups, in braised dishes and stir-fries. Its peppery pungency means that it is rarely eaten raw; cooking sweetens and mollifies its flavor. In this recipe, it is stir-fried with dou si (fermented black soybeans), two strong flavors that, together, mellow out and become an irresistible mouthful, especially when tossed with springy, chewy sweet potato starch noodles (the type used for the Korean dish japchae). Though it has a less pronounced flavor, regular celery works here, too—slice it finely into julienne to mimic skinny Chinese celery stems.

SERVES 4

10 ounces (300 g) sweet potato starch noodles

neutral oil

1 pound (450 g) Chinese celery (or regular celery; see recipe intro), cut into 2-inch (5 cm) pieces, tender leaves reserved

1 teaspoon sugar

1 teaspoon sea salt

1 tablespoon toasted white sesame seeds

2 green onions, finely sliced

Black bean sauce

2½ tablespoons black bean sauce

1 garlic clove, grated

4 teaspoons toasted sesame oil

2 teaspoons rice vinegar

Bring a large saucepan of salted water to a boil. Add the noodles and cook according to the package directions, until just tender. Drain and cool under cold water, then drain again.

To make the black bean sauce, combine all the ingredients in a bowl and whisk until smooth.

Heat a wok or large skillet over medium-high heat. When hot, add about 2 tablespoons of oil, along with the celery, sugar and salt. Stir-fry for 3–4 minutes, until the celery is softened and starting to char. Add the sauce and stir-fry with the celery for 1 minute. Add the noodles, along with any tender celery leaves, and toss to coat well. Cook for 2 minutes, until the noodles are heated through. Transfer to bowls and serve topped with the sesame seeds and green onion.

Gluten-free and vegan

Substitute • sweet potato starch noodles: mung bean vermicelli, rice noodles

Vegetable swap • celery: cauliflower, broccoli, zucchini

Celery Leaf Soup

When celery is at its freshest, it will come with a thick head of tender leaves, which should be eaten and enjoyed for their fresh, intense flavor. Celery leaves are highly perfumed, and can be used as an herb or tossed in salads. Or use them to make pesto, of the same ilk as my Fennel Frond Pesto on page 200. But my favorite way to eat them is in this soup, rich with the sweet flavor of green onions, with a hint of spice from ginger. The potatoes add heft and body while also countering the strong flavor of the celery leaves; add more potatoes if you prefer a heavier soup. Of course, if you don't have leaves, you could substitute celery stalks.

SERVES 4

extra-virgin olive oil

4 garlic cloves

6 green onions, roughly chopped, plus more, sliced, to serve

1-inch (2.5 cm) piece of ginger, peeled and finely sliced

2 large potatoes (about 1 lb/450 g), peeled and cut into ⅓-inch (1 cm) cubes

1 teaspoon sugar

sea salt and black pepper

6⅓ cups (1.5 liters) vegetable stock

7 ounces (200 g) celery leaves (or about 1 lb/450 g chopped celery)

chili oil or chili crisp, to serve

Heat a large saucepan over medium-high heat. When hot, add about 2 tablespoons of olive oil, then throw in the garlic, green onion and ginger. Cook for 2 minutes until they have taken on some color, then add the potato, sugar, 1 teaspoon of sea salt, a few turns of black pepper and the vegetable stock and cook for 10 minutes or until the potato is tender. Add the celery leaves and cook for 2–3 minutes, until completely wilted.

Blitz the soup either using a stick blender or by transferring it to a blender or food processor, until it is smooth and light. Taste and season with more sea salt and black pepper, to your liking.

To serve, scatter with sliced green onion and drizzle with chili oil or chili crisp.

Gluten-free and vegan

Marinated Celery
with Couscous and Pickled Golden Raisins

This salad will please crowds and surprise celery dissenters. Marinating the celery tames the strong grassy notes, bringing out a savory side and offering a tender and crisp bite. The pickled golden raisins are tart and fruity, bringing high and low acidic moments, delivering plump pops of tang with every mouthful. While feta is optional, it does bring a sharp saltiness that works beautifully with the other ingredients.

SERVES 4

4 celery stalks (about 8 oz/225 g), finely sliced (reserve any tender leaves)

1 garlic clove, grated

¼ teaspoon red pepper flakes

1 teaspoon cumin seeds or ½ teaspoon ground cumin

4 teaspoons apple cider vinegar

½ teaspoon sugar

extra-virgin olive oil

sea salt and black pepper

1 cup (240 ml) vegetable stock or water

1 cup (190 g) couscous

3½ ounces (100 g) feta, crumbled (optional)

handful of soft herbs (dill, parsley, cilantro, chives), torn

¼ cup roasted almonds, chopped

Pickled golden raisins

½ cup (70 g) golden raisins

¼ cup (60 ml) apple cider vinegar

¼ red onion or 1 shallot, sliced

½ teaspoon sea salt

½ teaspoon sugar

For gluten-free • replace the couscous with quinoa

Vegan

Substitute • couscous: quinoa, farro, pearl couscous • feta: shaved pecorino • golden raisins: sultanas, dried cranberries

Vegetable swap • celery: fennel, cauliflower

In a small bowl, combine the celery, garlic, red pepper flakes, cumin, apple cider vinegar, sugar and 2 tablespoons of olive oil. Season with 1 teaspoon of sea salt and a few turns of black pepper. Toss to combine and leave to marinate for 30–60 minutes at room temperature or overnight in the fridge.

To make the pickled golden raisins, combine all the ingredients in a small bowl. Toss to combine and set aside to pickle for 30 minutes.

Place the vegetable stock or water, 2 tablespoons of olive oil and ½ teaspoon of sea salt in a saucepan and bring to a boil. Remove from the heat and add the couscous to the pan. Stir, then cover and let stand for 5 minutes. Fluff the couscous with a fork and set aside.

In a large serving bowl, place the couscous, marinated celery and all the pickling liquid, the pickled golden raisins (drain off the the raisin pickling liquid but keep it in case the salad needs more acidity), feta (if using) and herbs and toss to combine. Drizzle with 2–3 tablespoons of olive oil, season with sea salt and black pepper and toss again. Taste and, if it needs more acid, add 1–2 tablespoons of the raisin pickling liquid. Top with the almonds and serve at room temperature.

Celery and Vermicelli Spring Rolls

These spring rolls are inspired by Vietnamese chả giò, which are made from rice paper wrappers (bánh tráng) and fried (they are also known as nem rán in northern Vietnam). Every family has their own version of the filling, but it usually includes ground meat mixed with crunchy vegetables. This celery-centric filling is inspired by my mother's voluptuous Chinese spring rolls, which burst with mung bean vermicelli. Chả giò are usually served with nước chấm, Vietnam's beloved salty, sweet and tangy sauce, but for those, like me, who don't eat seafood, my vegan "nearly nước chấm" hits all the familiar umami, zesty notes—make a double batch and use the extra for the Grilled Eggplant and Soba Noodle Salad on page 181. Thank you to Shirley Cai, who helped me get the flavors of this nearly nước chấm sauce right.

MAKES 12

neutral oil

6 celery stalks, finely diced

1 large potato (about 9 oz/250 g), peeled and cut into ¼-inch (6 mm) dice

3 garlic cloves, finely chopped

1-inch (2.5 cm) piece of ginger, peeled and finely chopped

2 teaspoons sugar

sea salt and white pepper

2 green onions, chopped

4 teaspoons soy sauce or tamari

1 teaspoon toasted sesame oil

3½ ounces (100 g) mung bean vermicelli, soaked in warm water for 20 minutes

twelve 8½-inch (22 cm) round dried rice paper wrappers (bánh tráng)

1 romaine lettuce, leaves separated

handful of Asian herbs (Thai basil, mint, Vietnamese mint, cilantro)

Nearly nước chấm (makes about ½ cup)

⅓ cup (80 ml) lime juice

2½ tablespoons brown sugar

4 teaspoons soy sauce or tamari

1 garlic clove, grated

1 fresh Thai red chile, finely sliced

½ teaspoon sea salt

Gluten-free and vegan

Substitute • rice paper wrappers: spring roll wrappers

Vegetable swap • celery: carrot, kohlrabi

Heat a skillet over medium-high heat. When hot, drizzle with 1–2 tablespoons of the neutral oil and add the celery, potato, garlic and ginger. Reduce the heat to medium, add 1 teaspoon of the sugar and ½ teaspoon of sea salt and cook for 3–4 minutes, until the potato is just tender. Turn off the heat and add the green onion, soy sauce or tamari, sesame oil and a pinch of white pepper. Taste and, if needed, add more salt—you want this mixture to be on the salty side because you'll be combining it with the vermicelli.

Drain the mung bean vermicelli and chop it up. Add to the celery mixture and toss well to combine.

In a wide shallow bowl, add about 1 cup (240 ml) of water and the remaining 1 teaspoon of sugar and stir to dissolve (sugar helps the rice paper brown when fried). Dip a rice paper wrapper into the water for about 15 seconds, making sure it's completely submerged. Lift it out, shaking off any excess water (it will be a bit firm but will soften as you work with it) and lay it on a clean flat surface. Place about 1 heaping tablespoon of the filling (don't overfill) close to the edge of the rice paper closest to you, then fold the bottom edge over the filling. Fold in both sides and roll up tightly. Repeat with the remaining wrappers, soaking and filling each one individually. Place the rolls on a plate in the fridge for 10–15 minutes to dry out.

To make the nearly nước chấm sauce, combine all the ingredients in a small bowl.

Heat a saucepan over medium-high heat and add enough oil to reach ¾–1¼ inches (2–3 cm) up the sides of the pan. Test the oil with a wooden chopstick or spoon (when it sizzles, it's ready), then drop 2 or 3 spring rolls into the pan, making sure they don't touch, and fry for 2–3 minutes on each side until golden. Remove from the oil and drain on paper towel. Repeat with the remaining spring rolls. Serve the spring rolls with lettuce leaves, herbs and the nearly nước chấm dipping sauce on the side.

Do ahead: These spring rolls can be fried and left for several hours at room temperature. Fry them again when you are ready to eat.

Tiger Salad with Green Tea Noodles

Take a walk on the bright side with this tiger salad, or lao hu choy (which translates to "tiger vegetables"). The name of this dish is said to refer to the fiery, untamed flavors, concurrently pungent yet fresh and tart. There are many variations of lao hu choy; some include green bell peppers, others cucumber. The tiger salad from Xinjiang, an autonomous region in the northwest of China, is made with tomato, red onion, green chile and cilantro. This recipe takes cues from the Northern Chinese version, celebrating the salty herbaceousness of celery and cilantro. The addition of noodles takes tiger salad from a palate-cleansing side dish to a bold main event. I've used green tea noodles as I love the green-on-green color, but any noodles will work here.

SERVES 4

7 ounces (200 g) green tea noodles

4 celery stalks (about 8 oz/225 g), peeled and finely sliced diagonally

1 small bunch of cilantro (about 1½ oz/40 g), leaves and tender stems cut into 2-inch (5 cm) lengths

1 fresh Thai red or green chile, finely sliced diagonally

4 green onions, finely sliced diagonally

sea salt

Tiger dressing

3 tablespoons rice vinegar

1 teaspoon sea salt

1 tablespoon sugar

2 teaspoons soy sauce or tamari

2 teaspoons toasted sesame oil

Bring a large saucepan of salted water to a boil. Add the noodles and cook according to the package directions until al dente. Drain and refresh under cold water, then drain again.

Meanwhile, make the tiger dressing by whisking together all the ingredients in a small bowl.

In a large bowl, combine the noodles, celery, cilantro leaves and stems, chile, and green onion. Pour the dressing over the top and toss to combine. Taste and season with more sea salt, if needed.

Serve at room temperature or chilled.

Do ahead: This salad can be served cold, so prep the ingredients the day before and store, tightly wrapped, in the fridge. When ready to eat, add the dressing.

Vegan

Substitute • green tea noodles: soba, wheat, egg or somen noodles

---

Vegetable swap • celery: cucumber, green bell pepper

Eggplant

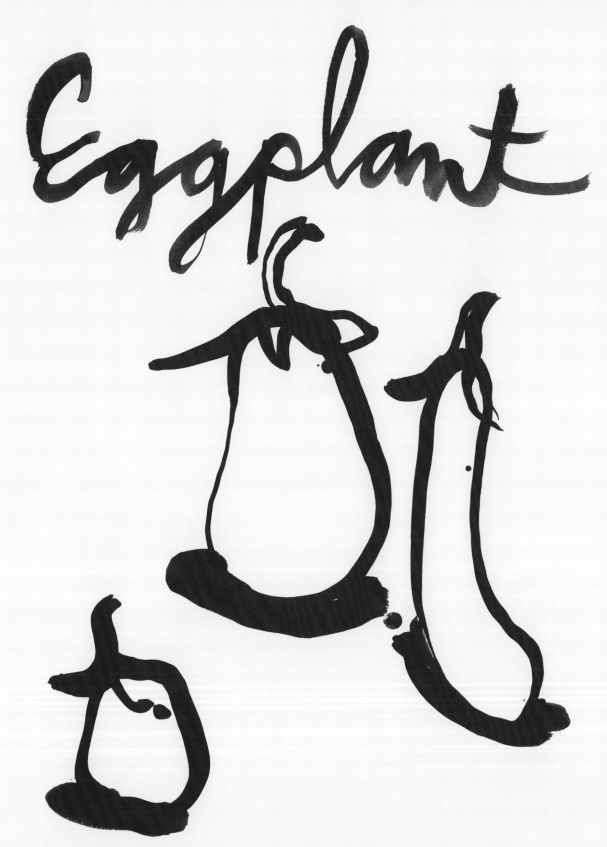

"To dream about eggplant is to wake up hungry. And perhaps in love, too?"

In Japanese culture, hatsuyume is the first dream of the new year, one that is said to foretell the luck of the dreamer for the year ahead. It is said that it is best to dream of *Ichi Fuji, Ni Taka, San Nasubi*—Mount Fuji, Hawk and Eggplant—which all symbolize soaring to great heights. Additionally, the Japanese word for eggplant is *nasu,* which is similar to the words for "to accomplish" or "to fulfill."

In the 16th century, Spaniards called eggplants *berengenas* or "apples of love," while botanists in Northern Europe called the species *mala insana,* or "mad apple" because they thought that eating it would make a person insane. Insanely in love, perhaps?

To dream about eggplant is to wake up hungry. And perhaps in love, too? Eggplants stand apart from the rest. They are completely unique in every way. A member of the nightshade family—along with potato, tomato and bell peppers—eggplants possess a sponge-like flesh that passionately absorbs flavors and becomes lusciously creamy. The flesh is meaty, robust but light, and open to endless adaptation—great in salads, in stews and braised, in pasta, with noodles and, surprisingly, in cake. I am particularly partial to eggplant that is smoky and spicy.

Many people still wonder about the need to salt eggplant prior to cooking. Traditionally, this was a method to draw out bitterness. I almost always skip this step because I find that modern domesticated eggplants no longer offer much bitterness. In a few cases, I will salt the eggplant to draw out moisture, which concentrates the eggplant flavor, while tenderizing it prior to cooking—I find this brings out sweetness, too.

A ripe eggplant will have a smooth, bright, shiny, taut skin. Choose one that is firm, but not so hard that the skin won't spring right back when you press on it. Eggplants that are heavy for their size are at their peak. Soft, soggy eggplants will likely be bitter from age.

Mapo Eggplant

Mapo tofu is one of the first dishes my mother adapted to my vegetarian diet. Her recipe is saucy and lively, with the sharp bite of ja choy (pickled mustard plant stem), delivering a salty, spicy, fermented element. I've adapted her recipe here, in a way that unexpectedly mimics the textures of the original porky dish, while subverting the role and intention of the ingredients. The eggplant becomes silky, replicating the delicate mouthfeel of silken tofu in the traditional dish, while the crumbled extra-firm tofu is robust and hearty, hugging the sauce in the way minced pork does. I like to use Chinese eggplant for this dish—it's less seedy and sweeter—but you could use regular eggplants here by cutting them into thick fingers. Dusting the eggplant in cornstarch and searing it is a crucial step, adding flavor, ensuring that the eggplant stays intact, while also thickening up the sauce.

SERVES 4

2 large Chinese eggplants
(about 14 oz/400 g), cut diagonally
into rounds ½ inch (1.25 cm) thick

1 tablespoon cornstarch

neutral oil

4 dried shiitake mushrooms,
rehydrated in 1½ cups (360 ml)
boiling water

16-ounce (450 g) block of extra-firm
tofu, roughly crumbled

1 teaspoon five-spice powder

sea salt

2 garlic cloves, finely chopped

1-inch (2.5 cm) piece of ginger,
peeled and finely chopped

2½ tablespoons doubanjiang or
black bean sauce

4 green onions, chopped into 2-inch
(5 cm) lengths

2 teaspoons soy sauce or tamari

1 teaspoon sugar

rice, to serve

Place the eggplant in a large bowl and sprinkle with the cornstarch. Using your hands or a large spoon, toss to coat.

Heat a large Dutch oven or deep skillet over medium-high heat. When it's hot, drizzle with oil and arrange as many eggplant rounds as you can fit in a single layer. Sear for 3–4 minutes, until lightly golden, then flip them over and fry the other side; they don't have to be completely cooked at this stage—we just want them to be lightly golden. Remove the eggplant from the pan and set aside.

Remove the shiitake mushrooms from the water, squeezing out any excess liquid. Keep the mushroom soaking water (if there is a lot of sediment in the water, pour it through a fine-mesh sieve to remove). Finely slice the mushrooms.

To the same pan, add 2 tablespoons of oil, along with the tofu, mushrooms, five-spice powder and about 1 teaspoon of sea salt. Cook for 3–5 minutes, stirring every now and then, until the tofu starts to brown. Add the garlic and ginger, stir and cook for 1 minute.

Add the doubanjiang or black bean sauce, green onion and soy sauce or tamari and sauté for 2 minutes until aromatic. Add the eggplant and mushroom soaking water (or substitute water), then reduce the heat to medium, cover and simmer for 5 minutes, until the eggplant is completely softened. Add the sugar and stir, then taste and season with more sea salt, if needed. Serve with rice.

Gluten-free and vegan

Substitute • dried shiitake
mushrooms: fresh shiitake, oyster
or cremini mushrooms

Vegetable swap • eggplant: zucchini

Grilled Eggplant and Soba Noodle Salad
with Nearly Nước Chấm

This recipe is inspired by the lively, fragrant grilled eggplant dishes in Vietnamese cuisine. Here, spongy eggplants are grilled until silky and tender, and then tossed with nearly nước chấm, my piquant vegan take on this foundational Vietnamese sauce. If you are grilling, the eggplant could also be cooked on a griddle for a smoky edge. Load this soba noodle salad with as many herbs as you can handle, for heightened vibrancy and fresh textures. As with all soba noodle salads, I recommend cooking the noodles a day ahead (or at least a few hours prior), tossing in some sesame or neutral oil and storing them in the fridge overnight, as this helps the noodles develop a firmer structure to stand up to the robust dressing.

SERVES 4

7 ounces (200 g) soba noodles

2 large eggplants (about 1¾ lb/800 g)

extra-virgin olive oil

½-inch (1.25 cm) piece of ginger, peeled and grated

1 garlic clove, grated

sea salt and black pepper

½ cup (120 ml) Nearly Nước Chấm (see page 171)

1 cup Asian herb leaves, such as Thai basil, Vietnamese mint, cilantro, green onions, perilla leaves, finely sliced

toasted sesame oil, for drizzling

½ cup roasted peanuts, roughly chopped

Position a rack so the food will be about 2 inches (5 cm) from the heat source and preheat the broiler to high.

Bring a large saucepan of salted water to a boil. Add the soba noodles and cook according to the package directions, until al dente. Drain immediately and run under cold water until the noodles are completely cold. Set aside to drain.

Slice the eggplants into discs ½ inch (1.25 cm) thick, then lay them flat and slice them into batons. Place the eggplant on a sheet pan, drizzle with 2–3 tablespoons of olive oil and add the ginger and garlic. Season well with sea salt and broil for 5 minutes, watching the eggplant closely so it doesn't burn. Flip the eggplant over and broil for another 4–5 minutes, again watching closely, until the eggplant is tender and golden. Remove from the broiler and transfer to a plate. While still warm, pour over the nearly nước chấm and toss to coat.

Combine the eggplant, noodles and herbs in a large bowl and season with sea salt and black pepper. Toss well. Drizzle with sesame oil and serve with the peanuts scattered over the top.

For gluten-free • use rice vermicelli or mung bean vermicelli

Vegan

Vegetable swap • eggplant: mushrooms

Smoky Eggplant and Lentil Stew
with Baked Feta

This oven-baked stew yields the most tender, fall-apart eggplant, bathed in a rich, smoky tomato stew. While I usually skip the salting of eggplants, a largely redundant technique to draw out bitterness and astringency—modern eggplant cultivars are much less bitter—here, salting fulfills a different function. Salt draws out some of the liquid, concentrating the eggplant flavor and seasoning it, while also bringing out its sweet fruitiness. Salt also gives the eggplant a head start on cooking, tenderizing the flesh and ensuring a creamy interior. Of course, if you're in a hurry to put dinner on the table, skip the salt—the results will still impress. The molten feta gets crisp at the edges and adds a tangy saltiness to this rich stew.

SERVES 4

1 pound (450 g) eggplant (any variety), peeled and cut into ¾-inch (2 cm) chunks

sea salt and black pepper

extra-virgin olive oil

2 yellow onions, diced

5 garlic cloves, finely chopped

2½ tablespoons tomato paste

one 28-ounce (800 g) can crushed tomatoes

1 cup (200 g) brown or green lentils

1 teaspoon smoked paprika

1 teaspoon harissa flakes or paste (or ½ teaspoon red pepper flakes)

1 tablespoon brown sugar or maple syrup

2 cups (480 ml) vegetable stock or water

8 ounces (225 g) feta, cut into slices ¼–⅜ inch (5 mm–1 cm) thick

handful of parsley or mint leaves (optional)

bread, flatbread, rice or mashed potatoes, to serve

Preheat the oven to 425°F (220°C).

Place the eggplant in a colander and sprinkle with 1 teaspoon of sea salt. Toss to coat and let drain for 10–15 minutes. Place the eggplant (no need to rinse) in a large deep baking dish, drizzle with 3–4 tablespoons of olive oil and roast for 20 minutes.

Meanwhile, heat a Dutch oven or large saucepan over medium heat. When hot, add 3 tablespoons of olive oil, along with the onion, and cook, stirring often, for 8–10 minutes, until translucent and soft (if the onion is turning golden too quickly, reduce the heat to medium low). Add the garlic and tomato paste and cook for 2 minutes. Add the crushed tomatoes, lentils, paprika, harissa, brown sugar or maple syrup and vegetable stock or water, then season with sea salt and black pepper and stir to combine. Remove the baking dish from the oven and pour the tomato and lentil mixture over the eggplant. Stir to combine and cover with foil. Place the dish on a sheet pan to catch any drips, then return to the oven for 35–40 minutes, until the lentils are plump and tender.

Remove the dish from the oven and turn the broiler to high. Top the stew with the feta slices, drizzle with olive oil and place under the broiler for 4–5 minutes, until the feta is molten and charred in spots—do not walk away; I sit in front of the oven and watch it like a hawk, to prevent the feta from burning.

Top with herbs (if using), and serve with your choice of bread, flatbread, rice or mashed potatoes.

Gluten-free

Veganize • use vegan feta or omit

Substitute • lentils: cooked legumes, such as chickpeas, cannellini beans, black-eyed peas, butter beans, or uncooked farro • feta: Halloumi, mozzarella, cheddar

Eggplant Balls
with Spicy Tamarind Tomato Sauce

This is my version of vegetarian "meatballs," though I rarely think of them this way. To me, they are balls of eggplant perfection, a satisfying snack served with something spicy (as they are here) or a robust addition to a sauced dish. While some people shy away from the slightly gelatinous texture of eggplant, it is this very viscosity that makes them perfect for meatless "balls." This might be the only recipe in which I will ever boil eggplant, but here it ensures that the eggplant is not oil-logged, with enough moisture to bind the other ingredients. The spicy tamarind tomato sauce is tart and slightly sweet, a perfect, tangy dipping sauce. Serve with a salad on the side or add the eggplant balls to a pasta sauce.

SERVES 4

2 large eggplants (about 1¾ lb/800 g), cut into 1-inch (2.5 cm) cubes

1 garlic clove, finely chopped

¼ cup (20 g) nutritional yeast or grated cheddar

½ cup chopped soft herbs, such as parsley, basil, dill or cilantro

1 large egg, lightly beaten or 1 flax egg (see Cook's Notes, page 30)

1 tablespoon Dijon mustard

sea salt and black pepper

3 cups (180 g) panko breadcrumbs

extra-virgin olive oil

rice, couscous or pasta, to serve

Spicy tamarind tomato sauce

extra-virgin olive oil

2 shallots, finely sliced

2 garlic cloves, finely chopped

1-inch (2.5 cm) piece of ginger, peeled and finely chopped

1 tablespoon black mustard seeds

4 teaspoons tamarind paste

¼–½ teaspoon red pepper flakes

one 14.5-ounce (411 g) can diced tomatoes

sea salt

2 teaspoons sugar, plus more to season

For gluten-free • use gluten-free breadcrumbs

Vegan

Substitute • tamarind: lime juice mixed with 1 teaspoon of sugar

Bring a large saucepan of salted water to a boil. Add the eggplant and cook, uncovered and using a wooden spoon to press the eggplant into the water every now and then to keep it submerged, for 10–12 minutes, until tender. When cooked, drain in a colander and use a wooden spoon to press out any excess water.

To make the spicy tamarind tomato sauce, place a saucepan over medium-high heat. When hot, add a generous drizzle of olive oil, along with the shallots. Reduce the heat to medium and cook for 4–5 minutes, until softened. Add the garlic, ginger and mustard seeds and cook for 1 minute. Add the tamarind paste and stir to combine, followed by the red pepper flakes, diced tomatoes, 1 teaspoon of sea salt and the sugar. Add ½ cup (120 ml) of water, then cover and cook for 15 minutes to allow the flavors to meld. When ready, taste and add more salt or sugar if needed—the sauce should be slightly sweet, salty, tangy and spicy.

Place the drained eggplant in a bowl and add the garlic, nutritional yeast or cheddar, soft herbs, egg or flax egg, Dijon mustard, about 2 teaspoons of sea salt, a few turns of black pepper and 2 cups of the breadcrumbs. Using your hands or a large spoon, press the mixture together until well combined. Roll into balls the size of golf balls, then roll each ball in the remaining 1 cup of breadcrumbs. You should get 16–18 balls.

Place a small deep saucepan over medium-high heat and add enough olive oil to come 1¼ inches (3 cm) up the sides of the pan. Test the oil with a wooden chopstick or spoon (when it sizzles, it's ready), then add a few eggplant balls and fry for 2 minutes on each side or until golden. Drain on paper towel. Continue until all the eggplant balls are cooked.

Serve the eggplant balls with the spicy tamarind tomato sauce and your choice of rice, couscous or pasta.

Eggplant Katsu

This eggplant katsu is my vegetarian take on the beloved Japanese dish of panko-encrusted meat cutlets, usually chicken but sometimes pork. It is traditional to use panko, a coarser-textured crumb, resulting in maximum crispiness (at a pinch, regular breadcrumbs will work, too). The eggplant is the perfect vegetable to give the "katsu" treatment—the super-crispy crumb beautifully complements the creamy flesh inside. The dish is usually served with a tonkatsu sauce, a thick brown sauce that is often sold in bottles and labeled as "fruit and vegetable sauce"—it is akin to a sweeter and thicker version of Worcestershire sauce. This quick homemade version is without Worcestershire (which contains anchovies) but just as complexly flavored. Turn this into an eggplant katsu curry by serving with the Japanese Turnip Curry on page 472.

SERVES 4

3 cups (180 g) panko breadcrumbs

sea salt and black pepper

½ cup plus 2 tablespoons (75 g) all-purpose or buckwheat flour

4 teaspoons cornstarch

1 teaspoon baking powder

2 large eggplants (about 1¾ lb/800 g), sliced into discs ⅜ inch (1 cm) thick

neutral oil

¼ head green cabbage (about 7 oz/200 g), finely sliced

1 lemon, quartered

2 green onions, finely sliced

white rice, to serve

"Tonkatsu" sauce

¼ cup (65 g) ketchup

1 teaspoon sugar

2 tablespoons soy sauce or tamari

¼ teaspoon garlic powder or 1 small garlic clove, grated

1 teaspoon balsamic vinegar

Place the panko breadcrumbs in a shallow bowl and add 1 teaspoon of sea salt and a few turns of black pepper. Toss to combine.

Prepare the batter by combining the all-purpose flour or buckwheat flour, cornstarch, baking powder and 1 teaspoon of sea salt in a bowl. Add ¾ cup (180 ml) of room temperature water and whisk until smooth.

Dip each piece of eggplant into the batter, holding it over the bowl to allow any excess batter to drip off, then place it in the breadcrumbs and toss to coat well. Place the eggplant on a plate and continue until all the eggplant is crumbed.

Heat a large, deep skillet over medium-high heat. When hot, add enough oil to generously cover the bottom of the pan and place a few slices of eggplant into the oil so they sit in a single layer—don't overcrowd (you will need to fry in batches). Reduce the heat to medium and pan-fry the eggplant for 2–3 minutes, until the bottom is golden and crispy. Flip over and repeat on the other side. Pan-fry the remaining eggplant.

Meanwhile, make the tonkatsu sauce by combining all the ingredients in a small bowl and mixing well.

Divide the cabbage and lemon wedges among four plates. Place a few pieces of eggplant katsu on each plate and top with the tonkatsu sauce and green onion. Serve with rice on the side.

For gluten-free • use gluten-free breadcrumbs and buckwheat flour

Vegan

Creamy Whole Roasted Eggplant
with Tomato and Lentil Sauce

This dish is engineered as a deconstructed moussaka, of sorts. It's a loose interpretation though—there's eggplant, a tomato and lentil sauce and a creamy element—but it's an easy-going dish that comes together rather effortlessly. Roasted whole at high heat, the eggplant stays moist and succulent, the flesh becomes melty. The skin acts like a protective force field, preventing flavor from escaping, keeping all the earthy goodness within, while also imparting a smokiness. The cashew cream is velvety yet light and adds a pleasing mellow sweetness. Apart from the brief hot soak, the cashew cream takes mere minutes to make, but if you are short on time or ingredients, see the time-saving notes below. This is a very eggplant-forward recipe that is also completely agreeable to eggplant fence-sitters. If you are enjoying this dish on its own, I recommend one eggplant per person; if you are eating it with rice, pasta, grains or bread, then one eggplant will be enough for two people—but allow your hunger to dictate.

SERVES 4

2–4 large eggplants (about 14 oz/400 g each)

extra-virgin olive oil

1 yellow onion, finely diced

4 garlic cloves, finely chopped

¼ cup chopped dill, plus sprigs to serve

½ teaspoon red pepper flakes

one 14.5-ounce (411 g) can crushed tomatoes

½ cup (100 g) brown lentils

2 cups (480 ml) vegetable stock

1 teaspoon sea salt

½ teaspoon sugar

mint leaves, to serve (optional)

1 lemon, halved

Cashew cream

1 cup raw cashews

1 cup (240 ml) boiling water

¾ cup (180 ml) vegetable stock

1 garlic clove, roughly chopped

sea salt and black pepper

Gluten-free and vegan

Substitute • dill: mint, parsley • lentils: chickpeas, cannellini beans, black-eyed peas

Vegetable swap • eggplant: zucchini

Soak the cashews for the cashew cream in the boiling water for 10–15 minutes while you prepare the other ingredients.

Preheat the oven to 425°F (220°C). Line a sheet pan with parchment paper.

Prick the eggplants all over with a fork and place on the prepared pan. Drizzle with olive oil, then transfer to the oven and roast for 45 minutes, turning the eggplants halfway through cooking.

Meanwhile, heat a large saucepan over medium-high heat. Add about 2 tablespoons of olive oil, along with the onion, and stir for 2–3 minutes, until softened. Add the garlic, dill and red pepper flakes and stir for 30 seconds. Add the tomatoes, lentils, vegetable stock, sea salt and sugar, then cover and reduce the heat to medium. Cook for 20–25 minutes, until the lentils are tender.

To make the cashew cream, drain the soaked cashews. Add them to a blender or food processor, along with the vegetable stock, garlic and about 1 teaspoon of sea salt and a few turns of black pepper. Puree for 30–60 seconds (or longer, it will depend upon how powerful your blender is), until completely smooth and silky. If it's too thick, add a touch of water. Taste and add more sea salt or black pepper, if required.

Remove the eggplants from the oven and allow to cool for a few minutes. Slice them lengthwise through the center and place them on a plate, cut-side up. Using a fork, rough up the flesh by dragging the fork up and down—this will loosen the flesh from the skin and allow the sauce to penetrate.

To serve, ladle some of the tomato and lentil sauce into each eggplant half and top with the cashew cream, a few dill sprigs, mint leaves (if using), a squeeze of lemon juice and a drizzle of olive oil.

Notes: Save time by skipping the cashew cream and topping the eggplant with crumbled feta or ricotta.

Another time-saver: skip the tomato and lentil sauce and simply combine a store-bought tomato-based pasta sauce with canned lentils.

I usually eat the eggplant flesh and topping only, discarding the skin. But you do you.

Eggplant, "Char Siu" Style

Char siu, the strips of barbecued roast pork with their signature crimson exterior, is a treasured Cantonese meat, and the most popular siu mei dish. Siu mei is a term that refers to the roasted meats popular in Hong Kong, but also commonly found in Chinatown windows around the world. Most city-dwelling Cantonese kids grew up eating siu mei—during my carnivorous youth, as my mother arrived home from the store, I would sidle up with my best good-daughter-face and charm a few slices of warm, juicy char siu and crispy pork crackling before dinnertime. In this recipe, eggplant is marinated, char siu style, in a fragrant, fruity barbecue sauce. Eggplant, a renowned carrier of flavor, greedily absorbs the sauce before it is roasted at high heat, emerging sweet and silky, imbued with lots of dark, caramelized notes. A note for gluten-intolerant cooks: make sure your hoisin sauce is gluten-free or use the homemade version on page 151. This marinade is incredibly versatile and can be used to marinate and roast firm tofu and other vegetables in the exact same way. This is best eaten with rice, of course, but it's also good stuffed into a crusty roll with cilantro, mint and salad greens, or used to make eggplant char siu bao (there's a bao recipe in *To Asia, With Love*).

SERVES 4

2 large eggplants (about 1 ¾ lb/800 g), sliced into discs ⅜ inch (1 cm) thick

extra-virgin olive oil

sea salt

rice, to serve

2 green onions, finely sliced, for topping

toasted white sesame seeds, to serve

Char siu sauce

2 small garlic cloves, grated

¼ cup (60 ml) hoisin sauce

4 teaspoons soy sauce or tamari

4 teaspoons maple syrup

2 teaspoons rice vinegar or Shaoxing rice wine

1 teaspoon five-spice powder

To make the char siu sauce, whisk together all the ingredients in a large bowl. Add the eggplant slices and marinate for 30–60 minutes or up to 4 hours in the fridge.

Preheat the oven to 400°F (200°C). Line a sheet pan with parchment paper.

Lay the marinated eggplant slices on the prepared pan, drizzle with olive oil and roast for 15 minutes. Remove the pan from the oven and flip the eggplant over. Using a pastry brush, baste each slice with the marinade and drizzle with more olive oil, then return to the oven and roast for another 15 minutes. When cooked, brush the tops of the eggplant slices with more of the marinade and season well with sea salt.

Serve the eggplant with rice, topped with the green onion and sesame seeds.

Gluten-free and vegan

Substitute • maple syrup: honey, brown sugar

Vegetable swap • eggplant: cauliflower, mushrooms, extra-firm tofu

Chocolate-Eggplant Brownie

Many years ago, a friend gave me an uncredited recipe printed from the internet for something called Chocolate Heartbreak Cake. The rich, super-moist chocolate cake tasted like any other, except it curiously contained a whole eggplant. I gleefully made this recipe for my family, buoyed by the knowledge that the cake was the keeper of secrets. I was never the parent to disguise vegetables in food for my kids, but with eggplant a polarizing vegetable to my then-young children, this felt like a victory. Years later, after some research, I discovered that this unusual chocolate cake recipe was from a cookbook by Harry Eastwood called *Red Velvet & Chocolate Heartache*, which used vegetables to replace the fats in recipes. This brownie is inspired by that cake, but I've gone even further and made it gluten-free and vegan. The result is a lush, fudgy brownie, fiercely chocolatey and irresistibly nutty from the almonds.

MAKES SIXTEEN 2-INCH (5 CM) SQUARES

1 large eggplant (about 14 oz/400 g)

1¼ cups (250 g) dark chocolate chips (vegan or regular)

¾ cup (150 g) brown sugar

1 cup (110 g) almond flour

½ cup plus 2 tablespoons (50 g) cocoa powder

1 teaspoon baking powder

1 teaspoon sea salt

½ cup (50 g) sliced almonds

Preheat the oven to 400°F (200°C). Grease an 8-inch (20 cm) square baking pan (or a smaller pan if you want thicker brownies) with cooking spray and line with parchment paper. Line a sheet pan with foil.

Prick the eggplant all over with a fork, then slice in half lengthwise through the stem. Place the eggplant, cut-side down, on the lined pan, then transfer to the oven and roast for 30–40 minutes, until the eggplant feels very soft to the touch. Remove from the oven and allow the eggplant to cool for a few minutes until you can handle it comfortably. Using a large spoon, scoop out the soft flesh and discard the skin. There are faster ways to cook your eggplant—you could peel, cube and steam it for 8–10 minutes, or microwave on high for 8 minutes.

Place the hot eggplant in a bowl and add 1 cup of the chocolate chips. Stir until the chocolate is melted. Add the brown sugar and stir vigorously until the sugar is dissolved and the mixture is glossy.

Place the almond flour, cocoa powder, baking powder and sea salt in a small bowl and whisk to combine.

Add the dry ingredients to the chocolate-eggplant mixture and fold well, until everything is combined. Pour the batter into the prepared pan and spread evenly. Top with the almonds and remaining ¼ cup of chocolate chips.

Transfer to the oven and bake for 30–35 minutes, until the sides of the brownie look puffed and the surface feels firm to the touch. Remove the pan from the oven and allow to cool completely, then cut into 16 squares. These brownies are soft and fudgy—place them in the fridge for a few hours or overnight for a firmer texture.

Storage: These brownies keep well in the fridge for about 4 days.

Gluten-free and vegan

Substitute • almond flour: other nut flour, almond meal, gluten-free all-purpose flour, all-purpose flour • flaked almonds: walnuts, hazelnuts

Vegetable swap • eggplant: sweet potato

Fennel

"Honestly, it was easy to fall head over heels for this charismatic bulb."

The town of Marathon in Greece is named after wild fennel—máratho or márathos in Greek—which grew abundantly in the area. Here, around 490 BCE, the Greeks won a momentous battle against the invading Persian army, a victory that gave rise to hundreds of years of Greek advancement. After the triumph, a herald named Pheidippides ran the 42 kilometers (26.1 miles) from Marathon to Athens to announce the victory, thus inspiring the idea of the modern marathon.

My love for fennel began later in life. I can't precisely recall my first time with fennel, but I surmise it was sometime in my twenties and it was most likely in the form of a salad, tossed with orange segments and black olives, and laved in olive oil. Honestly, it was easy to fall head over heels for this charismatic bulb. This dish remains one of the most-loved salads in our family.

Sweet with the flavor of mild anise, with a refreshingly crisp bite, fennel is edible from root to stem. The bulb and stalks can be eaten raw or cooked, and I'm particularly partial to pickling them. The frilly fronds (the leaves) can be used as you would any herb, as a fresh way to finish a dish, or to make herbaceous pestos or scented oils. I like to crisp up the fronds in a skillet—it's a great snack and a perfect way to finish a soup or salad.

Choose fennel bulbs that are heavy for their size—indicating lots of moisture—with a smooth outer layer. If your fennel isn't perfect on the outside, simply remove the outer layer. Fennel and baby fennel can be used interchangeably. Keep in mind, many people—including my kids—prefer raw fennel to cooked, which is sweeter and mellower.

Fennel Frond Pesto

Billowing, feathery fennel fronds can be transformed into a delicious pesto, with a mellow anise flavor that does not overpower. The first time I tried fennel frond pesto was during quarantine, when fresh vegetables became a precious commodity and using the whole vegetable was a necessity. During the first lockdown of 2020, my friend Lisa Marie Corso sent me her recipe for fennel frond pesto, and it was incredibly eye-opening—a vibrantly green, grassy sauce that didn't taste distinctly of fennel, much smoother than other "vegetable top" pesto mixes. I've been experimenting with different versions of fennel frond pesto ever since, sometimes with other herbs or leaves added, often without cheese, or with different nuts and seeds. This is my favorite recipe, incorporating toasted pumpkin seeds, which add a mild nuttiness and gentle sweetness. Serve with pasta, roasted vegetables, on grain bowls or as a salad dressing (see page 203).

MAKES 1½ CUPS

about 2½ cups (150 g) fennel fronds

4 garlic cloves, roughly chopped

½ cup toasted pumpkin seeds

sea salt

1 cup (240 ml) extra-virgin olive oil

1¾ ounces (50 g) hard cheese, such as cheddar, parmesan or pecorino, finely grated

Place the fennel fronds, garlic and pumpkin seeds in a blender and pulse a few times to chop everything up. Add about 1 teaspoon of sea salt, along with the olive oil, and blitz until you have a coarse paste. Transfer to a bowl and stir in the cheese. Taste and add more sea salt, if needed.

Storage: This pesto will keep in an airtight container in the fridge for up to 2 weeks, or freeze in a container or resealable bag for up to 3 months.

Gluten-free

Veganize • replace the hard cheese with 2–3 tablespoons of nutritional yeast or 1–2 tablespoons of miso

Substitute • pumpkin seeds: walnuts, pine nuts, sunflower seeds

Fennel and Gnocchi Salad
with Fennel Frond Pesto

Here is a lovely double fennel salad, a wonderful way to show how we can create an entire meal around one vegetable: crunchy shaved raw fennel is slathered in fennel frond pesto and tossed with crispy morsels of pan-fried gnocchi. This salad shows how anise flavors can be layered without overthrowing the other ingredients or dominating the overall dish. This is an adaptable recipe, too—add some roasted broccoli or cauliflower, incorporate a leafy green, such as baby spinach or watercress, or substitute a filled pasta like tortellini or ravioli for the gnocchi. You could also use a short pasta shape in place of the gnocchi. You can use either vacuum-sealed or frozen gnocchi—if using frozen, don't thaw it first! I like to use baby fennel in this salad because they are sweeter and more tender, but regular fennel works just fine.

SERVES 4

extra-virgin olive oil

1 pound 10 ounces (750 g) gnocchi

sea salt and black pepper

2 baby fennel bulbs (about 13 oz/375 g) or 1 regular fennel bulb (about 12 oz/350 g), finely sliced

¾–1 cup Fennel Frond Pesto (see page 200)

handful of grated parmesan, pecorino or cheddar

Place a large skillet over medium-high heat. When hot, drizzle in 2–3 tablespoons of olive oil, add the gnocchi and season with a pinch of sea salt. Pan-fry for 3–4 minutes, tossing the gnocchi often, until golden on both sides.

Transfer the gnocchi to a large serving plate, add the fennel and fennel frond pesto and toss until well coated. Serve with a handful of grated cheese on top.

For gluten-free • use gluten-free gnocchi

Veganize • use vegan cheese

Substitute • gnocchi: boiled or roasted potatoes • parmesan, pecorino or cheddar: nutritional yeast

Fennel and Black Olive Fried Rice

Fennel and olives are not obvious inclusions in fried rice, but together they add a lovely earthy saltiness to this dish. Black, wrinkly olives have a natural anise flavor, which make them a perfect match for fennel. The use of olives in fried rice originates from Thailand, with a dish called kao pad nahm liap. Olives are called *magok* in Thailand, and some believe that Bangkok is named after this fruit, which was brought to Southeast Asia by Chinese immigrants who settled in Thailand, the Malay Peninsula and Singapore. I love this rendition of fried rice, with a freshness and salad-like feel that comes from the sliced fennel, cucumber, chile, nuts and herbs.

SERVES 4

3 large eggs

sea salt and white pepper

extra-virgin olive oil

1 shallot, finely diced

1 fennel bulb (about 12 oz/350 g), finely diced, fronds reserved

3 garlic cloves, finely chopped

3½ ounces (100 g) black wrinkly olives, pitted and chopped

5 cups (750 g) cold cooked rice (leftover rice is perfect)

2 green onions, finely sliced

To serve

1 fennel bulb (about 12 oz/350 g), finely sliced

2 Persian (mini) cucumbers, finely sliced

1–2 fresh Thai green or red chiles, sliced

½ cup roasted cashews or peanuts

handful of cilantro leaves

Add the eggs to a bowl and whisk until the whites and yolks are well combined. Season with ½ teaspoon of sea salt and a pinch of white pepper. Heat a wok or large skillet over medium-high heat. When hot, add about 1 tablespoon of olive oil, then add the egg and let it sizzle for a few seconds. Move the egg around the pan until it is just set, then remove from the pan and set aside.

Place the same wok or skillet back over medium-high heat, then add a good drizzle of olive oil, along with the shallot. Stir-fry for 1 minute or until tender, then add the diced fennel, garlic and olives and stir-fry for 1–2 minutes, until the fennel is softened. Add the rice, drizzle with more olive oil, then reduce the heat to medium and stir-fry until the rice is hot and crispy in some parts. Add the egg to the rice, season generously with sea salt and white pepper and toss well. Turn off the heat and scatter with the green onion and fennel fronds.

Serve the rice alongside the finely sliced raw fennel, cucumber, chile, roasted cashews or peanuts and cilantro leaves.

Gluten-free

Veganize • omit the eggs

Substitute • egg: cubed extra-firm tofu

Vegetable swap • fennel: broccoli, cauliflower, Brussels sprouts

Fennel, Orange and Halloumi Grain Salad

Around our family table, the classic Italian pairing of fennel and orange is a salad that gets devoured without question. Alive with grassy anise and lively citrus notes, this recipe brings hearty grains and Halloumi to the mix, to make a substantial main meal. The texture of this salad is especially pleasing: juicy oranges, crunchy raw fennel, chewy grains and squeaky cheese combine in every bite to create a joyous mouthful. If you have one, use a mandoline to deliver the finest slices of fennel, and when in season consider using blood oranges to provide a tart, slightly bitter note. If you're looking for more punchiness, add a few black olives, shaved red onion, Belgian endive or radicchio leaves or top with pomegranate seeds.

SERVES 4

1 cup (200 g) pearl barley, farro or freekeh grains

sea salt and black pepper

3 blood or regular oranges

extra-virgin olive oil

8-ounce (225 g) block of Halloumi, drained, patted dry and cut into slices about ¼ inch (6–7 mm) thick

1 fennel bulb (about 12 oz/350 g), finely sliced, fronds reserved

handful of chopped or torn soft herbs, such as parsley, chives, green onions, dill or basil

Lemon dressing

1 garlic clove, grated

2½ tablespoons lemon juice (from 1 lemon)

¼ cup (60 ml) extra-virgin olive oil

2 teaspoons honey

½ teaspoon sea salt

Place the grains in a saucepan with 2–3 cups (480–720 ml) of water. Add 1 teaspoon of sea salt and bring to a boil over medium-high heat. Reduce the heat to low, cover and cook according to the package directions, until just tender. Drain and set aside to cool slightly.

To make the lemon dressing, whisk together all the ingredients in a small bowl.

Cut the top and bottom off the oranges, so they sit flat on a cutting board. Starting from the top, slice off a section of the peel, making sure to remove as much of the white pith as possible, and work your way around each orange until all the peel is removed. Lay the oranges on their side and cut them into rounds about ¼ inch (5–7 mm) thick. Reserve any juice from the cutting board.

Heat a skillet over medium-high heat. When hot, add a drizzle of olive oil and lay the Halloumi in the pan, in a single layer. Fry for 1–1½ minutes, until golden, then flip over and repeat. Remove from the pan and set aside.

In a large serving bowl, place the grains, orange slices and any reserved juice, the fennel and fennel fronds, herbs and the dressing. Toss to combine. Taste and season with sea salt and black pepper. Top with the Halloumi slices and serve immediately.

For gluten-free • replace the grains with quinoa or brown rice

Veganize • omit the cheese

Substitute • Halloumi: feta, mozzarella, burrata, shaved parmesan • lemon juice: white wine vinegar, apple cider vinegar

Fennel and Lentil Avgolemono Soup

Avgolemono, or egg–lemon, is the name for a group of sauces and soups made with eggs and lemon used to thicken and flavor a broth. Though widely regarded as a Greek dish, it has origins in Sephardic Jewish cuisines where it is known as agristada. Egg yolk–enriched sauces are also common in Turkish, Italian, Arabic and Balkan cuisines. Avgolemono soup is usually made with chicken and rice or orzo. This is my vegetarian version, a sunny, silky, lemon-scented soup, which sparkles with anise overtones of fennel. If you are lucky enough to have a fennel bulb with bountiful fronds, make the garlicky charred fronds to top the soup—they become crunchy and smoky, with a slight anise flavor, and are a beautiful way to finish this soup (they are also good enough to eat on their own). I adore the addition of lentils here, adding body and oomph, without the heaviness.

SERVES 4

extra-virgin olive oil

1 yellow onion, finely chopped

2 celery stalks (about 3½ oz/100 g), finely chopped

1 fennel bulb (about 12 oz/350 g), finely chopped, fronds reserved

3 garlic cloves, finely chopped

1 teaspoon dried thyme

1 teaspoon dried oregano

6⅓ cups (1.5 liters) vegetable stock

¼ cup (50 g) Puy (French) lentils

sea salt and black pepper

2½ tablespoons white (shiro) miso

3 large eggs

¼ cup (60 ml) lemon juice (from about 2 lemons)

Charred garlicky fennel fronds (optional)

extra-virgin olive oil

3½ ounces (100 g) fennel fronds

2 garlic cloves, finely chopped

sea salt and black pepper

Heat a Dutch oven or large saucepan over medium-high heat. Add 1–2 tablespoons of olive oil, along with the onion. Cook for 2–3 minutes, until softened, then reduce the heat to medium, add the celery, chopped fennel, garlic, thyme and oregano and cook for 2 minutes. Add the vegetable stock, lentils, 1 teaspoon of sea salt and season with black pepper. Cover and cook for 15 minutes, then check that the lentils are cooked; if not, cover again and cook for another 5–10 minutes over low heat, just until the lentils are tender.

If you have enough fronds to make the charred garlicky fennel fronds, heat a skillet over medium-high heat. Add 2 tablespoons of olive oil, the fennel fronds and garlic and stir occasionally, letting the delicate leaves char. Reduce the heat to medium and cook for 6–8 minutes, until most of the leaves are charred and crispy. Season with sea salt and black pepper.

When the lentils are tender, add the miso to the soup and stir well to combine. Taste and season with sea salt and black pepper.

Add the eggs to a spouted measuring cup or bowl. Whisk until the egg is frothy and slightly lighter in color, about 2 minutes. Add the lemon juice and whisk to combine well. Slowly add 3 tablespoons of the hot soup into the egg-lemon mixture, whisking constantly, to temper the egg (this will increase the temperature of the egg slightly and reduce the risk of curdling at the next step). Very carefully add the egg mixture to the soup, whisking vigorously and constantly, until completely combined. Reduce the heat to low and cook, stirring constantly, until the soup is thick enough to lightly coat a spoon, about 5 minutes; do not let the soup reach a simmer.

To serve, ladle the soup into bowls and top with the charred garlicky fennel fronds (if using) and a generous drizzle of olive oil.

Serving suggestion: Top with crumbled feta.

Gluten-free

Substitute • charred garlicky fennel fronds: fresh dill • lentils: cooked chickpeas

Vegetable swap • fennel: celery, celeriac, potato

Fennel Quickles

These fennel "quickles" (quick pickles) are tangy and slightly sweet, refreshingly jaunty as a snack or as part of a larger meal. Best of all, thanks to the thin shards of fennel, the pickling is swift and, in most cases, it will be ready by the time you have prepared the rest of your ingredients. A perfect addition to noodle bowls, sandwiches and grilled cheese, and salads.

MAKES 1½–2 CUPS

1 fennel bulb (about 12 oz/350 g), very finely shaved

½ cup (120 ml) rice vinegar or apple cider vinegar

2 teaspoons sea salt

2½ tablespoons sugar

1 teaspoon fennel seeds

1 teaspoon black mustard seeds

Place the fennel in a nonreactive (not metal) bowl or clean jar. Add the vinegar, sea salt, sugar, fennel seeds, black mustard seeds and ½ cup (120 ml) of water to a small saucepan. Set over medium-low heat, stirring, until the sugar dissolves. Take off the heat immediately and pour the pickling liquid over the fennel. Leave the fennel to pickle for a minimum of 15 minutes.

Use in salads (see page 212 for the Pickled Fennel Niçoise) and store in a jar in the fridge for up to 3 months (it will continue to pickle).

Gluten-free and vegan

Vegetable swap • fennel: finely shaved radish, turnip, cauliflower

Pickled Fennel Niçoise

Originating from Nice in the Provence-Alpes-Côte d'Azur region, salade niçoise is a mixed salad, traditionally featuring raw vegetables to showcase the quality of Provençal produce. Today, the salad has many faces, with additions that may include some, but not all, of the following: tomatoes, black olives, capers, green beans, boiled eggs and potatoes, and it is commonly served with tuna or anchovies. This version is definitely not traditional, but the briny-ness of the quick-pickled fennel and the caper vinaigrette feels right. The sharp fennel, salty olives and tangy dressing work well with the mellow beans, potatoes, eggs and cucumber. The Fennel Quickles (see page 210) take just moments to come together and will be ready in the time it takes you to prepare the vegetables and dressing.

SERVES 4

4 large eggs

sea salt

10 ounces (300 g) green beans, trimmed

1½ pounds (700 g) baby potatoes, peeled and halved

2 Persian (mini) cucumbers (about 7 oz/200 g), sliced diagonally

1 cup (150 g) black olives, pitted

Fennel Quickles (see page 210)

Caper vinaigrette

1 tablespoon capers, rinsed and finely chopped

1 garlic clove, grated

4 teaspoons lemon juice (from about ½ lemon)

¼ cup (60 ml) extra-virgin olive oil

½ teaspoon sugar

½ teaspoon sea salt

black pepper

Bring a saucepan of water to a boil. Add the eggs and set the timer for 8 minutes. As soon as you hear the timer, remove the eggs using a large slotted spoon (keep the water, don't pour it away) and either plunge the eggs into an ice bath or run them under cold water until completely cold. Peel them and slice.

To the same pan of water, add 2–3 teaspoons of sea salt. Add the green beans and cook for 3–4 minutes, until the beans are bright green and crisp-tender. Using tongs, remove them from the water and place in a colander in the sink. Run under cold water until the beans are cold.

Add the potatoes to the boiling water and cook for 10–12 minutes, until just tender. Remove the potatoes using a slotted spoon and place in the colander to drain.

To make the caper vinaigrette, combine all the ingredients in a bowl. Add 1 tablespoon of water and stir to combine.

To serve, place the green beans, potatoes, egg, cucumber, black olives and pickled fennel on a serving plate. Drizzle with the dressing and serve immediately.

Gluten-free

Veganize • omit the eggs

Substitute • potatoes: croutons, cauliflower • green beans: sugar snap peas, snow peas

Vegetable swap • fennel: finely sliced carrot, celery, daikon

Fennel and Black Pepper Ice Cream

Fennel has a mild sweetness that imparts a considered complexity to desserts. In this simple no-churn ice cream, a small fennel bulb is pureed with sweetened condensed milk, bestowing a whisper of anise, along with a delicate, understated herbaceousness. This dessert dances with savoriness—the black pepper adds just a hint of piquant earthiness, while a little extra-virgin olive oil delivers richness and a fruity edge.

SERVES 4–6

1 small fennel bulb (about 7 oz/200 g), finely sliced, fronds reserved to serve

1 teaspoon fennel seeds

½ teaspoon freshly ground black pepper, plus more to serve

one 14-ounce (395 g) can sweetened condensed milk (regular or vegan)

1 cup (240 ml) heavy cream or vegan coconut cream

1 tablespoon extra-virgin olive oil, plus more for drizzling

Place all the ingredients in a high-speed blender or food processor and whiz until smooth. Pour the creamy mixture into a small loaf pan or dish that measures approximately 8½ × 4¾ inches (22 cm × 12 cm), cover with plastic or reusable wrap and freeze for at least 3–4 hours, until firm.

To serve, let the ice cream stand at room temperature for 5 minutes (to make scooping easier) and top with a drizzle of olive oil, a few fennel fronds and a few turns of freshly ground black pepper.

Gluten-free and vegan

Ginger

"My mother had a mammoth jar of
pickling ginger in our laundry room."

My mother had a mammoth jar of pickling ginger in our laundry room. It sat in a nook, next to the barrel of potatoes. When I was younger, I would sit and stare at the jar, mesmerized by the knobbly, knotted roots suspended within clear fluid. I recently asked her about these pickles and she explained that they were ji geung (young ginger). Young ginger, sometimes called spring ginger, is an ephemeral treat of the seasons—it appears most commonly during the spring, but I've also seen varieties crop up in early autumn. Mild and tender, young ginger has a paper-like translucent skin that is so thin, it can be rubbed off.

I asked my mother for the recipe. In her own words:

The pickles must be made with young ginger. Rub or scrape off the skin and dunk the ginger into a pot of boiling water. Remove the ginger from the water with a slotted ladle and then immediately submerge the ginger back into the boiling water. This process prevents molding. Drain the ginger. In a large pot, heat some white vinegar, add some white sugar until sweet enough and then add some salt, too. The salt is crucial, to bring out the ginger flavor. Let the vinegar cool completely and then add the ginger to the pickling liqud. Transfer to a clean, sterilized jar. Seal tightly. Serve, thinly sliced with pidan (century egg). Stores for two years.

Note, there are no measurements. I didn't ask for more. I would feel my way with this one—you should, too.

Fried Ginger and Charred Green Onion
E Fu Noodles

E fu noodles, sometimes called yi mian or longevity noodles, are a distinctive noodle sold in prefried and dried cakes. When cooked, they become slightly chewy and spongy, a texture unlike other noodles. Cantonese in origin, and symbolizing long life, it is no surprise that e fu noodles are often served at formal dinners and celebrations. During the Chinese banquets of my youth, when our patience and waistlines were tested over eight or nine courses, we would be rewarded with a final savory course of saucy lobster, served on top of e fu noodles. The sweet lobster was the prize for many but, for me, I always dug deeper and went straight for the chewy ginger and green onion–scented noodles. At home, my mum makes a version with shiitake mushrooms and yellow chives (when they are in season). This recipe features golden fried ginger, which infuses the oil that is then used to fry the green onions and noodles. These noodles are fragrant, with a clear ginger flavor that does not overwhelm. E fu noodles are available from Chinese grocery stores, and if you can't find them, substitute with a thick egg or wheat noodle.

SERVES 4

7 ounces (200 g) dried e fu noodles (yi mian or longevity noodles)

3-inch (7.5 cm) piece of ginger (about 2 oz/60 g), peeled and finely sliced

¼ cup (60 ml) neutral oil

10 green onions, cut into 2-inch (5 cm) lengths, white and green parts separated

sea salt

toasted white sesame seeds, to serve

Seasoning sauce

2½ tablespoons vegetarian stir-fry sauce

4 teaspoons soy sauce or tamari

¼ teaspoon white pepper

½ teaspoon sugar

4 teaspoons toasted sesame oil

2 teaspoons Shaoxing rice wine

½ teaspoon sea salt

Vegan

Substitute • e fu noodles: hokkien, udon, thick egg or wheat noodles • green onions: leeks • vegetarian stir-fry sauce: oyster sauce for nonvegetarians

Vegetable swap • ginger: shiitake mushrooms

Bring a large saucepan of salted water to a boil. Add the noodles and cook according to the package directions until tender. Drain, run under cold water and drain again.

Meanwhile, to make the seasoning sauce, whisk together all the ingredients in a small bowl.

Build the ginger slices into a stack and finely slice them into razor-thin strips.

Heat a large skillet or wok over medium-high heat. Add the oil and heat for 30 seconds. Add the ginger and fry, stirring constantly, until most of it is golden and crispy, 3–4 minutes. Add the white part of the green onion and stir-fry for 1 minute, then add the green part and season with ½ teaspoon of sea salt. Toss for 2 minutes until the green onion is wilted and starting to char. Add the noodles, along with the seasoning sauce and toss for 1–2 minutes. Remove from the heat.

To serve, top with sesame seeds.

Ginger Jook
with Frizzled Ginger and Garlic

There is a common misconception that congee, which I know as jook, is just one dish. In fact, this is a dish that spans many countries in Asia, each region with its own rendition, which varies in ingredients, consistency, toppings and rituals. The dish is known as zhou in Mandarin, chok or khao tom in Thai, cháo in Vietnamese, hsan pyok in Burmese, bâbâr in Khmer, bubur in Malay and Indonesian, lúgaw in Tagalog and okayu in Japanese. But the commonly used term *congee* derives from India, and the Tamil word *kanji*. Even in my mother's kitchen we had three different styles of jook, which were served on different occasions. Her everyday jook was made with a less-rice-more-water ratio and was highly flavored, rich with pork bone, black-eyed peas, peanuts, jujube (red dates), lotus seeds, star anise, peanuts and shiitake mushrooms. Her baak jook (white congee) was made simply with water and lotus seeds, completely bland and flavorless, eaten during celebrations as a palate cleanser. Finally, there was her jook jai (little jook), a jook steamed in a clay vessel, which resulted in a thick, cloud-like consistency—my mother made this for me when I had a sore throat and this is also one of the first foods my children ate as babies. This recipe is close in texture to this thick jook, neutral in flavor but heavy in ginger. It is finished with beautiful, curly frizzled ginger and garlic, along with the scented oil.

SERVES 4

¾ cup (150 g) white rice, such as jasmine or medium-grain

4 teaspoons toasted sesame oil

sea salt

6⅓ cups (1.5 liters) water or vegetable stock

2 dried shiitake mushrooms (optional; see Notes)

1 small piece of kombu (optional; see Notes)

2 star anise

1½-inch (4 cm) piece of ginger (about 1 oz/30 g), peeled and finely sliced

2 green onions, finely sliced

Umami Crisp (see page 27) or Garlicky Chili Oil (see page 28), to serve (optional)

Frizzled ginger

3-inch (7.5 cm) piece of ginger (about 2 oz/60 g), peeled and finely julienned

2 garlic cloves, finely sliced

½ cup (120 ml) neutral oil

1½ teaspoons sea salt

Place the rice in a large saucepan and rinse well in water. Pour off the water and place the pan over medium-high heat. Add the sesame oil and 2 teaspoons of sea salt and stir to coat the grains. Add the water or stock, mushrooms (if using), kombu (if using), star anise and ginger. Bring to a boil, then cover with a propped-open lid (place a wooden chopstick on each side of the saucepan, then rest the lid on top of the chopsticks, leaving a gap for steam to escape). Reduce the heat to medium-low and simmer, stirring every now and then, for 1–1½ hours, until the rice has completely broken down and the jook is thick and fluffy. Give the jook a good stir, then add 2 teaspoons of sea salt and stir again. If you used kombu, you can either remove it or stir it vigorously through the jook to break it up (which is what I do). There's no need to remove the mushrooms—they can be eaten.

Meanwhile, to make the frizzled ginger, heat the ginger, garlic and oil in a small saucepan over medium-high heat until the oil starts to bubble around the edge. Reduce the heat to medium-low and cook, stirring often, until the ginger and garlic turn golden, about 15 minutes. Stir more often as the ginger and garlic start to caramelize, and watch carefully as they will burn quickly. Remove from the heat immediately and pour into a heatproof bowl. Stir in the salt.

To serve, ladle the jook into bowls and top with the frizzled ginger, making sure to spoon over some of the scented ginger oil. Top with the green onion and umami crisp or garlicky chili oil, if desired.

Notes: The use of kombu and shiitake are both optional (though recommended). If you aren't using them, I recommend using vegetable stock in place of water.

If you're not using umami crisp or chili oil, top with a splash of Maggi seasoning sauce.

Leftover frizzled ginger can be served on top of eggs, fried rice, noodles or roasted veggies.

Gluten-free and vegan

Ginger and Cilantro Noodle Pancake

It is interesting what manifests from scarcity, or the threat of scarcity. I spent the first two months of lockdown in Brooklyn devising all the ways I could use instant noodles; dishes that were an extension of the package instructions. I saw instant noodles as my ultimate quarantine food; inexpensive, with an unlimited shelf life and, most important, accessible—with the supermarkets cleaned out of canned beans and pasta, instant noodles remained in ample supply. I made kimchi noodle soups, peanut butter noodles, cacio e pepe noodles, noodle fry-ups, noodle salads and, most memorable of all, instant noodle cakes. This ramen pancake is one of the fun recipes I conceived during this time—flavored by a lively ginger-cilantro oil, the noodles are pan-fried until a crispy crust forms. Serve with the Stir-Fried Lettuce (see page 54), Ginger Jook (see page 222) or a green salad.

SERVES 4 AS A SNACK

3 packages instant ramen noodles (about 9 oz/250 g), soaked in warm water for 10 minutes

5 teaspoons soy sauce or tamari

1 tablespoon rice vinegar

2 tablespoons toasted white sesame seeds

big handful of cilantro leaves

1-inch (2.5 cm) piece of ginger (¾ oz/20 g), peeled and finely julienned

Ginger-cilantro oil

3-inch (7.5 cm) piece of ginger (2 oz/ 60 g), peeled and finely chopped

½ tightly packed cup cilantro, leaves and stems finely chopped

1 teaspoon sea salt

⅓ cup (80 ml) neutral oil

To make the ginger–cilantro oil, place the ginger, cilantro and salt in a small heatproof bowl. Heat the oil in a saucepan over medium-high heat for 2–4 minutes, until a wooden chopstick or spoon sizzles immediately when you place it in the oil. When it's ready, *very carefully* pour the oil over the ginger and cilantro mix—stand back, as it will spit and sizzle violently. Stir and set aside.

Drain the noodles in a colander, shaking it to remove excess water. Toss the noodles with your hands or tongs to loosen them. Transfer to a large bowl and add three-quarters of the ginger-cilantro oil (reserve the rest for topping), the soy sauce or tamari, rice vinegar and sesame seeds. Toss to combine.

Heat a large skillet that is approximately 9–10 inches (23–25 cm) in diameter over medium-high heat. When hot, add the noodles and cook, undisturbed, for 2–3 minutes to give the bottom a good sear and enough time to turn crispy (this helps the noodles hold together). Reduce the heat to medium and cook, again undisturbed, for another 5–7 minutes, until the bottom is golden all over. Using a spatula, lift parts of the noodle pancake to ensure that it is not burning—if the noodles get darker in one spot, move your pan around over the heat to ensure even browning. When it is ready, place a plate about the same size as the pan over the noodle pancake and swiftly flip it over. Slide the pancake, uncooked-side down, back into the pan and tuck the edges of the noodles in so that it is a neat round. Cook, undisturbed, for 4–5 minutes, until golden and crispy. Slide onto a plate.

To serve, cut into wedges and top with the remaining ginger-cilantro oil, cilantro leaves and ginger strips.

Vegan

Substitute • instant noodles: egg noodles • cilantro: green onions

Silken Tofu Pudding with Ginger Syrup

There are few desserts that excite my mother, but this one is her absolute favorite. Tofu fa (otherwise known as doufuhua or the shortened version douhua) is a tofu pudding, sweetened with sugar syrup. Thought to have originated in China during the Han dynasty, tofu pudding is now pervasive across Asia. There are many Chinese versions: some are served with a brown sugar syrup, others are infused with pandan leaves, while there are also savory renditions. In Indonesia, it is served with ginger syrup and peanuts; in the Baguio area of the Philippines, it is enjoyed with strawberry syrup; while in Vietnam, it is also served with a ginger syrup and is called tàu hũ nước đường. Traditionally, tofu fa is made with fresh tofu, but my recipe takes a shortcut with store-bought silken tofu, which makes this a quick breakfast, dessert or any-time-of-the-day snack.

SERVES 4

¾ cup (150 g) brown sugar

1½-inch (4 cm) piece of ginger (about 1 oz/30 g), peeled and finely sliced, plus a few extra slices to serve

1¾ pounds (800 g) silken tofu (about 2 blocks), drained

Place the brown sugar, ginger and 1 cup (240 ml) of water in a saucepan and heat gently over medium heat for 8–10 minutes, until the sugar has dissolved and the liquid is warm (it doesn't need to boil).

Place the silken tofu on a cutting board and, using a knife, diagonally slice off thick, irregular-sized chunks and divide them among four bowls (this gives you slices of tofu rather than larger chunks, but you can also cut them into cubes if you prefer).

Divide the ginger syrup among the four bowls, topping each with a few slices of ginger. Serve warm or place in the fridge and eat cold.

Gluten-free and vegan

Substitute • brown sugar: rock sugar, granulated sugar

Upside-Down Rhubarb
and Ginger Olive Oil Cake

Rhubarb perfectly captures the transience of time, the fickleness of the seasons. When this fugacious fruit makes its annual cameo during the spring, it means baking is imminent (though it can also be used in savory dishes). Rhubarb is naturally tart, but sugar will bring relief and extract its jaunty fruitiness. Ginger is a natural foil to rhubarb's astringency, bringing a touch of heat and spice. In this classic upside-down cake, the rhubarb is lightly stewed in a ginger syrup—take care not to overcook as you want the rhubarb to hold its shape. I use both fresh and ground ginger in this recipe—they each bring slightly different characteristics: the former adds texture and a bright spicy hum, while the latter has a stronger, more emphatic gingery kick.

SERVES 8

¾ cup (150 g) brown sugar

2 large eggs

¾ cup (150 g) sour cream

¾ cup (180 ml) extra-virgin olive oil

1 teaspoon ground ginger

1-inch (2.5 cm) piece of ginger
(about ¾ oz/20 g), peeled and grated

½ teaspoon sea salt

1 teaspoon vanilla paste or extract

1½ cups (185 g) all-purpose flour

1 teaspoon baking powder

½ teaspoon baking soda

powdered sugar, to serve (optional)

Stewed rhubarb

3 tablespoons (42 g) salted butter

6 tablespoons granulated sugar

1 teaspoon vanilla paste or extract

1-inch (2.5 cm) piece of ginger
(about ¾ oz/20 g), peeled and grated

10 ounces (300 g) rhubarb, trimmed
and cut into 2-inch (5 cm) strips

Preheat the oven to 350°F (180°C). Grease an 8-inch (20 cm) square cake pan with cooking spray and line with parchment paper.

To make the stewed rhubarb, heat a saucepan over medium heat and melt the butter. Add the sugar, vanilla and ginger and stir together. Add the rhubarb and stir to coat well. Reduce the heat to medium low and cook for 3–4 minutes, until the rhubarb has softened slightly but is still holding its shape (we don't want mush). Remove from the heat and pour the rhubarb (along with any syrup) into the prepared pan. Carefully arrange the rhubarb into neat rows, or in any pattern you like.

In a large mixing bowl, add the brown sugar, eggs, sour cream, olive oil, ground ginger, grated ginger, sea salt and vanilla and whisk together until well combined. Add the flour, baking powder and baking soda and whisk until just combined.

Pour the batter over the rhubarb, smoothing it evenly so that all the rhubarb is covered completely. Place on the middle rack of the oven and bake for 30–35 minutes, until an inserted skewer comes out clean. Remove from the oven and cool for 10 minutes, then very carefully invert the cake onto a plate or board. Dust with powdered sugar, if desired, and serve.

Storage: This cake is best eaten on the day it is baked, but it can be kept in an airtight container in the fridge for up to 3 days.

For gluten-free • use cup-for-cup
gluten-free all-purpose flour

Ginger and Coconut Mochi Cake

Growing up, my favorite Chinese desserts were always the chewy ones. The texture is unique, some say it's an acquired taste, but for me, these stretchy desserts represent childhood and home. Lo mai chi, the bouncy, coconut-coated balls filled with either peanuts, red bean or black sesame paste, is still my Chinese bakery must-have, while my mother's nian gao (New Year cake) is not-too-sweet and deliciously wobbly, a family celebration treat that is even better pan-fried. This mochi cake offers all the chew and gooeyness of my childhood treats, confidently accented with ginger and coconut. For those who are new to glutinous rice (mochi) desserts, note that this cake won't rise like a cake made with wheat flour. When it's cooked, it will still wobble a bit and will be difficult to slice, so let it cool completely. If you can't eat the whole cake within three days, I recommend freezing it (see below for instructions). I use Erawan or Mochiko brand of glutinous rice flour or sweet rice flour, which can be found at most Chinese or Asian supermarkets.

SERVES 8–10

4 large eggs

3¾ cups (450 g) glutinous (sweet) rice flour

two 13.5-ounce (400 ml) cans coconut milk

2¼ cups (440 g) granulated sugar

3 tablespoons (42 g) unsalted butter, melted

2-inch (5 cm) piece of ginger (1½ oz/40 g), peeled and grated

1 tablespoon ground ginger

6 tablespoons unsweetened shredded coconut, plus ¼ cup (20 g) more for topping

½ teaspoon fine sea salt

Preheat the oven to 350°F (180°C). Grease and line an 8½-inch (22 cm) square baking dish or similarly sized round cake pan. If you are using a springform pan, place it on a sheet pan while baking to catch any batter that may seep out.

Place the eggs in a large bowl and whisk well. Add the remaining ingredients and whisk for about 2 minutes, until completely smooth. Pour the batter into the prepared dish and bake for 30 minutes. Rotate the dish, top with the remaining ¼ cup (20 g) of shredded coconut and bake for another 25–30 minutes, until the edges are starting to brown and the top springs back when gently pressed.

Remove from the oven and allow to cool completely, about 30 minutes. Run a sharp knife around the perimeter of the cake to loosen it, then cut into slices or squares while still in the dish. If you have problems cutting through the sticky cake, let it cool for a while longer or lightly dust your knife with cornstarch—the longer it cools, the easier it will be to cut.

Storage: The cake can be stored in an airtight container in the fridge for up to 3 days; reheat in the oven or microwave until warm and soft. Mochi cake also freezes very well—simply store it in an airtight container, with individual pieces separated by wax paper. To eat, thaw slightly and reheat either in the oven or in the microwave.

Gluten-free

Ginger and Date Sticky Rye Puddings

Sticky date pudding, or sticky toffee pudding as it is known in some parts of the world, gets a little makeover with the addition of ginger, introducing a gentle heat to counter the deep, caramelly notes of the dates. I love the use of rye flour here—it brings a darker flavor and an earthy-nutty dimension that adds interest. There are many grades of rye flour, which will affect the density of the finished product; if you have the choice, opt for a light or medium rye, which adds complex flavor while ensuring that the crumb remains light and delicate. This moist pudding can also be made as a single slab cake (use an 8-inch/20 cm square cake pan) and cut into squares to serve. A fresh, creamy accompaniment, such as whipped cream, crème fraîche or mascarpone—or the vegan equivalent—is mandatory, in my opinion, helping to cut through the sweetness. Vanilla ice cream works, too.

MAKES 12 SMALL PUDDINGS

8 ounces (220 g) Medjool dates, pitted and roughly chopped

2-inch (5 cm) piece of ginger (1½ oz/40 g), peeled and roughly chopped

2 teaspoons ground ginger

2½ tablespoons ground flaxseeds

1⅓ cups (320 ml) oat, soy or regular whole milk

¾ cup (180 ml) extra-virgin olive oil

1⅔ cups (200 g) rye (or all-purpose) flour, preferably light or medium rye

scant ¾ cup (140 g) brown sugar

1 teaspoon baking powder

1 teaspoon baking soda

½ teaspoon fine sea salt

vegan or regular vanilla ice cream, or whipped coconut cream, to serve

Toffee sauce

4 tablespoons (56g) unsalted vegan or regular butter

1 cup (240 ml) thick coconut cream or regular cream

½ cup (100 g) brown sugar

¼ teaspoon flaky sea salt

½ teaspoon vanilla extract

Preheat the oven to 350°F (180°C). Grease a 12-cup standard muffin tin with cooking spray.

Place the dates, fresh ginger, ground ginger, flaxseeds and milk in a saucepan and heat over medium-high heat until it comes to a simmer. Reduce the heat to medium low and cook for 2–3 minutes, until the dates are soft. Using a stick blender, blender or food processor, blitz the date mixture until smooth. Add the olive oil and whiz again to combine. Set aside to cool.

In a large mixing bowl, add the flour, brown sugar, baking powder, baking soda and sea salt, and whisk to get rid of any lumps. Add the date mixture and stir together well. Divide the batter among the 12 muffin cups and bake for 18–20 minutes, until an inserted skewer comes out clean. Set aside to cool for 10 minutes.

To make the toffee sauce, in a saucepan, combine the vegan or regular butter, coconut cream or cream and sugar and bring to a simmer. Cook, whisking frequently, for 5–7 minutes, until the mixture thickens. Add the salt and vanilla and stir to combine.

While the puddings are still warm, remove them from the muffin tin. Place the puddings upside down on a plate and generously ladle on some of the toffee sauce. Finish with a dollop of ice cream or whipped coconut cream and serve immediately.

Storage: The puddings can be kept in an airtight container and stored in the fridge for up to 5 days. They can also be wrapped and stored in a tightly sealed bag or container in the freezer for up to 3 months. In both instances, reheat in the oven or microwave. The cooled toffee sauce can be refrigerated for up to 1 week and can be reheated in a pan on the stovetop or in the microwave.

For gluten-free • use cup-for-cup gluten-free all-purpose flour

Vegan

Kale

"The fertile greenness,
like the smell of grass after the rain,
is something that my body craves."

Kale came into my life at a time when I was flirting with all the ways to make a salad heartier, heftier, healthier. Kale is, in many ways, my perfect salad leaf. Its slight bitter edge mellows when cooked, but it retains its deep, robust flavor. I find kale's earthiness very enticing—the fertile greenness, like the smell of grass after the rain, is something that my body craves.

Kale is a descendant of wild cabbage, like many of our favorite brassicas. Even though it has experienced renewed popularity over the last decade, it is an ancient vegetable that is believed to have been grown and consumed for more than 2,000 years. Some call kale the "queen of greens." There are many varieties of kale, and while they can be used interchangeably, they each also have attributes that make them better in certain applications.

Curly kale is the garden variety—with thick, frilly leaves, fibrous stems and a slightly peppery flavor. It is great for pan-frying and roasting, and can stand up to longer cook times in braises, stews or sauces. Don't waste the stems—finely chop them and cook along with the leaves. Curly kale leaves can be tough, but I love to consume them raw, massaged in olive oil, acid and salt, which tenderizes them.

Multinamed Tuscan kale is also known as dinosaur kale, lacinato kale or cavolo nero. Its dark blackish-green dimpled leaves are thinner and sweeter. Slice it up for salads (the leaves are softer so require much less massaging), but I also love to pan-fry it with garlic for pasta dishes or add it to soups.

Red (or red Russian) kale looks like a cross between curly and Tuscan kale, with reddish-purplish-tinged flat leaves and stems that resemble oak lettuce leaves. It has a mild, sweet flavor and can be used like curly kale.

A Sesame-Infused Kale Salad

This is my favorite green salad, a lunchtime staple. It starts off with a whole bunch of kale leaves, which are rubbed with the toasty richness of sesame oil, sesame seeds, garlic and acid. The Midas touch comes from a ripe avocado that is squished through the leaves, leaving a creamy coating. The avocado trick (and really the salad itself) is one I learned from my friend Lukas Volger, who shares a similar salad in his brilliant book *Start Simple*. There are so many ways to build up the flavors in this recipe—add a spoonful of tahini to amplify the sesame flavor or add a drop of Umami Crisp (see page 27) for heat. While perfect as a light meal, this salad can also be used as a canvas for a heartier main meal—top with chickpeas, quinoa, sliced marinated tofu or roasted veggies, or serve alongside pan-fried dumplings.

**SERVES 4 AS A SIDE OR
2 AS A MAIN DISH**

6 ounces (180 g) kale leaves (from 1 bunch), torn

1 garlic clove, grated

2½ tablespoons lime or lemon juice

2½ tablespoons toasted sesame oil

4 teaspoons extra-virgin olive oil

1 avocado, roughly diced

1 teaspoon sea salt

3 tablespoons toasted sesame seeds (black, white or both)

2 green onions, finely sliced

1 mild chile (red or green), finely sliced (optional)

black pepper

Place the kale in a large bowl. Add the garlic, lime or lemon juice, sesame oil, olive oil, avocado and sea salt. Using clean hands, massage everything together, squeezing the avocado into the leaves, until the kale is completely coated and softened. Add the sesame seeds, green onion, chile (if using) and season with a few turns of black pepper. Serve immediately.

Gluten-free and vegan

Substitute • lime or lemon juice: rice vinegar, apple cider vinegar

Vegetable swap • kale: cavolo nero, Swiss chard

Kale and Orzo

This recipe is a reimagining of spanakorizo, the classic Greek dish made with spinach and rice. In this rendition, kale delivers all the leafy greenness of spinach, along with strong earthiness and a robust texture, while the rice is replaced with orzo, the charming rice-shaped pasta (known as risoni in some parts of the world). Though it is a pasta shape, I often mix things up by replacing rice with orzo—its greatest asset is that it cooks quickly so it can be used to make risotto-like dishes, in salads where you'd normally use brown rice and in one-pot dishes where it is simmered in a sauce along with other ingredients. It's a versatile ingredient to keep in your pantry, alongside your rice and other types of pasta. And while I love orzo, it is the emphatic dark leafiness of kale that keeps me coming back to this dish—with accents of lemon, dill and butter, it's a simple knockout meal.

SERVES 4

1 bunch of cavolo nero or regular kale (about 9 oz/300 g)

extra-virgin olive oil

1 yellow onion, finely diced

2 garlic cloves, finely chopped

2 cups chopped dill

3 green onions, finely sliced

1 teaspoon dried mint

1 teaspoon dried oregano

sea salt and black pepper

1 pound (450 g) orzo

32 ounces (1 liter) vegetable stock

4 tablespoons (56 g) regular or vegan butter

zest and juice of 1 lemon (¼ cup juice)

3½ ounces (100 g) feta, crumbled (optional)

Remove the cavolo nero or kale leaves from the stems. Chop the leaves and set them aside in a bowl. Finely slice the stems and place in a separate bowl.

Heat a deep skillet or Dutch oven over medium-high heat. Add ¼ cup (60 ml) of olive oil, along with the onion, then reduce the heat to medium low and sauté for 7–8 minutes, until soft and translucent. Add the garlic, two-thirds of the chopped dill and the green onion and cook for 1 minute. Toss in the cavolo nero or kale stems and cook for 1–2 minutes, just to soften them. Next, add the cavolo nero or kale leaves, mint and oregano and cook for 2–3 minutes, until the leaves are wilted. Season everything with 1 teaspoon of sea salt and a good turn of black pepper.

Add the orzo and stir to combine. Increase the heat to medium high, then add the stock and bring to a boil. Cover with a lid, reduce the heat to medium low and cook for 10 minutes. Lift the lid and carefully test a piece of orzo for doneness—you are looking for an al dente finish.

Turn off the heat and add the butter, lemon zest and juice and crumbled feta (if using) and season well with sea salt and black pepper. Stir to melt the butter, scatter with the remaining dill, then serve immediately.

For gluten-free • use long-grain rice, quinoa or a gluten-free small pasta shape (adjust cooking times accordingly)

Veganize • omit the feta or replace with vegan cheese

Substitute • orzo: rice, quinoa, bulgur, millet

Vegetable swap • cavolo nero or kale: spinach, Swiss chard

Torn Lasagna with Kale and Kimchi

Nothing beats a well-constructed, meticulously composed lasagna, but for times when you just want the taste of this dish, without the preparation time (and ingredients), this is a smart alternative. The dish is ready in three steps: wilt the kale, make a tomato sauce base and combine the torn fresh lasagna sheets with cheese. There is no construction at all, you just bring the elements together in a deep dish and bake until golden. I often turn to kimchi to inject fast flavor and complexity to a dish, and here it does the job neatly. Gochugaru brings a sweet smokiness to the sauce. If you prefer, you could omit both the kimchi and gochugaru, which would give you more traditional lasagna flavors. I like to eat this with a green salad.

SERVES 4

1 bunch of kale (about 9 oz/300 g)

extra-virgin olive oil

1 garlic clove, finely chopped

sea salt and black pepper

1 pound (450 g) lasagna sheets

15 ounces (425 g) ricotta

1 cup (115 g) grated cheddar

1 cup (200 g) regular or
vegan kimchi

Smoky gochugaru sauce

extra-virgin olive oil

4 garlic cloves, finely chopped

2½ tablespoons gochugaru

2 teaspoons smoked paprika

2 teaspoons dried oregano

1 teaspoon sugar

sea salt

one 28-ounce (800 g) can crushed
tomatoes

For gluten-free • use gluten-free
lasagna sheets

Veganize • use dairy-free ricotta
and cheddar

Substitute • fresh lasagna sheets:
tortillas, lavash bread

Vegetable swap • kale: cabbage,
spinach, Brussels sprouts

Preheat the oven to 400°F (200°C).

Separate the kale leaves from the stems. Tear the leaves and finely chop the stems.

Heat a skillet over medium-high heat, add a drizzle of olive oil, the kale stems and garlic and sauté for 1 minute. Add the kale leaves, season with sea salt and black pepper and cook for 3–4 minutes, until the kale is wilted but still bright green. Remove from the heat and set aside.

To make the smoky gochugaru sauce, heat a large saucepan over medium heat. Add 1–2 tablespoons of olive oil and the garlic and cook for 30 seconds until aromatic. Add the gochugaru, smoked paprika, oregano, sugar and about 1 teaspoon of sea salt and stir to combine. Pour in the crushed tomatoes and 2 cups (480 ml) of water (you can use the crushed tomato can by filling it about three-quarters full; this is also a great way of removing any leftover tomatoes and juices in the can) and stir. Cover with a lid and cook for 20 minutes, to allow the flavors to meld.

Tear the lasagna sheets into smaller but still large-ish pieces—ideally around 2–4 inches (5–10 cm) wide; they do not need to be uniform.

Place the ricotta in a large mixing bowl, add 2 tablespoons of water and whisk to loosen it up. Add half the cheddar, 2 tablespoons of olive oil and season with sea salt and black pepper. Fold in the wilted kale and kale stems. Finally, add the kimchi and torn lasagna sheets and stir to combine.

Pour the gochugaru sauce into a 12 × 8-inch (30 cm × 20 cm) (or thereabouts) baking dish. Add the cheese, kale and lasagna sheet mixture to the sauce and gently stir to combine. Top with the remaining cheddar and bake for 35–40 minutes, until bubbling and golden. Allow to sit for 10 minutes before serving.

Shortcut: Skip the smoky gochugaru sauce and use a store-bought tomato-based pasta sauce. You can add gochugaru and spices to the sauce or use it plain.

Matcha Kale Noodles

Over the past few years, I've really enjoyed dabbling in noodle-making, learning via a combination of YouTube videos and the occasional FaceTime lesson from my mother. These matcha kale noodles are the result of some experimentation—the noodles have deep flavors from the matcha powder and kale, with a rich, verdant hue. Homemade noodles may seem intimidating, but I have been buoyed by seeing so many home cooks mastering the knife-cut noodles in my book *To Asia, With Love*. This recipe offers a slight progression, with a flavored dough. Enjoy these in a noodle soup (try with the Mushroom and Ginger Broth on page 282) or in the Kale, Ginger and Green Onion Noodles on page 246.

SERVES 4

1 tightly packed cup kale leaves

3¾ cups (450 g) all-purpose flour, plus more for dusting

4 teaspoons (10 g) culinary-grade matcha powder

2 teaspoons sea salt

neutral oil

rice flour, for dusting

Vegan

Vegetable swap • kale: spinach, arugula, basil, cilantro

Place the kale leaves in a blender or food processor and add a 1 cup minus 1 tablespoon (225ml) of water of water. Blend until completely smooth.

In a large bowl, add the flour, matcha and sea salt and whisk to combine. Gradually add the kale mixture, a little at a time, stirring constantly until the flour comes together in a scraggly mass. The dough will look dry, but this is fine. Turn the dough out onto a floured surface and knead for 12–15 minutes, until it is soft and bounces back when poked (you can do all of this in a stand mixer using a dough hook; knead on medium speed for 8–10 minutes). Wrap the dough tightly and rest for 10 minutes.

Divide the dough into four equal pieces and roll each piece out into a rectangle that is a scant ¼ inch (5 mm) thick (it doesn't need to be exact). Brush both sides liberally with oil and place on a sheet pan lined with parchment paper (you can stack the dough as the oil will prevent the pieces from sticking together). Cover the whole pan with plastic wrap to prevent the dough from drying out. Rest for at least 2 hours or longer. The dough can also be refrigerated overnight—bring it to room temperature the next day by leaving it out on the kitchen counter for about 30 minutes.

Place each piece of dough on a clean surface and cut each piece into strips—to make wide noodles, cut them into pieces 1–1½ inches (2.5–4 cm) wide. For thinner noodles, cut into strips a scant ¼–⅜ inch (5–10 mm) wide.

Working with one strand of noodle at a time, hold the ends in each hand and slowly pull in opposite directions (don't pull too hard, as it may snap; if it does, that's fine, you'll just have a shorter noodle). If you like, you can gently bounce the noodle against the kitchen counter to help it stretch longer (this step isn't completely necessary but it's fun!). Set aside and dust with rice flour to prevent the noodles from sticking.

Bring a large saucepan of salted water to a boil. Add the noodles and cook for 1–2 minutes for thinner noodles and 2–3 minutes for thicker noodles, until they float to the top. Drain the noodles. If you are using them straightaway, place them directly into your sauce. If not, rinse them and drizzle with a little oil to prevent them from sticking together.

To freeze: Dust the stretched noodles in rice flour and place them in bundles on a sheet pan lined with parchment paper. Place in the freezer and, when hard, transfer them to a freezer bag or airtight container. To cook, plunge the frozen noodles straight into boiling water (do not thaw first) and cook until they float to the top.

Kale, Ginger and Green Onion Noodles

This is a comforting bowl of noodles helmed by my familiar childhood flavors of green onions and ginger. I never tire of the perfume of ginger and green onions—the aroma is intoxicating, a warm embrace from my mother far away, bringing me home. Noodles are quick meals, but to me they also represent Sunday lunches from childhood, the only day of the week when my father was home for lunch, back when there were five of us around the table. Sunday lunch wasn't formal, but it was the meal when my parents dared to indulge, a little. Sometimes my father would pick up McDonald's or Kentucky Fried Chicken, bringing it home to eat around the table (we never dined in). Most weeks, my mother made noodles—chow mein, chow mei fun, chow hor fun, Singapore noodles—along with jook, and it was always one of my favorite meals. Afterward, my father would "relax" by stripping down to his white vest undershirt, embarking on a long afternoon of ironing, de-crinkling his shirts for the week ahead, while the soundtrack of the horse racing crackled incessantly from his tiny transistor radio.

Any noodles will perform in this dish but, if you have the time and inclination, I highly recommend using the Matcha Kale Noodles on page 244 for some earthy yet bright kale-on-kale action. Noodles aside, this is a quick dish that can be whipped up in around 15 minutes, perfect for vegetable-led weeknight cooking.

SERVES 4

10 ounces (300 g) dried noodles (any variety) or Matcha Kale Noodles (see page 244)

neutral oil

1-inch (2.5 cm) piece of ginger, peeled and finely chopped

6 green onions, white and green parts separated and roughly sliced

4 garlic cloves, finely chopped

6 ounces (180 g) kale leaves (from 1 bunch), torn

sea salt and white pepper

2½ tablespoons soy sauce or tamari

2½ tablespoons toasted sesame oil

1 tablespoon toasted white or black sesame seeds

handful of cilantro leaves

Bring a large saucepan of salted water to a boil. If you are using dried noodles, add them to the water and cook according to the package directions, until al dente. If you are using the fresh matcha kale noodles, add them to the water and cook for 1–2 minutes for thinner noodles and 2–3 minutes for thicker noodles, until they float to the top. Drain and reserve about ½ cup (120 ml) of the noodle cooking water.

Meanwhile, heat a large skillet or wok over medium-high heat. When hot, add 1–2 tablespoons of oil, along with the ginger and white part of the green onion. Toss for 30–60 seconds, until fragrant, then add the garlic and kale leaves and any tender stems. Season with sea salt and white pepper and toss for 2–3 minutes, until the kale is wilted. Add the soy sauce or tamari, sesame oil and green part of the green onion and stir-fry for about 30 seconds. Add the drained noodles, along with a splash of the noodle cooking water, and toss for 1–2 minutes, until well combined. Turn off the heat and taste, adding more sea salt or white pepper as needed.

Serve topped with sesame seeds and cilantro leaves.

For gluten-free • use rice, sweet potato starch or other starch noodles

Vegan

Vegetable swap • kale: Swiss chard, Asian greens

Kale Dumplings
with Brothy Butter Beans

The champion of weeknight cooking, canned beans are the quickest way to turn vegetables into a meal. Brothy beans are commonly made with dried beans, cooked in a broth of onion, carrot and celery, but here I have opted for canned beans, which come together much quicker. Rather than a clear broth, I've gone for something tomatoey (a winner in my family), which is then topped with kale-specked dumplings—the other type of dumplings!—which puff up and steam on top of the brothy beans.

SERVES 4

extra-virgin olive oil

1 small leek, white and green parts finely sliced and washed well

5 garlic cloves, finely chopped

2½ tablespoons tomato paste

1 teaspoon paprika

¼–½ teaspoon red pepper flakes

one 14.5-ounce (411 g) can crushed or diced tomatoes

2 cups (480 ml) vegetable stock

3 cups (500 g) cooked butter beans (about two 15 oz/425 g cans, drained)

1 teaspoon sugar

sea salt and black pepper

scant 2 ounces (50 g) kale leaves

4 teaspoons red wine vinegar

handful of basil leaves

Kale dumplings

1¼ cup (150 g) all-purpose flour

2 teaspoons baking powder

sea salt and black pepper

3 tablespoons (42 g) butter, chopped

scant 2 ounces (50 g) kale leaves, finely chopped

¾ cup (85 g) grated cheddar

handful of basil leaves, chopped

1 large egg

½ cup (120 ml) whole milk

For gluten-free • use gluten-free all-purpose flour

Veganize • use vegan milk, cheese, butter and 1 flax egg (see page 30)

Substitute • leek: yellow onion, shallot • cheddar: parmesan

Vegetable swap • kale: spinach, Swiss chard

Heat a large Dutch oven or wide saucepan over medium-high heat. Pour in 2–3 tablespoons of olive oil and, when it shimmers, add the leek and stir for 2–3 minutes, until softened. Add the garlic, tomato paste, paprika and red pepper flakes and stir for 1 minute, until fragrant. Add the tomatoes, vegetable stock, beans and sugar and season with about 1 teaspoon of sea salt and a few turns of black pepper. Bring to a boil, then reduce the heat to medium, cover with a lid and cook for 10 minutes, to allow the flavors to meld.

Meanwhile, to make the kale dumplings, combine the flour, baking powder, 1 teaspoon of sea salt and a good grind of black pepper in a bowl. Rub the butter into the flour with your fingertips, until it feels like sand. Stir in the kale, cheese and basil and combine well. Beat the egg with the milk and fold this into the flour mixture, until just combined.

Add the kale leaves and red wine vinegar to the brothy beans and taste, adding more sea salt and black pepper, to your liking.

Using a large tablespoon or ice-cream scoop, form balls of dough the size of golf balls and carefully drop these into the beans (you should get 8–10 dumplings). They will expand during cooking so space them apart. Cover and cook over low heat for about 15 minutes, until the dumplings are puffed and an inserted toothpick or bamboo skewer comes out clean.

To serve, ladle the brothy beans into bowls along with one or two dumplings each, drizzle generously with olive oil and top with a few basil leaves.

Notes: Use a Dutch oven or a saucepan that is wide enough to accommodate the dumplings on top, as they also need room to expand. I recommend one that is 10–12 inches (25–30 cm) in diameter, or even larger. Try not to lift the lid during cooking as the steam helps the dumplings puff up.

Cheesy Kale and Rice Cake Bake

Rice cakes (either the rice sticks or the sliced ovals; see page 92) are a wonderful staple to keep in your pantry. When the carb cravings hit, they satiate that desire with exceeding efficacy. They are similar to the chee cheung fun (steamed rice noodle rolls) of my youth, but are chewier, with more bite. This bake is *very* loosely inspired by the irresistible Korean dish tteokbokki, a dish of stir-fried rice cakes in a spicy sauce of gochujang, gochugaru and, often, fish cakes. This version is less spicy and cheesier, baked until bubbling and golden. If you don't have rice cake sticks, you could substitute gnocchi (straight from the package, uncooked), a short pasta shape, such as penne or rigatoni (cooked 2 minutes less than the package directions), or even tortellini. The kale is the perfect green for this dish, robust and sinewy, even after baking.

SERVES 4

2 tablespoons extra-virgin olive oil

4 garlic cloves, finely chopped

1 tablespoon gochugaru

2 tomatoes (about 9 oz/300 g), roughly chopped

1 teaspoon sea salt

1 teaspoon sugar

32 ounces (1 liter) vegetable stock

2 pounds (900 g) rice cake sticks, rinsed in water to separate

6 ounces (180 g) kale leaves (from 1 bunch), torn

1½ cups (170 g) grated cheddar

7 ounces (200 g) fresh mozzarella, torn

2 green onions, finely chopped

Heat a deep 10-inch (25 cm) ovenproof skillet or shallow Dutch oven over medium heat. Add the olive oil and garlic and cook for 15–20 seconds, until fragrant. Add the gochugaru, tomato, sea salt, sugar and vegetable stock and stir to combine. Cover with a lid and allow it to bubble away for 10 minutes.

Preheat the oven to 400°F (200°C).

After 10 minutes, remove the lid and stir the sauce, squishing the tomato with the back of a spoon or spatula. Add the rice cake sticks, along with the kale, and stir until the leaves wilt. Add half the cheddar, half the mozzarella and the green onion and stir to combine. Top with the remaining cheddar and mozzarella and transfer to the oven, placing a sheet pan underneath to catch any drips. Bake for 15–20 minutes, until melty and golden.

Allow to sit for 5–10 minutes before serving.

Gluten-free

Substitute • rice cake sticks: gnocchi, parcooked pasta (see recipe introduction), tortellini • cheddar and mozzarella: use other melty cheese, such as fontina, Gruyère, Taleggio, provolone

Vegetable swap • kale: cabbage, broccoli, Swiss chard

Salt and Vinegar Kale Chips
with Fried Chickpeas and Avocado

For days when you are craving crispy, salty things for dinner, skip the bag of chips and opt for this salad-ish plate of crunchy goodness. These salt and vinegar kale chips feel decidedly "snacky," but teamed with fried chickpeas, avocado and an optional frizzled egg, they become a delightfully textural dinner. These take a bit longer to crisp up than regular kale chips because they are doused in vinegar (it is still important to make sure to dry your kale well after washing to encourage maximum crunch). Customize your kale chips by adding other seasonings—a sprinkle of paprika and harissa will add more intense flavors while nutritional yeast or grated parmesan (or cheddar) will add more umami. The key point to remember is that salt will make your kale soggy, so only sprinkle it on after roasting.

SERVES 4

6 ounces (180 g) kale leaves (from 1 bunch), washed and dried, then torn

extra-virgin olive oil

3 tablespoons apple cider vinegar or malt vinegar

1 garlic clove, grated

sea salt and black pepper

3 cups (500 g) cooked chickpeas (about two 15 oz/425 g cans, drained)

1 teaspoon paprika

1 teaspoon chile powder

4 large eggs (optional)

2 avocados, sliced

Preheat the oven to 275°F (140°C).

Place the kale leaves on a sheet pan and add 2–3 tablespoons of olive oil, the vinegar and garlic. Massage the kale to coat evenly, then spread the kale across two sheet pans, making sure the leaves aren't overlapping. Place the pans on the middle and lower racks of the oven and roast for 25–30 minutes, switching racks halfway through, until the kale is crispy (watch closely as it burns quickly). Remove from the oven and season well with sea salt.

Meanwhile, heat a large skillet over medium-high heat. Add 3–4 tablespoons of olive oil to the pan, along with the chickpeas, and fry for 15–20 minutes, until golden and crispy. Using a slotted spoon, transfer the chickpeas to paper towels to drain briefly. Place the chickpeas in a bowl, sprinkle with the paprika and chile powder, and season with sea salt and black pepper. Toss to combine.

If you're including eggs, wipe out the pan and return to medium-high heat. When hot, add a drizzle of olive oil and crack in the eggs, one at a time. Reduce the heat to medium and fry the eggs until the edges are frizzled, the white is set and the yolk is cooked to your liking. Season with a pinch of sea salt. Remove from the pan and set aside.

Divide the kale, chickpeas and avocado among four plates and top with an egg (if using). Serve as is, or top with Fish-Free Furikake (see page 359), a drizzle of Umami Crisp (see page 27) or dollop with Basil Caesar-ish Dressing (see page 504).

Gluten-free and vegan

Substitute • chickpeas: finely diced potatoes, white beans, such as cannellini

Mushrooms

"The kingdom of fungi is splendid,
varied and enchanting."

According to my mother, one of my first words was "doong gu," the Cantonese name for shiitake mushrooms. She says I called this out effusively after each bite, demanding more. It seems my adoration of mushrooms was immediate and enduring.

Dried shiitake mushrooms are a foundational ingredient in Chinese cooking. Packed with rich umami flavor, my mother's kitchen was joyfully perfumed with their delicious aroma. Most mornings, she would set out a bowl of water to rehydrate the dried mushrooms, ready for that day's meals. Dried mushrooms are best rehydrated with a long soak in cold water (up to 24 hours in the fridge), but for quicker results submerge them in boiling water for 20–30 minutes. When ready to use, squeeze out as much liquid as possible and you will be left with an instant umami stock, which can be used in cooking (make sure you discard any grit left in the soaking liquid).

The kingdom of fungi is splendid, varied and enchanting. Mushrooms are unlike any other vegetable—they exist as one part of an otherworldly ecosystem that allows trees to communicate: beneath an individual mushroom, there are thin threads known as mycelia, which connect plants in the forest. Plants provide fungi with carbon-rich sugars and, in return, fungi provide plants with nutrients taken from the soil. Mushrooms are a sustainable food, thriving in small spaces, even indoors (I have used kits to successfully grow varieties such as blue oyster and lion's mane). They require little energy or water to grow, and some species cultivate in the dark. Truly magical.

Mushroom, Leek and Walnut Pâté

I have no fear of brown food. I grew up eating it; some of my favorite childhood dishes were the color of dirt, wood and the earth. I'm not sure where the repudiation of brown food came from—perhaps it was born with the rise of social media and the need to ensure that food is always bright and beautiful, but, to me, some of the most delicious foods in the world are this earthy hue. Brown represents warmth, steadfastness, simplicity, and this is how I see this very brown, very tasty mushroom pâté. It is an everything food that is incredibly adaptable—spread it on crackers and in sandwiches, add it to dumpling fillings, wrap in filo pastry to make little triangles, serve with scrambled eggs or use it to make the Sesame Mushroom Toast on page 260. Experiment with different types of mushrooms to achieve slightly different results—button mushrooms will give you a pâté that is milder in both flavor and color, while wild mushrooms will yield a more intense spread.

MAKES ABOUT 1½ CUPS

extra-virgin olive oil

1 large leek, white and green parts finely sliced and washed well

1 ounce (30 g) dried porcini or Chinese shiitake mushrooms, soaked in hot water for at least 20 minutes

3 garlic cloves, finely chopped

1 pound (450 g) mushrooms (any variety), roughly chopped

1 teaspoon five-spice powder

½ teaspoon red pepper flakes

sea salt and black pepper

1 cup (100 g) walnuts, soaked in warm water for 10 minutes

Heat a large skillet over medium heat. When hot, add about 2 tablespoons of olive oil and the leek, then cook for 6–8 minutes, until softened.

Meanwhile, remove the dried mushrooms from their soaking water and squeeze to remove excess liquid. Roughly chop the mushrooms, then strain the soaking liquid through paper towel or a fine-mesh sieve to remove any grit and sediment. Set the liquid aside.

Add the garlic, chopped mushroom and rehydrated dried mushrooms to the pan and stir for 5 minutes, until softened. Add the five-spice powder and red pepper flakes and season well with sea salt and black pepper. Set aside to cool for 5–10 minutes.

Drain the walnuts and add them to a food processor or blender, along with the cooled mushroom mixture, and pulse about 10 times, using a rubber spatula or wooden spoon to scrape down the side. If the mixture is thick and hard to blend, add a little of the mushroom soaking liquid to get the motor going. Continue pulsing (this gives you more control over the final texture, but you could just press blend and let it go) until you have reached your desired consistency—I like it almost smooth, with a little texture. Traditional pâté is very smooth. Spoon into a bowl or jar. Consume immediately or chill in the fridge for 2 hours, to allow the flavors to mingle.

Storage: Keep the pâté in an airtight container in the fridge for 3–4 days. Freeze in a zip-seal bag for up to 1 month and thaw by allowing to come to room temperature.

Serving suggestions: Spread a generous layer of pâté on bread and top with finely chopped chives and olive oil (pictured), an egg (fried or soft-boiled), dots of quick-pickled shallot or onion, scattered goat cheese or a drizzle of Umami Crisp (see page 27) or chili oil. Use for the Sesame Mushroom Toast on page 260.

Gluten-free and vegan

Substitute • leek: yellow onion • walnuts: cashews, pecans, hazelnuts

Sesame Mushroom Toast

This recipe is inspired by fond memories of shrimp toast, a treat from childhood lunches at my uncle's Sydney restaurant, Lee's Fortuna Court. This beloved Cantonese snack features small triangles of bread, which are smeared with a paste made from minced shrimp, then dipped in sesame seeds and deep-fried. This mushroom version satiates my hunger, thanks to the rich, bold mushroom pâté on page 258, which I use as the paste for the bread. This "fried bread" is pure comfort food. If you're short on time, use store-bought mushroom pâté.

SERVES 4–6 AS A SNACK

6 thick slices of white bread

¾–1 cup Mushroom, Leek and Walnut Pâté (see page 258)

2 green onions, finely chopped, plus more to serve

sea salt

⅓ cup toasted sesame seeds (white, black or both)

extra-virgin olive oil

Sweet and sour sauce

4 teaspoons sugar

1 teaspoon apple cider vinegar

1 tablespoon soy sauce or tamari

2½ tablespoons ketchup

1 garlic clove, finely chopped

To make the sweet and sour sauce, place all the ingredients in a small bowl and whisk to combine. Set aside.

Lay out the bread slices and spread a thick layer of the mushroom pâté on all of them, extending all the way to the edges. Scatter with the green onion and a little sea salt and gently press the green onion into the pâté. Pour the sesame seeds onto a plate and press the bread, pâté-side down, into the sesame seeds to coat evenly.

Pour about ⅜ inch (1 cm) of olive oil into a large skillet and set over medium-high heat until hot. Add a tiny blob of pâté to the oil; if it sizzles, the oil is ready. Working in two or three batches, fry the toasts, pâté-side down, until golden and crisp, about 2 minutes, then flip and cook until the other sides are golden and crisp, about 1 minute. Transfer to a plate lined with paper towel to drain.

Cut each toast diagonally into quarters and top with more green onion, then serve with the sweet and sour sauce on the side.

For gluten-free • use gluten-free bread

Vegan

Mushroom Khao Soi

Khao soi is a rich coconut curry noodle soup originating from Northern Thailand, Myanmar and Laos, but there are also many regional variations of the dish, which differ in the protein base or the type of noodles used. My vegetarian version is bolstered by a slew of mushrooms, both in the curry paste and the broth, which lends incredibly deep umami flavors. As with most homemade curry pastes, the list of ingredients may seem long, but they are mostly pantry items, and the paste comes together seamlessly in a blender or food processor. Toppings bring texture to the dish, for example, crunchy noodles—I usually use store-bought—and a mélange of other crispy and fresh things like fried shallots, bean sprouts and cilantro leaves.

SERVES 4

¼ cup (60 ml) neutral oil

10 ounces (300 g) mushrooms (shiitake, oyster, cremini), torn or sliced

sea salt

two 13.5-ounce (400 ml) cans coconut milk

2 cups (480 ml) vegetable stock

4 teaspoons brown sugar

2½ tablespoons soy sauce or tamari

2 limes, halved

10 ounces (300 g) baby bok choy or other Asian greens, washed and patted dry

1 pound (450 g) fresh egg noodles or 10 ounces (300 g) dried thin wheat or egg noodles

Mushroom khao soi paste (makes about 1½ cups)

3–4 dried Thai chiles, soaked in water for 10 minutes, chopped

2 shallots, roughly chopped

5 garlic cloves, roughly chopped

2-inch (5 cm) piece of ginger, peeled and roughly chopped

4 makrut lime leaves, chopped

3½ ounces (100 g) mushrooms (shiitake, oyster or cremini), roughly chopped

1 tablespoon curry powder

2 teaspoons ground turmeric

2 teaspoons cilantro seeds

½ cup chopped cilantro leaves and stems

For gluten-free • use rice noodles or mung bean vermicelli

Veganize • use egg-free noodles

Substitute • Asian greens: broccoli, zucchini, snow peas, asparagus

To make the mushroom khao soi paste, add all the ingredients to a blender or small food processor. Pulse a few times to break everything up, then add ¼ cup (60 ml) of water and blend until the paste is smooth.

Heat a large saucepan over medium-high heat. When hot, add the oil, along with the mushrooms, and cook, stirring occasionally, for 4–6 minutes, until softened and starting to char. Season with a pinch of sea salt. Add about ¾ cup of the paste (you can add more or less, according to how spicy you want it) and cook for 1–2 minutes, until it is fragrant and starts to stick to the bottom of the pan. Add the coconut milk, vegetable stock, sugar and soy sauce or tamari and stir well to combine. Reduce the heat to low and cook for 8–10 minutes, until the broth is flavorful and thick. Taste and season with sea salt, if needed, and add the juice of 1 lime.

Meanwhile, bring a saucepan of salted water to a boil. Add the greens and blanch them for about 1 minute, just until bright green. Using tongs, remove from the pan immediately and drain in a colander, refreshing under cold water. Leave to drain. To the same pan of water, add the noodles and cook according to the package directions, until al dente. Using tongs, remove the noodles and place them straight into four serving bowls.

Cut the remaining lime halves into smaller wedges. Divide the Asian greens among the four bowls of noodles and add some broth to each bowl. Top with your chosen toppings—fried noodles, crispy fried shallots, bean sprouts and/or cilantro leaves—and serve immediately with a wedge of lime.

Optional but recommended toppings: One handful each of fried noodles, crispy fried shallots, bean sprouts and cilantro leaves.

Leftovers: This khao soi paste makes enough for eight people, so I usually freeze half of it for future meals.

Mushroom and Potato Coconut Chowder

When I came up with this dish, I had a chowder in mind, but the result is far from being overly heavy or creamy. It is a light dish, but the chowder-like quality it does possess is chunkiness, with hunks of potato and nuggets of mushroom bathed in the silky, aromatic coconut broth. You could add more oomph by adding a can of legumes (chickpeas would be nice), inject more greenery with peas or green beans, or perhaps load it up with more carbs by way of gnocchi or chunky croutons.

SERVES 4

2 tablespoons (28 g) regular or vegan butter

extra-virgin olive oil

1 large leek, white and green parts finely sliced and washed well

2 celery stalks, finely chopped

2 garlic cloves, finely chopped

10 ounces (300 g) mushrooms (any variety), roughly chopped or torn

2 thyme sprigs

sea salt and black pepper

1 tablespoon rice flour

one 13.5-ounce (400 ml) can coconut milk

32 ounces (1 liter) vegetable stock

1 pound (450 g) potatoes, peeled and cut into 1-inch (2.5 cm) pieces

freshly grated nutmeg

2 green onions or small handful of chives, finely sliced

cayenne pepper or other chile powder, to serve

1 lemon, halved

Gluten-free and vegan

Substitute • coconut milk: regular whole milk, soy milk, oat milk, cream • leek: onion

Vegetable swap • mushrooms: corn

Heat a large saucepan or Dutch oven over medium heat, add the butter, about 2 tablespoons of olive oil and the leek and cook for 2–3 minutes, until softened. Add the celery and garlic and cook for about 2 minutes, until soft. Toss in the mushroom and thyme and cook for 5–6 minutes, until softened and the mushroom has started to caramelize. Season with about 1 teaspoon of sea salt and a good grind of black pepper. Sprinkle with the rice flour and stir to ensure the mushroom is well coated. Pour in the coconut milk and vegetable stock and stir well. Add the potato, then grate in some fresh nutmeg (use more or less, according to your personal taste). Cover and cook over medium-low heat for 15–20 minutes, until the potato is soft.

To serve, top each bowl of chowder with a scattering of green onion or chives, a sprinkling of cayenne pepper or chile powder and a squeeze of lemon juice.

Pan-Seared King Oyster Mushrooms
with Whipped Almonds

King oysters are mushroom royalty, with a robust flesh that offers a substantial and satisfying chew. Known for their regal tree shape (they are called king trumpet mushrooms in some parts of the world), they are the perfect mushroom for pan-searing, the hot surface ensuring a swift char, while the flesh becomes juicy, with a distinct nuttiness. The thick stems are the meatiest part of king oysters and are often used to imitate meat in plant-based cooking. Here, they interplay joyfully with the creamy whipped almonds—a hummus-like sauce that is extra nutty. Almonds are a harder nut and don't blend as easily as cashews, so I work around this by using sliced almonds, which soften quicker. If you only have whole almonds, simply chop them up roughly before soaking. Serve with bread or flatbread to mop up the delicious whipped almond sauce.

SERVES 4

1 pound (450 g) king oyster mushrooms

extra-virgin olive oil

3–4 thyme sprigs

sea salt and black pepper

1 lemon, halved

handful of parsley leaves

handful of toasted sliced almonds

Whipped almonds

2 cups skin-on sliced almonds

2 garlic cloves, roughly chopped

2½ tablespoons tahini

⅓ cup (80 ml) lemon juice (from about 2 lemons)

¼ cup (60 ml) extra-virgin olive oil

½ cup chopped parsley

1 teaspoon sea salt

Soak the almonds for the whipped almonds in 1 cup (240 ml) of boiling water for 20 minutes.

I like to slice the mushrooms two different ways to create a visually interesting dish. Cut half of the mushrooms lengthwise into "tree-shaped" slices and cut the other half crosswise to create discs ⅓–⅜ inch (8–10 mm) thick.

You will need to cook the mushroom in batches. Heat a large skillet over medium-high heat, add a generous drizzle of olive oil and lay out the mushrooms in a single layer (as many as you can fit). Top with a few thyme sprigs and, using a spatula, press the mushrooms down into the hot pan and cook, undisturbed, for 5–7 minutes, until seared and golden. Flip the mushrooms over and cook the other side until golden (if the pan starts to smoke too much, reduce the heat to medium). When the mushrooms are ready, transfer to a plate and season with sea salt, black pepper and a squeeze of lemon. Place the skillet back over the heat and cook the remaining mushrooms.

Meanwhile, to make the whipped almonds, add the almonds and their soaking water, the garlic, tahini, lemon juice, olive oil, parsley and sea salt to a blender or food processor and blitz. It may take 5–10 minutes (depending on how powerful your machine is) to get the almonds really smooth and creamy. If it's too thick, add a little more water and adjust the sea salt, black pepper and lemon to your liking.

Dollop the whipped almonds onto a plate and place the mushrooms on top. Finish with the parsley leaves, toasted sliced almonds, a squeeze of lemon juice and a drizzle of olive oil. Season with sea salt and black pepper and serve.

Gluten-free and vegan

Substitute • almonds: cashews

Vegetable swap • king oyster mushrooms: sliced Chinese eggplant

Southern Fried Mushrooms

While I've never been a fake meat fan and believe there are enough delicious plant-based foods in the world without the need to replicate meat flavors and textures, I do love the sheer playfulness of this dish that unapologetically mimics the physicality of fried chicken. Clusters of mushrooms—maitake (hen of the woods), shimeji (beech), oyster mushroom—work best for this recipe, but you could also use king oyster, halved lengthwise. The chickpea flour batter adds lots of nuttiness, while the polenta coating provides impressive crunch. I have given two cooking methods below—baking and shallow-frying—and to my surprise, both methods yield similar results. I love to eat these wrapped in lettuce leaves, with a blob of spicy mayonnaise—completely irresistible.

SERVES 4

Scant 2 cups (225 g) chickpea flour (besan)

1¼ teaspoons smoked paprika

¼ teaspoon chile powder

½ teaspoon garlic powder or 1 small garlic clove, grated

sea salt and black pepper

1 pound (450 g) maitake, shimeji or oyster mushrooms (preferably in clusters)

1¾ cups (240 g) finely ground or coarse yellow polenta

extra-virgin olive oil

1 head of romaine, butter or iceberg lettuce, leaves separated

Spicy mayonnaise

¾ cup (180 g) vegan or regular mayonnaise

½ teaspoon garlic powder or 1 small garlic clove, grated

1–2 tablespoons Umami Crisp (page 27), Garlicky Chili Oil (page 28) or regular chili crisp

Gluten-free and vegan

Vegetable swap • mushrooms: Chinese eggplant, firm tofu

In a large bowl, combine the chickpea flour, paprika, chile powder, garlic, 1 teaspoon of sea salt and a few turns of black pepper. Pour in 1⅓ cups (320 ml) of water and whisk to combine. Set aside to rest for a few minutes while you prepare the rest of the ingredients.

To make the spicy mayonnaise, place all the ingredients in a small bowl and stir to combine.

Keeping the mushrooms in clusters, gently tear them into chunks.

Place the polenta in a wide bowl and season with sea salt and black pepper.

Line two sheet pans with parchment paper or silicone baking mats. Dip one of the mushroom chunks into the chickpea flour batter, holding it momentarily over the bowl to allow any excess batter to drip off, then place straight in the bowl with the polenta. Carefully turn the mushroom in the polenta to coat. Place the battered mushroom chunk on one of the prepared pans, then repeat until all the mushrooms are coated.

To bake: Preheat the oven to 450°F (230°C). Generously drizzle the battered mushrooms with olive oil and bake for 10 minutes or until golden on the underside. Take the pans out of the oven and flip the mushrooms over, then return to the oven for another 5–10 minutes, until golden and crispy all over.

To shallow-fry: Heat a skillet over medium-high heat and add ½–¾ inch (1.5–2 cm) of olive oil. When the oil is hot, add as many of the battered mushrooms as you can fit, laying them as flat as you can in the oil. If the oil is smoking, reduce the heat a little. Fry for 2–3 minutes, until the undersides are golden, then flip the mushrooms over and cook until golden and crispy all over. Transfer the mushrooms to a plate lined with paper towels to drain.

To serve, scatter the lettuce leaves on a large plate or serving board. Top with the crispy mushrooms and serve with the spicy mayonnaise on the side. To eat, I like to wrap a piece of lettuce around the mushrooms, add a dollop of mayo and enjoy like a sang choy bao.

Black Sesame Mushrooms
with Soba Noodles

This dish is dark in hue and flavors. The black sesame sauce is a powerful ingredient here, imparting a rich, toasty flavor that intensely permeates the noodles. Made of ground black sesame seeds, black sesame paste is the lesser-known sister of tahini—it has a similar nuttiness but a stronger flavor. Sometimes called black tahini, it can be used in both savory and sweet dishes. It tends to have a slightly bitter aftertaste, which counterbalances sweet dishes well; in savory dishes like this, the bitterness is undetectable, but rather imparts an earthy umami.

SERVES 4

10 ounces (300 g) soba noodles

2 tablespoons extra-virgin olive oil

2 teaspoons toasted sesame oil

9 ounces (250 g) shiitake or cremini mushrooms, trimmed and halved

2 garlic cloves, finely chopped

2 cups baby spinach leaves

2 tablespoons black sesame seeds

sea salt and black pepper

2 green onions, finely chopped

Black sesame sauce

2½ tablespoons black sesame paste (black tahini)

2½ tablespoons black vinegar

2½ tablespoons soy sauce or tamari

2 teaspoons maple syrup or brown sugar

2 teaspoons toasted sesame oil

½–1 teaspoon chili oil (optional)

Bring a saucepan of salted water to a boil and add the soba noodles. Cook according to the package directions, until al dente. Drain and rinse under cold water until completely cool (or place in a bowl of iced water). Drain and set aside.

Meanwhile, heat a skillet over medium-high heat. When hot, add the olive oil and sesame oil, along with the mushrooms, and cook for 3 minutes or until they have some color. Reduce the heat to medium, add the garlic and cook, tossing often, for another 3 minutes until the mushrooms are tender and charred in parts. Remove from the heat and set aside to cool slightly.

To make the black sesame sauce, whisk together the black sesame paste and black vinegar, then gradually add the soy sauce or tamari, mixing until smooth. Add the remaining ingredients and whisk again until smooth.

Combine the mushrooms, noodles, spinach and sesame seeds. Add the sauce and use chopsticks or tongs to toss until everything is well coated. Taste and season with sea salt and black pepper, if needed, then top with the green onion and serve.

For gluten-free • use thick rice noodles

Vegan

Substitute • black sesame paste: tahini • black vinegar: apple cider vinegar • soba noodles: udon or ramen noodles • mushrooms: cabbage, tofu

Creamy Mushroom Udon Noodles

Tofu cream is a revelation. It's silky and lush, clings affectionately to each strand of noodle, yet is also feather-light. Creamy noodles can be bland if left to their own devices, but this dish is lifted by the fleshy mushrooms, which are deglazed in black vinegar (or soy sauce/tamari) to bring a tart finish. This tofu cream is also a versatile recipe to add to your repertoire—add some nutritional yeast and fresh herbs to make a silky pasta sauce or blitz it up with garlic, lemon juice and herbs for a ranch-esque dip. I recommend using firm tofu, as it has more body and makes for a heartier sauce.

SERVES 4

1¾ pounds (800 g) fresh cooked or vaccum-sealed udon noodles (or 10 oz/300 g dried)

extra-virgin olive oil

1 leek, white and green parts sliced and washed well

2 garlic cloves, finely chopped

1 pound (450 g) assorted mushrooms, such as shiitake, oyster, enoki, cremini, or button, cut in half or torn

1 tablespoon black vinegar or soy sauce/tamari

sea salt and black pepper

1 green onion, finely sliced

Tofu cream

1 pound (450 g) block of firm tofu, drained and roughly crumbled

1 garlic clove, roughly chopped

2½ tablespoons white (shiro) miso

1 teaspoon sea salt

black pepper

Bring a large saucepan of salted water to a boil. Add the udon noodles and cook according to the package directions until al dente. Drain and reserve 1 cup (240 ml) of the noodle cooking water. Rinse the noodles under cold water and drain again. Set aside.

Heat a large skillet over medium-high heat and drizzle with 1–2 tablespoons of olive oil. Add the leek, reduce the heat to low and cook for 10–12 minutes, until the leek is very soft and starting to caramelize. Increase the heat to medium and add the garlic and mushrooms, along with another drizzle of olive oil, then cook, stirring every now and then, for 6–8 minutes, until the mushrooms are tender and browned. Add the black vinegar or soy sauce/tamari and deglaze the pan (this extracts any bits of mushroom and leek stuck to the base of the pan). Turn off the heat and season with sea salt and black pepper.

To make the tofu cream, place the tofu, garlic, miso, sea salt, a few turns of black pepper and ½ cup (120 ml) of the reserved water in a blender or food processor. Blend for 30–60 seconds, until very smooth. The consistency should be creamy and pourable like cream. If it's too thick, add a touch more water.

Add the tofu cream to the mushroom mixture and stir to combine. Combine the mushroom sauce and noodles. Drizzle with olive oil and serve warm, topped with the green onion.

For gluten-free • use rice noodles

Vegan

Substitute • black vinegar: rice vinegar • udon noodles: ramen, wheat or egg noodles, spaghetti or other long pasta

Mushroom Cheung Fun

Cheung fun, bursting with shrimp, beef or mixed vegetables, is a dim sum staple. It is also a dish we often ate at home, for breakfast or a light lunch. After visits to the Chinese supermarket, my mother would arrive home with multiple packets of premade rolled rice noodles, called chee cheung fun, which she pan-fried and smothered with sweet soy sauce. Often these rice noodle rolls came laced with green onions and har mai (dried baby shrimp). In the 1980s, my mother learned to make her own rice noodles, which she cooked in the microwave (I have used this cooking method to great success).

Homemade cheung fun is relatively simple to make but it does take some patience. Your first, second or third batch may not be perfect, but it's worth persisting. The greatest challenges are in mastering a thin, smooth dough, getting your timings right and finding your rhythm with the steaming.

After years of trialing and making lots of errors in my own recipes, I abandoned my efforts and asked my mum for her cheung fun recipe. It is silky but sturdy and perfect for enjoying either steamed or pan-fried.

My essential cheung fun tips:

- I use fine rice flour (Erawan brand, which is the most common brand at Asian supermarkets), which produces a smoother noodle. Regular rice flour works, too, but I have noticed it feels less silky—for regular rice flour use 1 cup plus 1 tablespoon (170 g).

- I find that a ⅛ sheet pan that measures 9½ × 6½ inches (24 cm × 16.5 cm) or a similar size of rectangular/square plate works best, but explore sizes according to your pots and pans. I steam in either a large, oval Dutch oven or my wok (preferred) with a dome lid.

- Oil your pan generously and **wait for the rice noodles to cool (1–2 minutes) before rolling**. Hot rice noodles are more prone to tearing.

- Set up your station—have a small bowl of oil and a brush ready, with your mushrooms (or other fillings) and herbs close by.

- Whisk your batter every time before adding to the steaming pan as it tends to separate when allowed to sit.

- I use a 4¾-inch (12 cm) pastry bench scraper to roll the rice noodles. The rolling technique takes a while to master; it is more of a "lift and flick." The noodles might break as you're doing this, but don't worry, keep going.

- The rolls are easier to roll without any filling. So consider practicing a few times without the mushroom and green onion filling to get a feel for the dish.

Alternative serving suggestion: To pan-fry, wait until your cheung fun is completely cool (it will become a lot firmer and easier to handle). Heat a nonstick skillet until very hot. Add a drizzle of oil and add the cheung fun, then reduce the heat to medium and cook for 2–3 minutes on each side, until golden and crispy. Drizzle with some sesame paste (tahini is fine) and hoisin sauce, and top with sesame seeds.

MAKES TEN 5-INCH (13 CM) ROLLS

1 cup plus 1 tablespoon (115 g) fine rice flour (I use Erawan brand, available from Asian supermarkets)

1 teaspoon cornstarch

1¾ cups (420 ml) room temperature water

1 teaspoon neutral oil, plus more for brushing

cilantro leaves, to serve

toasted white sesame seeds, to serve

sesame paste or tahini, to serve (optional)

Mushroom filling

extra-virgin olive oil

5 ounces (150 g) shiitake mushrooms (or other variety), finely sliced

1 garlic clove, finely chopped

1 teaspoon soy sauce or tamari

sea salt and black pepper

2 green onions, very finely sliced

small handful of cilantro, leaves picked

Sweet soy sauce (optional)

2½ tablespoons brown or granulated sugar

¼ cup (60 ml) boiling water

4 teaspoons dark soy sauce (or regular soy, tamari or kecap manis)

2 teaspoons soy sauce or tamari

Gluten-free and vegan

To make the mushroom filling, heat a skillet over medium-high heat, add a drizzle of oil and toss in the mushrooms and garlic. Reduce the heat to medium and cook for 3–4 minutes, until the mushrooms are tender and wilted. Turn off the heat, add the soy sauce or tamari and season with sea salt and black pepper. Set aside.

To make the sweet soy sauce, combine all the ingredients in a small bowl and whisk until the sugar is fully dissolved. Set aside.

Combine the rice flour, cornstarch, water and oil in a bowl and whisk together until there are no lumps.

Prepare your steamer. Place a trivet inside a wok or wide saucepan/ Dutch oven that will fit your chosen cooking vessel, or any other type of steamer that can be fully enclosed with a lid. Fill your wok or pan with 2 inches (5 cm) of water and turn the heat to high. Bring the water to a rolling boil.

You will need two small sheet pans or heatproof plates—I use a ⅛ sheet pan that measures 9½ × 6½ inches (24 cm × 16.5 cm). Brush both pans or plates with oil, stir the batter and ladle about ¼ cup (60 ml) of the batter into the pan, swirling it around and using a spoon or chopstick to coax the batter to cover the entire pan in a thin layer. Place the pan onto the trivet inside the wok and dot with two or three slices of mushroom along the shorter end of the batter (no need to wait for it to become solid), then scatter with a little green onion and cilantro. Cover with a lid and steam for 2 minutes (or longer, depending on how thick your batter is), until the batter is bubbling and has turned slightly translucent. Make sure the water is boiling rapidly so the flour mixture doesn't congeal and taste starchy.

Once the first cheung fun is cooked, remove the pan from the steamer and cool for 1–2 minutes, until it is easier to handle (see "My essential cheung fun tips" opposite). Check for water in the pan and top it up if you need to. Stir the batter again and ladle ¼ cup (60 ml) into your second oiled pan or plate. Add this pan to the steamer, repeat the above steps with the mushrooms, green onions and cilantro, then cover and steam.

Once your first pan is cool enough to handle, use a pastry bench scraper or rubber spatula to carefully coax the rice noodle sheet from the bottom edge (if your pan is rectangular, roll from the shorter side) and gently roll it into a log—the action is like a "lift and flick." The noodle sheet may tear as you roll it, particularly in the spots underneath the mushrooms, but persist, as most of the imperfections will be covered up by the time it is rolled up.

Continue this cheung fun assembly line until you have used all the batter and mushroom filling.

To serve, drizzle with the sweet soy sauce (or just regular soy sauce) and top with cilantro leaves and sesame seeds. I also like a little bit of sesame paste or tahini drizzled over the top.

Pictured overleaf ›

Mushroom Cheung Fun

Miso Mushroom Ragu with Baked Polenta

With a mixture of fresh and dried mushrooms, this saucy dish imparts both bright and deeper umami moments, along with contrasting textures. The technique of adding the stock gradually, allowing the liquid to reduce before adding more, allows the mushroom flavors to develop slowly and become more concentrated. The baked polenta is a savior, predominantly hands-off and foolproof. As always, ensure that the polenta is warm when you are ready to serve as it becomes hard as it cools. Store leftover polenta in the fridge; the next day, cut it into fingers and pan-fry. You could also serve this mushroom ragu with pasta or rice.

SERVES 4–6

extra-virgin olive oil

1 yellow onion, finely chopped

4 garlic cloves, finely chopped

2 celery stalks, finely chopped

¾ oz (20 g/about ½ cup) dried porcini mushrooms, soaked in 1 cup (240 ml) boiling water for 20 minutes

2½ tablespoons tomato paste

1 pound (450 g) mixed mushrooms, trimmed and torn

1 thyme sprig

sea salt and black pepper

2 cups (480 ml) vegetable stock

2½ tablespoons white (shiro) miso

4 teaspoons red wine vinegar or balsamic vinegar

handful of chopped parsley

Oven-baked polenta

1¼ cup (170 g) polenta (not quick cooking)

4¼ cups (1 liter) vegetable stock or water

1 teaspoon sea salt

¼ cup (60 ml) extra-virgin olive oil

½ cup (120 ml) nondairy or regular whole milk

Preheat the oven to 350°F (180°C).

To make the oven-baked polenta, place the polenta, stock or water and salt in a baking dish (about 7 × 9½ inches/18 cm × 24 cm) and stir. Place in the oven (with a sheet pan underneath) and bake for 30 minutes. Remove from the oven, add the olive oil and milk, then stir and return to the oven for another 30 minutes.

Heat a large Dutch oven or deep skillet over medium-high heat. Add a good drizzle of olive oil, along with the onion, and cook for 3–4 minutes, until softened and starting to turn golden at the edges. Add the garlic and celery and stir for 1 minute.

Drain the porcini and squeeze out excess moisture, reserving the soaking liquid. Strain the liquid through paper towel or a fine-mesh sieve to remove any sediment.

Add the tomato paste to the onion mixture and stir for 1 minute, then add the porcini, mushrooms, and thyme. Cook, stirring occasionally, for 5 minutes. The mushrooms will become caramelized and then soft. Reduce the heat to medium, add the porcini liquid and season with ½ teaspoon of sea salt. Add 1 cup (240 ml) of the stock and allow this to cook and bubble for 4–5 minutes, until it's reduced. Add the remaining 1 cup (240 ml) of stock and cook for another 9–10 minutes, until it's reduced—the liquid should be quite thick, the consistency of gravy. Stir in the miso and vinegar. Taste and season with sea salt and black pepper.

Serve the baked polenta alongside the mushroom ragu and top with parsley.

Gluten-free and vegan

Substitute • porcini mushrooms: dried shiitake mushrooms • red wine vinegar or balsamic vinegar: lemon juice

Mushroom and Ginger Broth
with Soba and Lime

This broth is gentle yet fiercely flavored, a restorative pick-me-up for moments when your mind, body and soul are seeking a quiet bowl of comfort. Buttery shiitake mushrooms, either fresh or dried, provide the foundation for the broth, with garlic and ginger delivering an extra boost. I've used soba noodles for their delicate, nutty flavor and hearty texture, but you could also use rice vermicelli or a thinner noodle, such as somen. Don't skimp on the lime, as it adds vitality to the broth. In the summer, try this as a cold dish by adding a few ice cubes.

SERVES 4

14 ounces (400 g) soba noodles

4 teaspoons soy sauce or tamari

2 limes, halved

1 green onion, finely sliced

1 small head of broccoli (about 9 oz/250 g), cut into small florets

sea salt and white pepper

Mushroom and ginger broth

9 ounces (250 g) fresh or 2 ounces (60 g) dried shiitake mushrooms, trimmed

2½ tablespoons toasted sesame oil

2 garlic cloves, finely chopped

1-inch (2.5 cm) piece of ginger, peeled and finely sliced

½ teaspoon sea salt

pinch of white pepper

½ teaspoon sugar

6⅓ cups (1.5 liters) vegetable stock

If you are using dried shiitake mushrooms for the broth, soak them in 1 cup (240 ml) of boiling water for at least 30 minutes. Remove the mushrooms, squeezing out excess moisture, and reserve the soaking liquid for the broth, straining it through paper towel or a fine-mesh sieve to remove any sediment. If you are using the soaking liquid, you will only need 5¼ cups (1.25 liters) of vegetable stock.

To make the mushroom and ginger broth, heat a large saucepan over medium heat, add the sesame oil, garlic and ginger and stir for 1 minute, until aromatic. Add the whole shiitake mushrooms and sauté for 3–4 minutes, until everything has softened. Add the sea salt, white pepper, sugar and stock (if you are using the mushroom soaking liquid, add it now), then increase the heat and bring to a boil.

In a separate saucepan, bring some salted water to a boil. Add the soba noodles and cook according to the package directions, until al dente. Drain and run under cold water to stop them from cooking any further. Drain again and divide among four bowls. Drizzle each bowl of noodles with 1 teaspoon of soy sauce or tamari and the juice of ½ lime. Scatter with the green onion.

When the broth is boiling, add the broccoli, season with salt and white pepper and cook for 2 minutes, until bright green and just tender. Divide the broth and broccoli among the four bowls of noodles. Eat immediately.

For gluten-free • use rice vermicelli

Vegan

Substitute • broccoli: Asian greens, iceberg lettuce

Not Your Traditional Sunday Roast

A Sunday roast, reinterpreted. Mushrooms, the "meatiest" of all the vegetables, confidently assume their place as the centerpiece of this dish, simply seasoned with a woodsy sage butter, roasted until golden and crisp and served alongside your favorite vegetables. Flavor the butter as you like—use thyme leaves for a gentle perfume, lemon pepper for a tangy kick or turmeric for a golden glow. You could season the butter with a warm spice blend, such as harissa, ras el hanout or shawarma, and then drizzle the entire roast with a lemon tahini sauce. As it is, I've left my mushroom roast unadorned as I often just crave the purity of pared-back vegetables, but there are plenty of sauces and dressings in this book that could be served alongside this dish, such as miso-maple vinaigrette (see page 292), herby lemon oil (see page 294), soy tahini (see page 41), guasacaca sauce (see page 329) and many more. I've used a cluster of oyster mushrooms as they are sturdy and absorbent, but you could also use another "shroom bundle," such as shimeji (beech), maitake (hen of the woods) or lion's mane. If you can't find a cluster of mushrooms, opt for a giant portobello cap, pine or some chunky king oysters.

SERVES 4

5 tablespoons (70 g) salted regular or vegan butter, melted

sea salt and black pepper

10–15 sage leaves, finely chopped

2 pounds (900 g) roasting vegetables of your choice, such as potatoes, sweet potatoes, turnips, carrots, Brussels sprouts, parsnips

12 ounces (350 g) oyster mushrooms (preferably a cluster)

extra-virgin olive oil

5 rosemary sprigs

1 red or yellow onion, cut into wedges

1 head of garlic, cut in half horizontally

1 lemon, cut into 3–4 thick slices, seeds discarded

Preheat the oven to 425°F (220°C).

Season the melted butter with sea salt, black pepper and the sage.

Scrub your choice of vegetables clean or peel them, then cut into evenly sized pieces that are 1¼–1½ inches (3–4 cm) (if you cut them too large, they will not cook in time).

Remove any woody stems from the mushrooms. Generously drizzle a sheet pan or dish with olive oil and place the rosemary sprigs in the middle to create a bed for the mushrooms. Sprinkle the rosemary with some sea salt. Place the mushrooms on top of the rosemary, then nestle the roasting vegetables, onion wedges, garlic and lemon slices around the mushrooms. Drizzle the sage butter all over the mushrooms, making sure to distribute well into all the crevices. Now drizzle the vegetables with olive oil and season the whole pan with sea salt and black pepper. Place in the oven and roast for 40–50 minutes, until the mushrooms are golden and crispy around the edges.

When cool enough to handle, pop the roasted garlic out of its skins and scatter it all over the vegetables. Squeeze the roasted lemon slices all over too, then drizzle everything with a little olive oil. Serve as is, or with your favorite sauce or dressing.

Gluten-free and vegan

Substitute • sage: thyme, rosemary, lemon zest (see introduction above for other ideas) • onion: leek, shallots

Vegetable swap • mushrooms: small whole cauliflower or cabbage (adjust roasting times)

Stir-Fried Black Fungus and Cucumber

Black and wood ear fungus are staples of my mother's daily cooking. They are a textural delight, springy and crisp, with a jelly-like feel that carries flavors well. Black and wood ear fungus are very similar but differ slightly—black fungus is smaller and slightly thinner, while wood ear has a small coarse "stem" that needs to be trimmed off. Barring those differences, they can be used interchangeably. Here, black fungus is cooked with cucumber, a wonderful ingredient for stir-frying. Across Asia, cucumber is incorporated into many cooked dishes, including soups. My mother often stir-fries cucumber—cooked quickly over high heat, it becomes juicy, with a silky texture and a defined crunch. The trick to cooking cucumber is brevity—you only want to cook it long enough to highlight its flavor and crisp texture, to extract its fresh nectar, but not so much that it becomes limp and tasteless.

SERVES 4

3 Persian (mini) cucumbers, halved lengthwise

1 ounce (35 g/about 1 cup) black or wood ear fungus, soaked in water for 30–60 minutes

neutral oil

1 fresh Thai red chile (or 1 dried chile), finely chopped (seeds removed if you prefer less spice)

½ teaspoon ground Sichuan peppercorns

2 garlic cloves, finely chopped

1 tablespoon soy sauce or tamari

1 teaspoon sea salt

4 teaspoons black vinegar

handful of cilantro leaves

white rice, to serve

Using a spoon, scrape out the seeds of the cucumber and discard. Slice the cucumbers diagonally into ½-inch (1.25 cm) pieces. Drain the black or wood ear fungus.

Heat a skillet over medium-high heat, add 1 tablespoon of oil, along with the chile and Sichuan peppercorns, and sauté for 15–30 seconds, until fragrant. Add the black or wood ear fungus and garlic and toss for 2 minutes—the fungus will crackle and snap loudly in the pan.

Throw the cucumber into the pan, along with the soy sauce or tamari and sea salt, and stir-fry for 2 minutes until the cucumber is only slightly tender, but still very crisp (you definitely want to err on the side of crispy rather than soft!). Take off the heat and add the black vinegar.

Top with cilantro and serve with rice.

Gluten-free and vegan

Substitute • cucumber: zucchini
• ground Sichuan peppercorns: five-spice powder, red pepper flakes

Peas

"Perhaps this is controversial
to say, but I love frozen peas
more than fresh."

Perhaps this is controversial to say, but I love frozen peas more than fresh. To me, fresh peas feel like a lot of work—they require shelling, are only seasonal for a moment and run the risk of being chalky. Frozen peas, on the other hand, are consistent, our dependable best friend. My love of frozen peas comes from my mother, of course. She was, and still is, a big fan of frozen food. From her freezer she could whip out shrimp, squid, whitebait, meat, homemade wontons and more. And there were always bags of peas, along with corn and "mixed vegetables," the pea, corn and carrot mix that she used exclusively for fried rice and macaroni soup. In weeknight cooking, we are best not to forget the flexibility, and power, of the freezer.

Snow peas and sugar snap peas are, by contrast, wonderful when fresh. Snow peas, known as mangetout (French for "eat all") in France and the UK, are a staple in Chinese cooking. But interestingly, they are not native to China. In Cantonese, they are called hor lan do, which means "holland pea." It is believed that snow peas were developed in Holland in the 16th century, traveling to England and then on to China. They became so popular in Chinese cuisine that they are sometimes referred to as "Chinese peas."

Snow peas and sugar snaps are affable legumes. They require only minimal cooking and handling to coax out their natural greatness. Cooked at high heat, they bring a wonderful crunch and vibrancy to stir-fried dishes. They are equally pleasing when eaten raw. Both snow and sugar snap peas can be finely sliced for salads—this is one of my favorite ways of eating them.

And if you are lucky enough to come across pea shoots in the spring, nab them. Known as dou miu in Cantonese, these tender and sweet leaves, stems and twisty tendrils can be eaten raw, but they also spring to life when stir-fried with garlic over high heat.

Miso-Maple Sugar Snap Pea, Turnip and Strawberry Salad

I love the crunch of sugar snaps that have been pan-fried, just enough. *Just enough* is key—it draws out some sweetness, amplifies the sugar snaps' firm exterior, releases their naturally vibrant hues. They should offer resilience to your bite, but yield with minimal effort, offering the eponymous *snap*. You could also leave the sugar snaps raw, just finely sliced. This will offer a different experience, one that is greener, more spring-like. Miso and maple bring out all sides of the sugar snaps—the savory notes, along with earthy sweetness. It's a jaunty dressing, too, one that could be adapted to many vegetable situations. The strawberries complete this story, adding surprising moments of fruitiness and acidity.

SERVES 4

1 cup (200 g) white or mixed quinoa

2 cups (480 ml) vegetable stock or water

extra-virgin olive oil

1 pound (450 g) sugar snap peas, trimmed

sea salt and black pepper

2 small turnips (about 3½ oz/100 g), such as Harukei, peeled and finely shaved

5 ounces (150 g) strawberries, hulled and quartered

handful of mint leaves

Miso-maple vinaigrette

4 teaspoons white (shiro) miso

¼ cup (60 ml) extra-virgin olive oil

4 teaspoons maple syrup

4 teaspoons rice vinegar

1 garlic clove, grated

Place the quinoa and vegetable stock or water in a saucepan and place over medium-high heat. Bring to a boil, then reduce the heat to a simmer, cover and cook for 15–18 minutes, until all the liquid has been absorbed and the quinoa is translucent. Turn off the heat and let cool while you prepare the rest of the salad.

To make the miso-maple vinaigrette, add all the ingredients to a small bowl, along with 4 teaspoons of water. Whisk until smooth and well combined.

Heat a large skillet over medium-high heat. Drizzle with olive oil and add the sugar snap peas, season with sea salt and black pepper and toss for 2–3 minutes, until the sugar snaps turn bright green. Add 1–2 tablespoons of the vinaigrette to the peas and toss for 30 seconds. Allow to cool for 3–5 minutes.

Scoop the quinoa into a large bowl. Add the sugar snaps, turnip, strawberries, mint leaves and the remaining vinaigrette and toss to combine. Serve warm or at room temperature.

Do ahead: The quinoa and sugar snaps can be made several hours ahead of time and left at room temperature (or stored overnight in the fridge). Add the strawberries, turnip and vinaigrette just before you are ready to eat.

Alternative serving suggestion: If you are looking for a lighter dish, you can omit the quinoa and double the amount of sugar snap peas, adding in some baby spinach leaves. You could also use raw sugar snaps—simply slice them finely.

Gluten-free and vegan

Substitute • strawberries: blueberries, blackberries • turnips: radishes

Vegetable swap • sugar snap peas: green peas, snow peas, green beans

Peas and Burrata

My vision for this dish is as simple as its name, peas and burrata. A mound of seasonal sweet sugar snaps, peas and curly pea shoots, hugging a ball of creamy, oozy burrata. Available for the briefest of spring moments, pea shoots (also known as pea tendrils) are leaves from the pea plant, usually the snow or sugar snap pea varieties; they taste potently of peas, crossed with baby spinach. Pea shoots are versatile—while they are most often eaten raw in salads, they can also be stir-fried; I like to add pea shoots to fried rice. For sugar snap peas, a quick blanch brings out their gentle sweetness but, to add more crunch, you could also finely slice them and use them raw in this dish. If you have some toasted pine nuts on hand, they make a nice topping for this dish.

SERVES 4

generous 1 cup (150 g) peas (fresh or frozen)

10 ounces (300 g) sugar snap peas, trimmed

2 balls of burrata (10 oz/280 g)

3½ ounces (100 g) pea shoots (tendrils), torn into smaller pieces

sea salt and black pepper

crusty bread or sourdough, to serve

Herby lemon oil

4 teaspoons chopped mint leaves

4 teaspoons chopped basil leaves

1 small garlic clove, grated

¼ cup (60 ml) extra-virgin olive oil

4 teaspoons lemon juice (from about ½ lemon)

½ teaspoon sea salt

To make the herby lemon oil, place all the ingredients in a bowl and stir to combine. Set aside.

Bring a saucepan of salted water to a boil. If you are using frozen peas, cook them together with your sugar snaps. Add the sugar snaps and frozen peas and cook for just 1–2 minutes, until the sugar snaps are bright green but still have a nice crunch. Remove with a slotted spoon and run under cold water to prevent overcooking. If you are using fresh peas, add them to the same pan of water and blanch for 2–3 minutes, until tender. Drain and run under cold water.

Place the burrata on a serving plate. Arrange the pea shoots around the balls of burrata, then add the sugar snaps and peas. Spoon the herby lemon oil all over the peas and burrata and season everything with sea salt and black pepper. Serve immediately with crusty bread or sourdough.

Shortcut: Don't have time to make the herby lemon oil? Use a good-quality store-bought pesto and finish the dish with a squeeze of lemon juice.

Gluten-free

Veganize • use vegan mozzarella or other nondairy soft cheese

Substitute • burrata: fresh mozzarella, bocconcini, feta, whole-milk ricotta • pea shoots: baby arugula, baby spinach • sugar snap peas: snow peas, green beans

Tingly "Cacio e Pepe" Snow Peas
with Rice Noodles

This is no ordinary cacio e pepe. It comes with a potent three-peppercorn mix—black, white and Sichuan—which brings pungency, heat, fruitiness and mouth-numbing deliciousness. I got the idea for this boundary-bending dish when I was writing an article about the variety of peppercorns found around the world, and how these would taste in different applications. The combination of cacio (sharp pecorino) and pepe (black pepper) is one of the world's most flawless flavor pairings, but this little tweak, with the addition of white and Sichuan peppercorns, is also quite intriguing. I use whole peppercorns and pound them using my mortar and pestle for the freshest flavor. Everyone has a different level of tolerance to Sichuan peppercorns, so I encourage you to add as much or as little as you can enjoy (without losing feeling in your mouth), adding more black or white pepper if you prefer. When I made this dish for my kids, my son Dash happily ate three-quarters of the bowl before he came running into the kitchen for water—the numbing sometimes takes a little while to set in. The snow peas are a real treat here—finely sliced and cooked briefly, they stay crisp, providing a fresh relief from the spice. Timing is everything in this recipe—start the sauce just as your noodles are almost ready; that way, you can add the noodles straight into the sauce without having to drain them and rinse in cold water (which washes off the starch that helps bind the noodles to the sauce, giving a silky finish).

SERVES 4

1 pound (450 g) wide rice noodles

5 tablespoons (70 g) salted regular or vegan butter

9 ounces (250 g) snow peas, trimmed and finely sliced

2 ounces (60 g) pecorino, parmesan or other hard cheese, finely grated (preferably on a Microplane)

sea salt

Three-pepper mix

½–1 teaspoon Sichuan peppercorns, to your liking

½–1 teaspoon black peppercorns

½–1 teaspoon white peppercorns

1 teaspoon sea salt flakes

To make the three-pepper mix, place all the peppercorns and the salt flakes in a mortar. Pound with a pestle until finely ground.

Bring a saucepan of salted water to a boil. Add the rice noodles, stir well and cook for 2 minutes less than the package directions—the noodles should be slightly undercooked, with more of a bite than al dente. Try to time this so that the noodles can be dragged straight into the sauce. Reserve ½ cup (120 ml) of the noodle cooking water.

About 2 minutes before the noodles will be ready, heat a large skillet over medium heat. Melt 3 tablespoons (45 g) of the butter and when it's foamy, add about 2 teaspoons of the pepper mix, along with the snow peas. Toss for 1–1½ minutes, until the snow peas transform from a dull to a vibrant green and the pepper smells fragrant. Pour in half of the reserved noodle cooking water, then add the noodles and the remaining butter. Turn off the heat, add half the pecorino and season with a little sea salt. Toss the noodles until the cheese melts and the noodles are well coated (if they look dry, add some more of the reserved cooking water).

To serve, top with another 1–2 teaspoons of the pepper mix (add as much or as little as you like, according to how spicy you want it) and scatter with the remaining cheese. Serve immediately.

Tip: To slice the snow peas, stack a few together and slice them diagonally.

Gluten-free

Veganize • use vegan cheese

Substitute • three-pepper mix: freshly ground black pepper
• pecorino: ricotta salata, cheddar
• rice noodles: spaghetti, linguine, fettuccine

Pea Egg-Drop Macaroni Soup

My love for macaroni soup runs deep. It's an evocative dish, a reminder of my mother's devotion to cooking hearty breakfasts every morning and the quick lunches we would share when it was just the two of us at home. It is also a dish that captures her time in Hong Kong, where she lived for several years before her passage to Australia was made possible. Macaroni soup is the quintessential breakfast served in Hong Kong's cha chaan teng (this translates to "tea restaurants"), where eclectic Asian-style Western meals are served. It comes with a variety of toppings, including thick slices of ham, often with a fried egg on top. Some versions feature a tomato-based soup (there's a recipe in my book *To Asia, With Love*). My mother's version is simple: macaroni swimming in a stock made with chicken bouillon cubes, dotted with frozen three-vegetable mix (peas, corn and carrot) and cubes of Spam, topped with Maggi seasoning sauce (of course). I adore the sweet, plump peas in this version, which pop with each spoonful of macaroni and soup. I've added an egg drop here, which not only thickens the broth, but adds a richer finish. However, it's fine without it or if you want to go vegan.

SERVES 4

2 cups (200 g) elbow macaroni or other small pasta

4 teaspoons toasted sesame oil

1-inch (2.5 cm) piece of ginger, peeled and finely chopped

2 garlic cloves, finely chopped

6⅓ cups (1.5 liters) vegetable stock

4 large eggs

sea salt and white pepper

2¼ cups (300 g) frozen peas, thawed (or use fresh)

2 green onions, finely chopped

Optional toppings

toasted white sesame seeds

Umami Crisp (see page 27)

Maggi seasoning sauce

chili oil

Bring a saucepan of salted water to a boil. Add the pasta and cook according to the package directions, until al dente. Drain and refresh in cold water. Leave to drain.

Heat a large saucepan over medium heat. Add the sesame oil, ginger and garlic and stir for 30–60 seconds, until fragrant. Pour the stock into the pan, increase the heat to medium high and bring to a boil.

Meanwhile, break the eggs into a spouted measuring cup or a bowl with a spout. Season with about ½ teaspoon of sea salt and a pinch of white pepper. Whisk well.

Once the broth is boiling, season with sea salt and a little white pepper. When you are happy with the seasoning, add the pasta and peas and increase the heat to high. When the broth comes to a boil again, very slowly trickle the egg into the soup (no need to stir). Cook the egg until set, which should take 30–60 seconds.

Ladle the soup into bowls and top with the green onion and whatever optional toppings you prefer.

For gluten-free • use gluten-free pasta

Veganize • omit the eggs

Vegetable swap • peas: carrot, corn

Pea and Kimchi Falafel with Pea Tahini

During the arduous year-plus-long lockdown of 2020, I, like many people around the world, cooked like my life depended on it. And in more ways than one, it did. Planning for how, where and when we could buy groceries punctuated our days. Our time in the kitchen multiplied exponentially, our obsession with the next meal felt oppressive at times and cooking became a way to sustain us, both physically and mentally. Many people hoarded dried beans, or pasta and flour. I stocked up on kimchi, peas and tahini. This is one of the meals I cooked in quarantine. Frozen peas were a childhood favorite, but it was during lockdown that I truly began to appreciate their versatility. I used them in curries, salad dressings, pasta dishes, soups, savory pancakes, dumplings and more. In this untraditional take on falafel, the peas are spectacularly sweet and earthy, the perfect counter to the effervescence of kimchi. Soaked dried chickpeas will give you the best results (see shortcut about using canned or cooked chickpeas), while chilling the falafel before frying helps them stay together and gives a crispier finish. There are a few elements to this dish, but they are all very simple and, in the end, you have a complete, balanced meal that is full of bold, satisfying flavors and textures. Please note, reheated falafel is always drier in texture and is best eaten fresh. If you don't think you'll eat the full quantity, halve this recipe—for reference, this quantity is enough to feed a hungry family of five, three of whom are teenagers.

SERVES 5–6

1½ cups (300 g) dried chickpeas, soaked in cold water for 5–6 hours

1 cup (200 g) vegan or regular kimchi, drained and chopped

generous 1 cup (150 g) frozen peas, thawed

4 green onions, chopped

4 garlic cloves, roughly chopped

⅔ cup whole walnuts or almonds, roughly chopped

1 heaping cup parsley, cilantro, mint or dill, roughly chopped

1½ teaspoons sea salt, or to taste

½–¾ cup (75–90 g) rice flour or chickpea flour (besan), plus more if needed

1 teaspoon baking powder

1 tablespoon toasted white sesame seeds

neutral oil

extra-virgin olive oil (if baking)

4 or more round flatbreads (gluten-free or wheat)

Continued ▸

Drain the chickpeas and place them in a food processor, along with the kimchi, peas, green onion, garlic, nuts, herbs and sea salt and pulse several times to break everything up. Blitz until it's chunky—you want the mixture to be textured, not completely smooth.

Place the chickpea mixture in a bowl. Add the rice flour or chickpea flour, baking powder and sesame seeds and stir to combine. The mixture shouldn't be too wet and needs to be sturdy enough to hold its shape (add more flour if the mixture feels too soft to form into a medium-firm ball). Taste and make sure you are happy with the seasoning—add more salt if needed. Using your hands or a small ice-cream scoop, form the mixture into balls the size of golf balls (you should get 35–40). Place on a plate and chill in the fridge for 30 minutes (or up to 24 hours, covered).

Pour ¾–1¼ inches (2–3 cm) of neutral oil into a deep skillet or small, narrow saucepan. Place over high heat and, when the oil is hot enough—it will sizzle when you insert a wooden chopstick or spoon into the oil—reduce the heat to medium and carefully drop three or four falafel into the oil. Fry for 1–2 minutes on both sides, until golden. Watch the heat and adjust up or down according to how quickly the falafel browns. Remove and place on paper towels to drain, then continue until all the fritters are cooked. You can also bake them—place the balls of dough on a sheet pan lined with parchment paper, flatten them slightly and drizzle generously with olive oil. Bake in a preheated 425°F (220°C) oven for 15 minutes, then flip over and bake for another 15 minutes.

Pea tahini (makes about 1 cup)

generous ¾ cup (115 g) frozen peas, thawed

¼ cup (60 g) tahini

3 tablespoons chopped parsley or mint

1 garlic clove, roughly chopped

2½ tablespoons lemon juice (from about ½ lemon)

½ teaspoon sea salt

Tomato and herb salad

2 large tomatoes (about 1 lb/450 g), chopped into ¾-inch (2 cm) chunks

handful of parsley, cilantro, mint or dill

sea salt and black pepper

extra-virgin olive oil

To make the pea tahini, place all the ingredients in a blender or food processor, add ¼ cup (60 ml) of water and blitz until smooth.

For the tomato and herb salad, combine the tomato and herbs, season with sea salt and black pepper, drizzle with olive oil and stir to combine.

If your flatbreads aren't fresh, dry-fry them in a hot skillet until they are soft with some charring.

Place the flatbreads on plates and top with some of the tomato and herb salad and a few falafel. Drizzle with the pea tahini and serve.

Shortcuts: You can skip the pea tahini and tomato and herb salad if you're short on time. Serve the falafel with store-bought hummus and sliced tomatoes.

To use canned or cooked chickpeas, you will need two 15-ounce (425 g) cans or 2¾–3 cups (450–500 g) of cooked chickpeas. Canned chickpeas are much wetter than soaked dried chickpeas, so you will need to double the flour (at least) to absorb the additional moisture.

Leftovers: Extra falafel can be frozen for up to 3 months. To reheat, let them come to room temperature, then reheat in the oven. They can also be stored in the fridge for up to 3 days.

Troubleshooting: If your falafel fall apart, they are too wet. Test one ball first—if that cooks without coming apart, then you are good to go. If it falls apart, I recommend remixing the balls with more flour.

Pictured overleaf ▸

Gluten-free and vegan

Substitute • rice flour or chickpea flour (besan): all-purpose flour, gluten-free all-purpose flour

Pea and Kimchi Falafel with Pea Tahini

Thai Curry Snow Pea Stir-Fry

The minimal effort in making this light but gratifying stir-fry is not commensurate with the immense pleasure I find in eating it. A bowl of aggressively seasoned, crunchy snow peas feels too simple to be a meal, but it's the crunch, the texture and the persuasive flavors that keep me coming back for more and more. This completely effortless dish is redolent of my mother's almighty vegetable stir-fries—her sweet, crisp greens, glazed in a rich sauce or seasonings, are always a confident accompaniment to white rice (or noodles). Here, I use store-bought Thai curry paste, a weeknight workhorse, as a cheat that buys both time and flavor, adding flair to these tender pods in no time at all.

SERVES 4

1 tablespoon neutral oil

10 ounces (300 g) snow peas, trimmed and sliced in half diagonally

2 garlic cloves, finely chopped

2½ tablespoons vegan Thai red or green curry paste

2½ tablespoons coconut cream, plus more to serve

sea salt

handful of cilantro or basil leaves (or both), to serve

handful of roasted peanuts, roughly chopped

1 lime, quartered

rice or noodles, to serve (optional)

Heat a large skillet over medium-high heat and add a drizzle of oil. Add the snow peas and garlic and stir-fry for 1 minute until the snow peas are bright green. Add the curry paste and coconut cream, then season with sea salt and stir-fry for another 1–2 minutes, until the snow peas are crisp-tender and still vibrantly green.

Remove from the heat and transfer the snow peas to a serving plate. Drizzle with a little more coconut cream (2–3 tablespoons) and scatter with the herbs and peanuts. Serve with lime wedges and eat on its own as a side dish, or with rice or noodles as a complete meal.

Gluten-free and vegan

Substitute • coconut cream: coconut milk, cream

Vegetable swap • snow peas: sugar snap peas, green beans, asparagus

Smushy Spiced Peas
with Any Roasted Vegetables

These are not the overcooked frozen peas you remember from childhood. Smashed, and only a bit mushy, these "smushy" peas are a brazen reinterpretation of the Australian and British classic, where mushy peas collide with zhoug, the spicy cilantro sauce of Yemenite origin that you also find in Syria and Israel. Frozen peas do the job here, bringing lots of natural sweetness, smashed up in the company of cardamom, cumin, chile and plenty of fresh cilantro. What emerges is an enchanting condiment-slash-sauce, which provides a verdant canvas for roasted or grilled vegetables; any type you like. You could also stir these smushy peas into warm potatoes or pasta.

SERVES 4

2¼ cups (300 g) frozen peas

2 garlic cloves, finely chopped

¼ teaspoon ground cardamom or seeds from 2 pods, ground

½ teaspoon cumin seeds or ground cumin

1–2 jalapeño or serrano chiles, roughly chopped

1 small bunch of cilantro (about 1¾ oz/50 g), roughly chopped

⅓ cup (80 ml) extra-virgin olive oil

sea salt and black pepper

roasted or grilled vegetables, to serve

handful of soft herbs of your choice, such as cilantro, mint, dill, parsley

1 lemon, quartered, to serve

Bring a saucepan of salted water to a boil. Add the frozen peas and blanch for 1 minute, until bright green. Drain, refresh under cold water and drain again.

Place the peas in a food processor or blender, along with the garlic, cardamom, cumin, chile and cilantro. Pulse eight to ten times, until everything is mashed up, but not smooth. You want this mixture to be chunky. Add the olive oil and pulse again, three or four times, just until everything has come together. Season well with sea salt and black pepper.

Serve with your choice of roasted or grilled vegetables, topped with your herbs of choice, and with a wedge of lemon on the side.

Gluten-free and vegan

Substitute • jalapeño or serrano chile: fresh Thai red chile, red pepper flakes • lemon: lime

Vegetable swap • frozen peas: broccoli, potato, eggplant

Potato

"A beloved staple across
countless cultures"

In the late 18th century, Queen Marie Antoinette wore potato flowers in her hair to help popularize the scorned potato among French society, who still preferred wheat and bread. It worked, and soon after potatoes gained favor among the cognoscenti. Acreage was given for the growing of potatoes. The rise of the potato in French cuisine was well timed—in 1785, when famine struck Northern France, starvation was avoided thanks to this humble tuber.

Indeed, potatoes changed the world in many ways, but, most important, they made it more delicious. They are a beloved staple across countless cultures. Growing up, my mother used potatoes in omelets, stir-fries, saucy braises and in the classic regional dish from my family's native Zhongshan, si jai gao (steamed potato cakes). Made with a rice flour batter dotted with potato, har mai (dried baby shrimp) and siu yuk (roast pork), we devoured these savory cakes during cultural and family celebrations.

There are countless varieties of potatoes, and many wonder about the right potato for specific dishes.

Starchy, or baking potatoes, such as russets (aka Idahos), are best for frying or baking. The flesh becomes fluffy while the exterior crisps up. Starchy spuds don't hold their shape well, so they aren't great for salads; they are okay for mash, but their high starch content means they can become gluey, so don't overwork.

Waxy potatoes, such as new potatoes, red bliss, fingerlings and pee wee, have a creamy, firm and moist flesh and hold their shape well; they are perfect for boiling, roasting, in gratins and in salads.

All-rounders, such as Yukon Golds, possess the right combo of starch and moisture to hold up to nearly any cooking technique; a great option for boiling, roasting, baking, mashing and fries.

Roasted Potato and Lentil Salad
with Black Sesame Aioli

While it is easy to love a potato salad, this one inspires even wilder affection because of the delicious black sesame aioli. The sauce has all the garlicky creaminess we love about aioli, while also introducing nuttiness and earthiness from the black sesame seeds and sesame oil. This aioli is a wonderful all-rounder to add to your cooking repertoire—it's good with any and all roasted veggies and it's great in sandwiches, too. While waxy potatoes are usually best for boiled potato salads, I prefer an all-purpose variety here—medium-starch potatoes, such as Yukon Gold, get wonderfully crispy and caramelized, while the interior remains creamy.

SERVES 4

2 ¾ pounds (1.25 kg) all-purpose potatoes, such as Yukon Gold, peeled and cut into ¾–1 ¼-inch (2–3 cm) pieces

extra-virgin olive oil

sea salt and black pepper

1 cup (200 g) Puy (French) or black lentils

1 garlic clove, peeled

1 large carrot (about 5 oz/150 g), coarsely grated

4 green onions, finely chopped

handful of toasted black sesame seeds, to serve

Black sesame aioli

2 ½ tablespoons black sesame seeds

½ cup (125 g) vegan or regular mayonnaise

1 garlic clove, grated

4 teaspoons extra-virgin olive oil

4 teaspoons toasted sesame oil

sea salt and black pepper

Preheat the oven to 400°F (200°C).

Place the potato on a sheet pan, drizzle with extra-virgin olive oil and season with sea salt and black pepper. Roast for 20–25 minutes, until the potato is tender and golden.

Meanwhile, place the lentils and garlic in a saucepan of water and season with sea salt. Bring to a boil over medium-high heat, then reduce the heat to a simmer and cook for 20–25 minutes, until the lentils are just tender. Drain and stir the garlic into the lentils (it will break up).

To make the black sesame aioli, add the sesame seeds to a high-powered blender, small food processor or spice grinder and blend to a rough powder. Place in a bowl, add the mayonnaise, garlic, olive oil and sesame oil and whisk to combine. Add about 1 tablespoon of water to loosen it up. Taste and season with sea salt and black pepper.

Combine the potato, lentils, carrot and three-quarters of the green onion in a large bowl, add half the black sesame aioli and fold it in. To serve, dollop the remaining aioli over the top, scatter with the remaining green onion and finish with a few black sesame seeds.

Gluten-free and vegan

Substitute • lentils: chickpeas
• carrot: cabbage

Vegetable swap • potato: Brussels sprouts, parsnip, rutabaga, Jerusalem artichoke

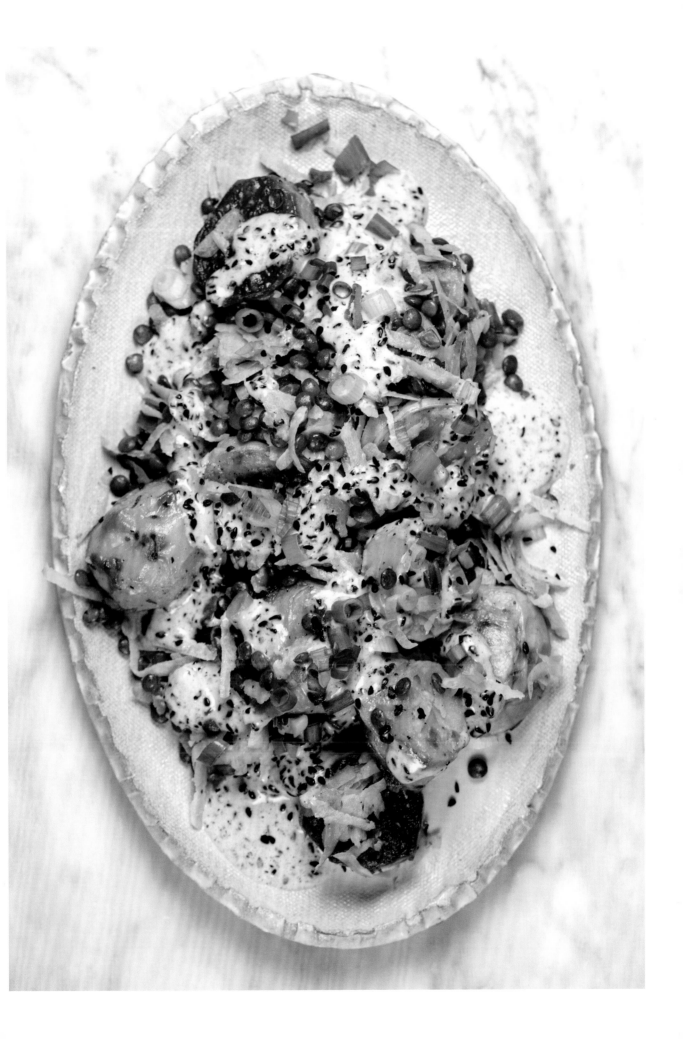

Hazelnut Hasselback Potato Gratin

Potatoes are essential to our holiday and celebration table, and for the past few years, this has been our chosen dish. This rich vegan gratin is perfumed with leeks and rosemary, and smothered in a velvety hazelnut cream. While you can use store-bought hazelnut milk, I always make my own (see Notes below for instructions)—I like the pronounced nuttiness of homemade hazelnut milk, which delivers a creamy béchamel-like sauce that is still light. Use the whole leek, including the green leaves that many recipes ask you to discard—these are slightly tougher than the tender whites, but this dish cooks in the oven for over an hour, plenty of time for them to soften.

**SERVES 4 AS A MAIN OR
6–8 AS A SIDE**

3 tablespoons (42 g) regular or vegan butter

3 tablespoons (30 g) rice flour or all-purpose flour

3 cups plus 2 tablespoons (750 ml) hazelnut milk (see Note)

1 garlic clove, finely chopped

pinch of freshly grated nutmeg

1 sprig of rosemary, leaves picked and finely chopped

1 tablespoon soy sauce or tamari

sea salt and black pepper

1 leek, white and green parts finely sliced and washed well

extra-virgin olive oil

3 pounds 5 ounces (1.5 kg) potatoes (any variety), scrubbed

15–20 sage leaves

Gluten-free and vegan

Substitute • hazelnut milk: cashew milk • leek: yellow onion • sage: rosemary

Vegetable swap • potato: sweet potato, taro

Preheat the oven to 350°F (180°C). You'll need an ovenproof dish—I use an 8½-inch (22 cm) square baking dish, but you can size slightly up or down.

Heat a saucepan over medium heat and melt the butter. Gradually add the flour, a tablespoon at a time, whisking constantly to prevent burning or clumps. When well combined with the melted butter, add the hazelnut milk and 1 cup (240 ml) of water and whisk constantly for 2–3 minutes, until creamy and slightly thicker (you want the consistency of heavy cream). Whisk in the garlic, nutmeg, rosemary, soy sauce or tamari and season well with sea salt and black pepper. Remove from the heat and set aside.

Place the leek in the ovenproof dish, drizzle with some olive oil, season with sea salt and black pepper and toss. Press the leek into an even layer, then add ½ cup (120 ml) of the hazelnut cream and smooth it out with the back of a spoon.

Next, finely slice the potatoes using a mandoline or sharp knife (a mandoline makes this job so much easier and quicker). As you are slicing, try to keep the potatoes in a neat stack. Arrange the stacks of potato in the dish, edge-side up, until the dish is full. I usually like to place the stacks in an alternating crisscross pattern, but you can simply line them up across the dish or in a circular pattern—it's up to you. The potato should be tightly packed.

Pour the remaining hazelnut cream over the potatoes, drizzle with olive oil and season with sea salt and black pepper. Place the dish on a sheet pan to catch any drips, then cover with foil and bake for 1 hour.

Meanwhile, place the sage leaves in a small bowl, drizzle with olive oil and season with a pinch of salt.

After 1 hour, remove the foil from the potato and scatter on the sage. Increase the oven temperature to 420°F (230°C) and bake for another 15–20 minutes, until the potatoes are golden and bubbling, and the sage leaves are crispy.

Serve with a green salad or steamed veggies.

Note: To make your own hazelnut milk, soak 1 cup of hazelnuts in boiling water for 30 minutes. Drain, then place the hazelnuts in a high-powered blender or food processor. Add 1 grated garlic clove and 2 cups (480 ml) of water (or vegetable stock, if you want more flavor) and blend until completely smooth. A high-powered blender will give you the smoothest results. This will yield 3 cups plus 2 tablespoons (750 ml) of hazelnut milk, enough for this recipe.

Spiced Double Potato Noodles

Made of potato starch, these handmade noodles are very different from homemade wheat-based noodles. Starches contain no gluten, so the raw dough is very supple. When cooked, the potato starch noodles become translucent, bouncy and rewardingly chewy. These noodles come together quickly—simply mix, knead and roll. The short noodles are similar in look and texture to Chinese silver needle noodles, which are known for their short tapered shape (they are also called rat's tail noodles in some Asian countries), and which are steamed rather than boiled, as I have done here. The stir-fry can be made with any type of large potato—cooked briefly at high heat, even starchy potatoes like russets won't fall apart. If you're looking for a shortcut, skip the homemade noodles and serve this potato stir-fry with store-bought sweet potato starch noodles or mung bean vermicelli for a similar stretchy noodle experience.

An important note: you need to use potato *starch* for these noodles, not potato flour.

SERVES 4

2 cups plus 2 tablespoons (340 g) potato starch, plus more for kneading

neutral oil

¾ cup plus 4 teaspoons (200ml) boiling water

1 pound (450 g) potato (any variety), peeled and finely julienned

½ teaspoon sea salt

½ teaspoon sugar

4 garlic cloves, finely chopped

4 green onions, white and green parts separated, finely chopped

¼ cup (60 ml) soy sauce or tamari

2½ tablespoons toasted sesame oil

1–2 tablespoons chili oil or chili crisp, plus extra to serve

1½ teaspoons ground cumin

2 handfuls of green leaves of your choice (such as garlic chives, baby bok choy, cabbage, spinach, kale), shredded

2 tablespoons toasted white sesame seeds, plus more to serve

2½ tablespoons black vinegar

Place the potato starch and 2 tablespoons plus 2 teaspoons of oil in a large bowl and stir together. Add the boiling water and, using a wooden spoon or spatula, stir to combine. It should look lumpy and a bit translucent. Cover with a plate or lid and leave to steam for 5 minutes. After 5 minutes, the dough should be cool enough to handle. Knead it with your hands in the bowl until it comes together. Scatter your work surface with a little potato starch and plop your dough on top. Knead for 4–5 minutes, until it is smooth and stretchable. If it feels dry and is cracking, add a touch more boiling water. If it feels sticky, dust with more potato starch. It should feel smooth and neither dry nor sticky.

Divide the dough into two equal pieces. Put one piece aside and cover with a damp tea towel. With the first piece of dough, break off ⅜–½-inch (1–1.5 cm) pieces, roll them into small balls until smooth, then roll them between your palms or on a clean work surface (they shouldn't stick) until you have short noodles that are 2–3⅛ inches (6–8 cm) long—they should be thicker in the middle, with tapered ends. The noodles don't all have to be the same size. Place the noodles on a surface that has been lightly dusted with potato starch and cover with a damp tea towel while you roll the second piece of dough into noodles.

Prepare an ice bath: fill a large bowl halfway with cold water and add some ice cubes.

Bring a large pot of salted water to a boil over high heat. Add the noodles—they will float to the top after 1 minute, then cook for another 3–4 minutes, until the noodles become swollen. This will take longer if your water isn't rapidly boiling so try to maintain a high heat. Using a large slotted ladle, remove the noodles and plunge them straight into the ice bath—they will become translucent in the cold water. Leave the noodles in the water while you prep the stir-fry ingredients.

Heat a wok or large skillet over medium-high heat until it is very hot. Add 2½ tablespoons of neutral oil, then add the potato strips, sea salt and sugar. Cook, tossing constantly, for 4–5 minutes, until the potato is just tender but still a little crisp. Reduce the heat to medium and add the garlic, white part of the green onion, soy sauce or tamari, sesame oil, chili oil or chili crisp, cumin, shredded greens and sesame seeds. Stir together for 1–2 minutes, then drain the potato noodles and add them to the wok or pan, tossing until they are completely hot. Add the black vinegar and toss to combine. Check the seasoning and add more sea salt, if needed.

To serve, top with the green part of the green onion and extra sesame seeds or chili oil, if you like. Eat either hot or warm.

Do ahead: The noodles can be cooked and stored in the ice bath for several hours. They can be drained and added to the potato stir-fry as instructed above, but they will need to cook for 1–2 minutes longer to warm them all the way through.

Pictured overleaf ›

Gluten-free and vegan

Vegetable swap • potato: taro, sweet potato

Spiced Double Potato Noodles

Potato and Olive Oil Flatbread

The first time I tried potato and rosemary pizza, I was a six- or seven-year-old fish-out-of-water at a teenager's house party. My sister, several years my senior, had brought me along to a friend's party and, when I arrived, I was promptly herded into the kitchen, into the embrace of Nonna, the grandmother of the house. Nonna smelled like garlic and rosemary, warmth and love. She sat me down at the small kitchen table and plucked hot pizzas from the oven. She fed me potato and rosemary pizza and it was sublime, unlike any pizza I had ever tasted (in fact, this might have been the first pizza I ever tried). The potato was as thin as silk, and meltingly tender, heavily showered with rosemary leaves. The base was without sauce, steeped in olive oil, crusty and crisp. Nonna's perfect pizza is the inspiration for this potato and olive oil flatbread, made with an unleavened yogurt dough, rather than a traditional pizza dough (see shortcut below).

MAKES ONE 12-INCH (30 CM) FLATBREAD

1¾ cups plus 2 tablespoons (225 g) all-purpose flour, plus more for dusting

1 teaspoon fine sea salt

2 teaspoons baking powder

⅔ cup (160 g) plain or vegan yogurt

1 large potato (about 9 oz/250 g), scrubbed

1 garlic clove, grated

extra-virgin olive oil

sea salt and black pepper

5 ounces (150 g) mozzarella, roughly chopped (optional)

1–2 rosemary sprigs, leaves picked

Veganize • use vegan yogurt and mozzarella

Substitute • rosemary: sage

Vegetable swap • potato: zucchini, sweet potato

Place the flour, salt and baking powder in a bowl and whisk to combine. Add the yogurt and mix with a wooden spoon until you have a stiff dough. Turn out onto a lightly floured work surface and knead the dough until it comes together cohesively—it will still look a little lumpy at this stage. Place in a lightly floured bowl, cover with a clean tea towel and allow to rest while you prepare the remaining ingredients. (The ideal resting time is 20–30 minutes. The dough can also be made a day ahead and rested in the fridge overnight. Bring back to room temperature before rolling out.)

Preheat the oven to 425°F (220°C).

Set up a large bowl of cold tap water. Using a mandoline, the slicing disc on a food processor or a sharp knife, finely slice the potato (leave the skin on) and place the slices straight into the bowl of water to prevent them from browning.

On a lightly floured surface, roll the dough into an oval-ish shape that is approximately 12 inches (30 cm) long and 8 inches (20 cm) wide—this does not have to be exact. Transfer the dough to a piece of parchment paper.

Place the garlic in a small bowl, drizzle with about 2 tablespoons of olive oil and stir to mix well. Pour the garlic oil over the dough and use the back of a spoon to spread it evenly. Sprinkle with sea salt. If you are using mozzarella, scatter it over the dough. Drain the potato in a colander and press with a clean tea towel to remove excess water. Arrange the potato slices, slightly overlapping, over the dough, leaving a scant ¼-inch (5–6 mm) border around the edge, and scatter with the rosemary. Season with more sea salt and a few turns of black pepper, and drizzle with some more olive oil. Bake for 22–25 minutes, until the flatbread edges are golden and the edges of the potato are crispy. If your potato is not as golden as you'd like, you could move the pan up to the top rack and broil for 2–3 minutes—but watch it like a hawk as it will burn quickly.

Cool for 5 minutes, then cut into slices and serve.

Shortcut: Replace the yogurt flatbread dough with a store-bought uncooked pizza dough or precooked crust.

Baked Potato Dinner

Growing up, with rice and a Cantonese banquet as our daily dinner, my mother's sai chaan, or "Western meal," was a rare treat. Usually comprising a well-done T-bone steak served alongside roast potatoes, blanched peas and boxed gravy, this meal felt like a window into another world, a momentary reprieve from the perceived cultural shackles of my upbringing. My favorite part of my mother's sai chaan was the roast potatoes, golden and crispy-edged, simply seasoned with salt and white pepper. Here, the baked potatoes of my youth become the star of this weeknight-friendly sheet-pan meal. A giant baked potato is a blank canvas for toppings—fill with legumes, pesto, tahini, kimchi, chili oil, wilted greens, your favorite cheeses or a simple flavored butter, as I've done here. While whole potatoes take a while to cook, it is mostly hands-off cooking. Serving some vegetables and salty cheese alongside the potatoes turns this into a complete, hearty, vegetable-packed meal.

SERVES 4

6 large starchy potatoes (about 3 lb 5 oz/1.5 kg), such as russets, scrubbed

extra-virgin olive oil

sea salt and black pepper

3 garlic cloves, unpeeled

6 tablespoons (84 g) regular or vegan butter, at room temperature

1 green onion, finely chopped

10 ounces (300 g) broccolini or broccoli

9 ounces (250 g) Halloumi, drained and cut into slices a scant ¼ inch (5–6 mm) thick

Gluten-free

Veganize • use vegan butter and substitute vegan feta or extra-firm tofu for the Halloumi

Substitute • broccolini/broccoli: green beans, Brussels sprouts, baby bok choy

Vegetable swap • potato: sweet potato

Preheat the oven to 400°F (200°C).

Place the potatoes on a sheet pan and cut a slit in the middle, down the length of each potato (this is where you'll split the potato when it's cooked). Drizzle with some olive oil and sprinkle with sea salt. Add the garlic cloves to the pan. Roast the potatoes for 1½–2 hours, until the skins are crispy and the interiors are completely tender and fluffy.

After 20 minutes, remove the garlic cloves and allow to cool. When cool enough to handle, remove the skin and place the garlic in a bowl, along with the butter. Mash until smooth, then add the green onion and season with sea salt and black pepper.

Cut the broccolini or broccoli into similar-sized pieces—if some stems are thicker than others, slice them lengthwise so they are thinner. Place in a bowl, along with the Halloumi, and drizzle with some olive oil.

Remove the potatoes from the oven. Carefully slice through the same slits you cut in each potato before they were baked. Using a clean tea towel to protect your fingers, carefully squeeze both sides of the potatoes to pop them open—the potatoes will be scorching hot so take care. Using a fork, carefully mash some of the potato flesh inside to fluff it up. Place a dollop of the roasted garlic and green onion butter (about a tablespoon) into each potato and let it melt into the flesh. Now dot the broccolini and Halloumi around the potatoes, making sure they are in a single layer to ensure even cooking. Return the pan to the oven for 15–20 minutes, until the broccolini is crisp-tender and the Halloumi is turning golden.

Remove from the oven and serve while still hot.

Mum's Velvet Potatoes

My mother made many dishes that we considered to be "signatures," and her saucy pork chops with potatoes is one we absolutely adored growing up. It is a dish I watched her make a lot, and even as a young vegetarian adult, I still asked my mother to teach me how to make it. Starting with hefty bone-in pork chops, use the blunt side of a cleaver or knife to repeatedly slash at the meat in a crisscross pattern to tenderize it. The chops then go into a large bowl, along with sliced potatoes, soy sauce, Shaoxing rice wine, salt, sugar, cornstarch, a splash of water; toss together. A wok is heated, a few cloves of smashed garlic go in to perfume the oil, then the pork chops, potatoes and all the juices are added to the pan. A lid goes on. It is tossed every now and then. When it is ready, the pork and potatoes are unthinkably tender and juicy. Recently, I learned that this home-style technique of dredging meat in cornstarch is called *velveting*, a rather regal name for such a simple technique. I've used my mother's velveting craft for these potatoes, a simple dish that is silky and flavorful, an elegant, luxurious way to enjoy this humble vegetable.

SERVES 4

¼ cup (35 g) cornstarch

2 tablespoons Shaoxing rice wine

2 tablespoons soy sauce or tamari

2¼ pounds (1 kg) potatoes (any variety), peeled and sliced into discs a scant ⅓ inch (8 mm) thick

neutral oil

2 shallots, finely sliced

2 garlic cloves, peeled and smashed but left whole

sea salt and white pepper

2 green onions, sliced

rice, to serve

Make a slurry by combining the cornstarch, Shaoxing rice wine and soy sauce or tamari in a large bowl. Add 2 tablespoons of water and whisk to combine. Add the potato and toss well to coat. Set aside.

Heat a wok or large skillet over medium-high heat. When hot, drizzle generously with oil and add the shallot and garlic cloves. Allow to sizzle for 15 seconds, then reduce the heat to medium and cook for 3–4 minutes, until softened and starting to caramelize. Add the potato, along with the cornstarch slurry, and ¾ cup (180 ml) of water. Stir and toss the potato well to prevent lumps, then, when it bubbles, reduce the heat to low, cover with a lid and cook for 20–25 minutes, tossing every 5 minutes or so, until the potato is tender and glistening (it may cook quicker if your potato slices are smaller, so check the potato often for doneness). Taste and season with sea salt and white pepper.

Transfer the potato to a serving bowl and top with the green onion. Serve with rice.

For gluten-free • replace the Shaoxing rice wine with dry sherry or water

Vegan

Substitute • shallot: 1 yellow onion

Big Potato Pancake
with Quick-Pickled Apple Salad

While I did not grow up celebrating Christmas in the traditional, cultural or religious sense, my dad loved Christmas and he made sure that we were able to experience at least some of what this holiday means in the West. He bought us synthetic Christmas trees, baubles and tinsel, sent out Christmas cards to family and friends and, as he became more familiar with conventions, he ensured that Santa visited me. Since then, I've been Christmas obsessed. During the years that my husband and I lived in London, we often visited the Christmas markets that take over European cities during December. This potato pancake is inspired by our family visit to Nuremberg's famed Christkindlesmarkt, which takes place during Advent. While there, the rest of my family enjoyed Nuremberg bratwurst and all varieties of German sausages, while I devoured fried potato cakes with applesauce—for three days straight (the vegetarian offerings were slim).

Use a starchy potato for maximum crunch, though waxy potatoes work, too. The key to a pancake that is crispy on the outside, soft on the inside and not laden with oil is to get the pan and fat very hot before you add the potato.

SERVES 4

2¼ pounds (1 kg) potatoes, preferably russet, peeled

1 teaspoon sea salt

6 tablespoons (84 g) ghee (or 3 tablespoons extra-virgin olive oil plus 3 tablespoons butter)

Quick-pickled apple salad

1 garlic clove, grated

2½ tablespoons apple cider vinegar

sea salt and black pepper

½ teaspoon sugar

1 apple, such as Fuji

1 celery stalk, finely sliced

3–4 handfuls of baby arugula or salad greens

handful of chopped chives

3 tablespoons extra-virgin olive oil

¼ cup (50 g) sour cream (optional)

¼ cup toasted sliced almonds

Gluten-free

Veganize • use olive oil, vegan butter and omit the sour cream

Vegetable swap • potato: taro

Grate the potatoes using the largest holes on a box grater—I like to hold my potato lengthwise so I can grate it into long strands. Grab handfuls of the potato and squeeze it tightly using both hands to draw out as much liquid as possible. Place the potato in a bowl, add the sea salt and toss to combine.

Heat a nonstick or well-seasoned cast-iron skillet (mine is 8½ inches/ 22 cm) over high heat. When hot, add 3 tablespoons of the ghee (or 1½ tablespoons of olive oil and 1½ tablespoons of butter) and allow to melt and heat up. Add the potato and, using a spatula, tidy up the potato around the edges by tucking them in (this makes the final pancake neater). Reduce the heat to medium low and cook for 10–12 minutes, until the potato is golden brown and crispy on the bottom.

Now we are ready for the flip. If you are worried about your potato sticking, carefully run a silicone spatula underneath just to make sure it's not stuck. You can flip the potato onto a plate or small wooden board (something with a handle helps a lot)—whatever you use, make sure it's not heavy. Place the plate or board over the skillet and quickly and confidently flip the pan over so that the crispy potato bottom is facing up on the plate or board. Add the remaining 3 tablespoons of ghee (or 1½ tablespoons of olive oil and 1½ tablespoons of butter) to the pan and let it melt. Gently slide the pancake back into the pan and cook for another 10–12 minutes over medium-low heat, until crispy and golden.

Meanwhile, make the quick-pickled apple salad. In a large bowl, add the garlic, vinegar, ½ teaspoon of sea salt and the sugar and stir to combine. Cut the apple into quarters and remove the core. Slice each quarter into ¼–⅓-inch (7–8 mm) pieces. Place in the vinegar mix and toss to combine. Let sit for 5–10 minutes, while you wait for the pancake to finish cooking. When ready to serve, add the celery, arugula or salad greens, chives, olive oil, sour cream (if using) and almonds to the quick-pickled apple, and season well with sea salt and black pepper. Toss well.

Slide the potato pancake onto a serving board or plate, cut into wedges, and serve alongside the apple salad.

Crispy Potato Wedges
with Lentils and Guasacaca Sauce

Potato wedges go from fast food to a hearty salad in this delightfully textured dish. Soaking your potatoes in hot water before baking removes excess starch and allows them to absorb moisture, leading to a crispy exterior with an internal flesh that stays moist and fluffy. If you are short on time, you can simply rinse your potatoes to remove at least some of the starch. Guasacaca is a bright and tangy avocado sauce from Venezuela, a versatile condiment, which can be served with empanadas, arepas or roasted vegetables (it works with seafood and meat, too, if you are so inclined). It's part dip, part dressing, and is a lively accompaniment that lightens up the heft of the potatoes and lentils.

SERVES 4–6

6 large starchy potatoes (about 3 lb 5 oz/1.5 kg), such as russet, scrubbed

extra-virgin olive oil

1 teaspoon garlic powder

1 teaspoon paprika

sea salt and black pepper

1 cup (200 g) Puy (French) lentils

handful of cilantro or parsley leaves

lime wedges, to serve

Guasacaca sauce (makes 1½ cups)

1 small red onion or shallot, roughly chopped

1 garlic clove, roughly chopped

1 ripe avocado (about 8 oz/220 g), chopped

1 jalapeño or fresh Thai green chile, roughly chopped

½ cup chopped cilantro (leaves and stems)

½ cup chopped parsley (leaves and stems)

1 tablespoon rice vinegar or white vinegar

zest and juice of 1 lime (about ¼ cup/60 ml juice)

sea salt

2½ tablespoons extra-virgin olive oil

Gluten-free and vegan

Substitute • garlic powder: harissa powder • Puy (French) lentils: cooked chickpeas

Vegetable swap • potato: sweet potato

Cut each potato in half lengthwise, then halve again into quarters. Finally, halve each quarter, so you have eight wedges per potato that are about the same size. Place in a bowl and cover with hot water (the hottest tap water is fine) for 10 minutes.

Preheat the oven to 400°F (200°C). Line two sheet pans with parchment paper.

Drain the potato and pat dry with paper towels. Divide the potato wedges between the prepared pans, drizzle with olive oil and sprinkle with the garlic powder and paprika. Season well with sea salt and black pepper and, using your hands, toss until the potato is well coated. Lay the wedges out with one cut side facing up and place on the middle and bottom racks of your oven. Roast for 30 minutes. Remove both pans from the oven and flip the wedges over onto the other cut side. Swap the pans and place the one that was on the middle rack on the bottom rack, and vice versa. Roast for another 25–30 minutes, until deeply golden and crispy.

Meanwhile, bring a saucepan of salted water to a boil. Add the lentils and cook for 20–25 minutes, until just tender. Drain. Place the warm lentils in a bowl and drizzle with 1–2 tablespoons of olive oil and season with sea salt and black pepper.

To make the guasacaca sauce, place the red onion or shallot, garlic, avocado, chile, cilantro, parsley, vinegar, lime zest and juice and 1 teaspoon of sea salt in a food processor or blender (you can also use a mortar and pestle) and blitz until coarsely ground. Add the olive oil and puree until the sauce is smooth and creamy.

To serve, I like to layer the sauce, lentils and potato. Spread some of the guasacaca sauce on a large serving platter (or individual serving plates), top with a handful of lentils, a few potato wedges and a few smaller dollops of sauce. Repeat this again—lentils, potato and sauce—until you have a nice stack. Season everything with sea salt and black pepper, shower with cilantro or parsley leaves and serve with lime wedges.

Shortcut: For a time-saver, use canned lentils.

Crispy Potato Tacos

Potato tacos, or tacos de papa as they are known in Mexico, is the perfect meal for those times when you find yourself with an excess of potatoes (often) and a package of tortillas on hand (always). Tortillas are an endlessly versatile pantry item and here they are stuffed with potato and cheese for a deeply satisfying meal or light snack. I like to cook the potatoes whole, with the skin on, which not only prevents them from absorbing too much water, but the skin also adds a nice texture to the filling. Using small potatoes will ensure that they cook faster. If you have leftover mashed potatoes, use them for the filling.

SERVES 4

1½ pounds (700 g) small potatoes, scrubbed

1½ cups (165 g) grated cheddar

1 small garlic clove, finely chopped

1 teaspoon ground cumin

1 teaspoon paprika

handful of cilantro, leaves and stems finely chopped

1 teaspoon sea salt

16–18 corn tortillas

neutral oil

finely sliced lettuce or cabbage, to serve (optional)

½ small red onion, very finely sliced, to serve (optional)

sour cream, to serve (optional)

Spicy red salsa

3 tomatoes (about 1 lb/450 g), chopped

1 garlic clove, chopped

½ red onion, roughly chopped

small handful of cilantro, leaves and stems roughly chopped

½–1 fresh Thai red chile (seeded if you prefer less spice)

1 teaspoon ground cumin

1 teaspoon dried oregano

1 teaspoon sugar

1 teaspoon sea salt

¾ cup (180 ml) vegetable stock

Gluten-free

Veganize • use vegan cheese (or omit) and omit the sour cream

Substitute • cheddar: grated feta or Halloumi • fresh tomatoes: canned whole tomatoes

Bring a large saucepan of salted water to a boil. Add the potatoes and cook for 15–20 minutes, until tender. Check them by inserting a fork or knife into the largest potato in the pan—if it goes in and out easily, the potato is ready. Drain and allow to cool for a few minutes.

To make the spicy red salsa, place all the ingredients except the vegetable stock in a blender or food processor and blend until completely smooth. Pour the puree into a saucepan, add the vegetable stock and bring to a boil. Reduce the heat to low and simmer for 15–20 minutes, while you prepare the remaining ingredients.

Place the potatoes in a bowl and roughly mash them (it does not have to be smooth; a chunky texture is great). Add the cheddar, garlic, cumin, paprika, cilantro and sea salt and mix to combine.

Place a skillet over medium-high heat and, working in batches, add the corn tortillas and heat until soft and pliable. Remove from the pan and cover the tortillas with a clean tea towel to keep them warm. Fill each tortilla with 1–2 tablespoons of the potato mixture, then fold in half and press down lightly.

In the same skillet over medium-high heat, add enough oil to cover the bottom of the pan. Place three or four tacos in the oil, pressing down lightly with a spatula so that the edges are in the oil, and fry for 1–2 minutes, until golden and crispy. Flip them over and repeat on the other side. Repeat with the remaining tacos.

Serve the tacos with the spicy red salsa and any of the optional serving suggestions.

Do ahead: The potatoes can be cooked and mashed 2 days ahead and stored in an airtight container in the fridge. The salsa can be made 2 days ahead and kept in the fridge.

You can freeze assembled tacos by wrapping them tightly and storing in a freezer bag or airtight container. To cook, no need to thaw, fry them straight from frozen.

Shortcut: If you are short on time, skip the red salsa and serve the tacos with a store-bought salsa or slices of avocado.

Salt and Pepper Tater Tots

As a teenager, I got my first taste of independence and freedom at my local shopping center. On Saturdays, my sister and I would take the bus there, spending our pocket money on new clothes, magazines or records. While there, I snacked on tater tots (which we call potato gems in Australia). We never got to eat things like this at home, so a whole bag of hot, greasy tater tots was an absolute treat. Tater tots are now a hot commodity in our house—for birthdays or celebrations my kids request macaroni and cheese topped with tater tots, reminiscent of hot dish, the classic one-dish dinner from Minnesota and North Dakota. I'll also use them in place of potatoes when making a Spanish tortilla. Here, I've stir-fried them with an aromatic base of green onions and red chile, topped with Chinese salt and pepper seasoning.

SERVES 4

1¾ pounds (800 g) frozen tater tots (potato gems)

2 tablespoons neutral oil

1 fresh Thai red chile, finely chopped

3 green onions, finely chopped

Salt and pepper seasoning

2 teaspoons sea salt

½ teaspoon sugar

1 teaspoon white pepper

¼ teaspoon ground ginger

½ teaspoon five-spice powder

Preheat the oven to 425°F (220°C). Place the tater tots on a sheet pan and bake for 25–30 minutes, until golden and crispy. Remove from the oven and set aside.

To make the salt and pepper seasoning, place all the ingredients in a bowl and mix well.

Heat a large skillet over medium-high heat. Add the oil and, when it starts to shimmer, toss in the chile and green onion. Stir-fry for about 1 minute, until fragrant, then add the baked tater tots and toss for 2 minutes, until the gems are well coated.

Transfer to a serving dish and serve scattered with the salt and pepper seasoning.

Note: The salt and pepper seasoning can be used to top roasted vegetables and battered tofu. Make a double batch and store in an airtight jar, at room temperature.

Gluten-free and vegan

Vegetable swap • tater tots: roasted potatoes, frozen French fries or wedges

Pumpkin & squash

"Stable, modest and comforting"

Iconic Japanese artist Yayoi Kusama observed that pumpkins don't always inspire much respect, but yet, she was enchanted by their "generous unpretentiousness."

Generous unpretentiousness perfectly conveys how I see winter squash and pumpkins—stable, modest and comforting. While we may not often hear people muttering "ooh, I really feel like winter squash tonight," or see them mentioned among food trends, winter squashes are stalwarts, quietly sneaking their way into our shopping baskets and onto our plates. They are the unplanned addition to pasta that has us humming with joy, they bring depth and heart to salads, and sweet richness to stews and curries. And they know how to command in soups.

During autumn and winter, squashes brighten our senses with their sunny golden hue and perky sweet savoriness. They pair well with spices, particularly warming ones like nutmeg, cinnamon and ginger, and spark up when teamed with a potent flavor, such as salty cheese, zesty lemon, vinegar, chile, fermented pastes such as miso, bitter leaves like radicchio and earthy herbs such as rosemary and sage.

There are many varieties of winter squash, varying in skin color, flesh density and sweetness but, as a rule, they are interchangeable in recipes. When they are in season, experiment with different types to experience the nuances in texture and flavor.

Kabocha Miso Soup with Ramen Noodles

This is a delicate soup, with deep umami flavors and a pronounced sweetness from the kabocha squash. Kabocha, sometimes called Japanese pumpkin, is one of the sweetest in the winter squash family, with a velvety texture that lends a smooth creaminess to this soup. Here, its sweet flesh plays happily with the salty miso, creating a rich soup base for noodles. If you're out of noodles, you could also blend this base to make a thick, silky bowl of squash goodness. You could easily substitute butternut squash for the kabocha.

SERVES 4

32 ounces (1 liter) Vegan Dashi (see page 360) or vegetable stock

neutral oil

1 yellow onion, finely sliced

1 pound (450 g) kabocha squash, peeled and cut into ⅜-inch (1 cm) thick slices

sea salt

1 pound 5 ounces (600 g) fresh ramen noodles (or 10 oz/300 g dried instant noodles)

14 ounces (400 g) medium tofu, drained and cut into ¾-inch (2 cm) cubes

⅓ cup (80 g) white (shiro) miso

4 green onions, finely sliced

rayu (Japanese chili sesame oil) or chili oil, to serve (optional)

Place the dashi or vegetable stock in a large saucepan and bring to a simmer over medium-low heat.

Heat a large skillet over medium heat. When hot, add 1 tablespoon of oil, along with the onion. Cook, stirring frequently, for 8–10 minutes, until softened and turning golden. Add the kabocha to the pan, season with 2 teaspoons of sea salt, then drizzle over 1–2 tablespoons of oil. Cook, stirring often, for 6–7 minutes, until some of the sides of the squash have turned a nice golden color (it does not need to be golden all over). Transfer the onion and squash to the simmering pan of dashi or vegetable stock, cover with a lid and simmer for 10 minutes (if the soup comes to a boil, reduce the heat to low).

Meanwhile, bring a large saucepan of salted water to a boil. Add the noodles and cook according to the package directions, until al dente. Drain, rinse with cold water and drain again. Divide the noodles among four bowls.

After 10 minutes, the squash should be tender. Add the tofu and miso and stir very gently to blend the miso into the soup—the squash and tofu will break up a little and that is fine. Taste and check the seasonings—it won't be too salty. If you prefer more seasoning, add a little extra salt.

Divide the soup among the four bowls, ladling it over the noodles. Serve, topped with the green onion and, if you like, a few drops of rayu or chili oil.

For gluten-free • use rice vermicelli, glass noodles or 100% buckwheat soba noodles

Vegan

Substitute • onion: leek, shallots

Vegetable swap • kabocha: sweet potato

Roasted Delicata and Radicchio with Date Vinaigrette

Delicata squash, the mottled-skinned cylindrical fruit, is one of my favorite winter squash varieties, delicately sweet, yet with a robust flesh that cooks quickly. I am particularly attracted to its delicate rind, which is thin enough to be eaten, making this a very easy vegetable to prepare. If you enjoy pumpkin seeds, roast the squash with the seeds in (they'll get crunchy), but remove them if you prefer. The bitterness of the radicchio is happy to hang with the mellow sweetness of delicata and caramelly sweetness of the date syrup. Finishing with shards of hard cheese is not mandatory, but I like the salty notes it brings to round out the dish.

SERVES 4

1 large delicata squash (about 1 lb/450 g), trimmed, cut into slices a scant ¼ inch (5 mm) thick

1 radicchio (6 oz/180 g), trimmed, cut into 8 wedges

1½ cups (250 g) cooked chickpeas (about one 15 oz/425 g can, drained)

extra-virgin olive oil

2 teaspoons baharat spice

sea salt and black pepper

3 cups (75 g) salad greens, baby spinach or baby arugula

¼ cup toasted pumpkin seeds

1¾ ounces (50 g) Manchego, shaved (optional)

handful of mint leaves

Date vinaigrette

1 garlic clove, grated

2½ tablespoons lemon juice (from ½ lemon)

5 teaspoons date syrup

¼ cup (60 ml) extra-virgin olive oil

¼ teaspoon sea salt

black pepper

Gluten-free

Veganize • omit the cheese or use vegan cheese

Substitute • date syrup: maple syrup, honey • radicchio: cabbage • baharat spice: ground cumin, ground coriander, smoked paprika

Vegetable swap • delicata squash: butternut squash, sweet potato

Preheat the oven to 400°F (200°C).

Place the delicata, radicchio and chickpeas on a sheet pan. Drizzle generously with olive oil, then scatter on the baharat spice. Season with sea salt and black pepper and toss to coat. Transfer to the oven and roast for 20–25 minutes, until the radicchio is golden and crispy and the delicata squash is tender.

Meanwhile, to make the date vinaigrette, combine the garlic, lemon juice, date syrup, olive oil and sea salt in a bowl and whisk to combine. Season with a few turns of black pepper.

Combine the squash, chickpeas, radicchio, salad greens and half the pumpkin seeds. Drizzle with the date dressing, season with sea salt and black pepper and toss to combine. Transfer to a serving plate, scatter with the cheese (if using) and mint leaves, and top with the remaining pumpkin seeds.

Miso-Roasted Kabocha
and Chickpeas with Kale

Miso with winter squash is one of my go-to flavor pairings. Together, they perfectly straddle that irresistible fine line between salty and sweet. Here, the miso works its magic with the squash, amplifying its sweetness, savoriness and earthy nuttiness. The mirin in the glaze is subtle, but it adds some welcome acidity. This is a light salad, but you could add more heft by adding some quinoa, couscous or brown rice.

SERVES 4

3 tablespoons white (shiro) miso

4 teaspoons mirin

extra-virgin olive oil

4 teaspoons maple syrup or brown sugar

2¼ pounds (1 kg) kabocha squash, peeled and sliced into wedges ¾ inch (2 cm) thick

3 cups (500 g) cooked chickpeas (about two 15 oz/425 g cans, drained)

sea salt and black pepper

7 ounces (200 g) kale leaves (from 1 bunch), roughly torn

zest and juice of 1 lemon (2–3 tablespoons juice)

¼ cup toasted pumpkin seeds (see page 347 to make your own)

Preheat the oven to 400°F (200°C).

Place the miso paste, mirin, 3 tablespoons of olive oil and the maple syrup or brown sugar in a large bowl and whisk until you have a thick paste. Add the squash and chickpeas, toss to coat, then transfer to a sheet pan. Season with sea salt and black pepper and roast for 25–30 minutes, until the squash is tender and golden.

Meanwhile, place the kale in a large bowl, then add the zest and juice of the lemon, 2–3 tablespoons of olive oil and about 1 teaspoon of sea salt. Massage the leaves for 1 minute, then leave them to sit until the squash is ready.

To serve, place the massaged kale leaves in a bowl and top with the squash and chickpeas and squash seeds. Season everything with sea salt and black pepper and a final drizzle of olive oil.

Gluten-free and vegan

Vegetable swap • kabocha: sweet potato

Butternut Squash "Lasagna"

I love the reimagination of a dish or an ingredient, and this recipe does both. Inspired by the classic flavors and fastidious construction of lasagna, I've replaced the pasta sheets with thin slices of butternut squash. This substitution is not a gimmick, nor is it due to a dislike of the unparalleled original, but is driven purely by curiosity and a desire to unlock the sweet, salty, earthy possibilities of butternut. The squash is roasted first, to help release the natural sugars in the flesh, and is then combined with a tangy, subtly spiced tomato sauce and creamy ricotta and mozzarella, which takes this sweet vegetable far into the savory side. There are many ways to customize this recipe: add some pesto between the layers, dot with black olives or capers, slip some chickpeas in for extra heartiness or include some wilted spinach or kale to create an even taller stack.

SERVES 4–6

1 butternut squash (about 2 lb 13 oz/1.3 kg), peeled

extra-virgin olive oil

sea salt and black pepper

1 yellow onion, finely diced

4 garlic cloves, finely chopped

3 tablespoons tomato paste

½ teaspoon red pepper flakes

one 28-ounce (800 g) can crushed tomatoes

1 cup (240 ml) vegetable stock

1 teaspoon sugar

1¾ cups (400 g) ricotta

2¼ ounces (65 g) hard cheese, such as cheddar, pecorino or parmesan, finely grated, plus more to serve

12 ounces (350 g) fresh mozzarella, finely sliced or torn

handful of basil leaves, to serve

Gluten-free

Veganize • use vegan ricotta, hard cheese and mozzarella

Substitute • mozzarella: feta, Halloumi

Vegetable swap • butternut squash: zucchini, sweet potato, potato, eggplant

Preheat the oven to 400°F (200°C).

Separate the "neck" of the butternut from the rotund body. Slice both sections in half lengthwise. Slice the neck into slices ⅜ inch (1 cm) thick. Remove the seeds and membrane from the body (keep the seeds and roast them, see page 347) and slice into half-moons ⅜ inch (1 cm) thick. Arrange the squash across two sheet pans, drizzle with olive oil and season with sea salt and black pepper. Position on the middle and lower racks of the oven and roast for 20 minutes, switching racks halfway through cooking. Remove from the oven and set aside.

Meanwhile, heat a large saucepan over medium-high heat. Add 2 tablespoons of olive oil, along with the onion, and cook for 2 minutes until softened, then add the garlic, tomato paste and red pepper flakes and cook for 2 minutes longer. Pour in the crushed tomatoes, vegetable stock, 1 teaspoon of sea salt and the sugar, then cover with a lid and simmer over medium heat for 10 minutes.

Combine the ricotta and grated cheese in a bowl. Season with sea salt and black pepper.

Spread a little of the tomato sauce in a baking dish (I use a 10-inch/ 25 cm square dish, but you could use a slightly larger or smaller dish; rectangular dishes work great, too). Start layering: lay one-third of the squash slices on the tomato sauce, dollop with one-third of the ricotta mixture (it won't spread as it's thick, so I just dot little blobs), then add one-third of the remaining sauce and top with one-third of the mozzarella. Repeat these layers two more times— butternut, ricotta, sauce, mozzarella. You should finish with a layer of mozzarella.

Bake for 30–40 minutes, until the mozzarella is golden and the sauce is bubbling around the edges.

Wait for 10 minutes before serving. Serve topped with torn basil leaves and extra grated cheese.

Do ahead: Make the tomato sauce and roast the butternut the day ahead.

Shortcut: Use store-bought pasta sauce.

Garlicky Sweet and Salty Pumpkin Seeds

My mother never wasted one pumpkin seed. She went the extra mile, leaving them to dehydrate completely under the sun before roasting them, guaranteeing optimum crunch. I skip the sun-drying process in this recipe as I lack easy access to outdoor space, but if you're not in a hurry to eat, you could simply leave the seeds to dry out overnight on your kitchen counter. Cleaning the seeds takes some patience—it's easiest to do this by soaking the seeds in a bowl of water to encourage separation from the slimy membrane. You can really flavor your seeds any way you like—I have opted to go the classic sweet and salty route, but you could mix things up by adding different spices, such as curry powder or harissa, or lean heavily into autumn flavors with a pumpkin pie spice blend, or cinnamon and sugar.

MAKES ½ CUP

½ cup pumpkin or squash seeds (from 1 pumpkin or winter squash)

1 teaspoon soy sauce or tamari

2 teaspoons sugar

2 teaspoons extra-virgin olive oil

pinch of flaky sea salt

⅛ teaspoon garlic powder

Preheat the oven to 350°F (180°C).

Remove the membrane from the seeds and place them in a bowl of water. Rinse them well, using your hands to help separate the seeds from the remaining membrane. Drain, then pat dry with paper towels.

Spread the seeds out on a sheet pan. At this stage, you can leave the seeds to dry overnight on your kitchen counter, or you can proceed to the next step (the extra drying time will give you a crunchier finish, but you still get good results without it). Add the soy sauce or tamari, 1 teaspoon of the sugar and the olive oil and toss to coat the seeds. Place the pan on the middle rack of the oven and roast for 25–30 minutes, tossing every 5 minutes, until the seeds are golden brown and crispy (they will crisp up further as they cool). Watch the seeds closely and take them out if they start to brown sooner.

Remove the seeds from the oven and scatter with a little flaky sea salt, the remaining 1 teaspoon of sugar and the garlic powder, then toss to distribute the seasoning evenly. Allow to cool completely before eating. They can be enjoyed as a snack or tossed over salads.

To store: If you haven't eaten these all in one go, store in an airtight jar in the pantry for up to 2 weeks.

Gluten-free and vegan

Pumpkin Egg Custard Tarts

Originating in Guangzhou, Guangdong Province, during the early 20th century, daan tat (egg custard tart) is the quintessential Cantonese dessert, a delicate, flaky pastry filled with a smooth, lightly sweetened egg custard. Influenced by Guangzhou's trade and interaction with Britain, Chinese pastry chefs at Western-style department stores and restaurants were tasked with inventing a dessert to appeal to British palates. The result was this iconic tart, less creamy and eggier than the British custard tart. Though I adore the original, this pumpkin-laced version, which I call faan gwa daan tat or pumpkin egg custard tart, is an exciting reinterpretation. The pumpkin gives the custard body and richness. If you like, you could add a little spice, such as nutmeg or cinnamon, to the custard. The condensed milk acts as the sweetener, but you can substitute the same quantity of cream and add ½ cup (100 g) of sugar. I use puff pastry for ease and speed, but you could use your favorite homemade puff pastry or flaky pie dough, both of which are used in tarts served at dim sum, Chinese bakeries and cha chaan teng in Hong Kong.

MAKES 12

6 large egg yolks

¾ cup (180 g) pumpkin puree (see Note)

½ cup (150 g) sweetened condensed milk

½ cup (120 ml) oat milk or whole milk

2 teaspoons vanilla extract

two 10-inch (25 cm) square sheets of puff pastry (about 1 lb/450 g), thawed

½ teaspoon ground cinnamon

Preheat the oven to 400°F (200°C). Grease a 12-cup standard muffin tin with nonstick oil spray.

Combine the eggs, pumpkin puree, sweetened condensed milk, oat or whole milk and vanilla extract in a bowl and whisk until completely smooth. Set up a bowl with a fine sieve on top. Pour the custard through the sieve, leaving it to strain through—there will be bits of pumpkin flesh left over, so press the flesh to extract as much of the liquid as possible, but don't press the flesh through the sieve. Set aside.

Place a sheet of puff pastry on a clean work surface. Sprinkle with ¼ teaspoon of the ground cinnamon and use your fingers to spread it out and lightly press into the pastry. Take the side closest to you and gently roll the pastry into a log. Cut this log into six pieces, then stand the pieces on one end (so you can see the coil) and press down with your hand to form six discs. Now, working with one disc at a time and using your fingers, press the discs into rounds 3½–4 inches (9–10 cm) in diameter. Repeat with the second sheet of pastry. You should have 12 rounds in total. Press each round into a muffin cup, pressing the pastry into the bottom of each cup so it reaches up the sides. The pastry should be just slightly higher than the top of the muffin tin, as it will shrink as it cooks. This next step is optional, but I enjoy it as it reminds me of Cantonese egg tarts—with a fork, gently press into the very edge of each pastry round to form a pattern.

Pour the custard into each pastry shell, almost to the top of the rim (take care not to overfill as this will make transferring to the oven difficult). Place in the oven and bake for 20–22 minutes, until the pastry is golden on the sides and the custard is puffed like a dome—it will deflate as the tarts cool. Remove from the oven and set aside to cool.

Note: For the pumpkin puree, use canned pumpkin puree or follow the notes on page 351 to make your own.

For gluten-free • use gluten-free puff pastry

Spiced Pumpkin Doughnuts

My youngest, Huck, declared these "the best doughnuts I've ever eaten" while middle child, Dash, who is not a pumpkin fan, muttered "you can make anything taste good." Doughnuts have long been crowd-pleasers, but the best ones are usually deep-fried. This baked version is not lacking—the pumpkin delivers not only flavor, but also a moist crumb and a beautiful golden hue. The classic autumnal flavors of pumpkin pie spice give just the right amount of warmth and the oil keeps everything light. Best of all, it's a fuss-free recipe (no electric mixer needed!). A nonstick doughnut pan is required, but if you don't have one, use a 12-cup muffin tin to make "doffins" (doughnut-muffins), making sure to bake them for slightly longer, about 18–20 minutes.

MAKES 12

2 cups plus 1 tablespoon (250 g) all-purpose flour

1¼ teaspoons baking powder

¼ teaspoon baking soda

2 teaspoons pumpkin pie spice (see Notes)

½ teaspoon sea salt

⅔ cup (160 ml) neutral oil

1 tightly packed cup (200 g) brown sugar

1 teaspoon vanilla extract

2 large eggs

1 cup (250 g) pumpkin puree (see Notes)

4 tablespoons (56 g) butter, melted

Pumpkin pie spice sugar

1 cup (220 g) granulated sugar

2 teaspoons pumpkin pie spice (see Notes)

For gluten-free • use gluten-free all-purpose flour

Vegetable swap • pumpkin puree: sweet potato puree, parsnip puree

Preheat the oven to 350°F (180°C). Grease a 12-cavity (or two six-cavity) nonstick doughnut pan with cooking spray.

In a bowl, add the flour, baking powder, baking soda, pumpkin pie spice and sea salt and whisk to combine.

Place the oil, sugar and vanilla extract in a large bowl and whisk to combine. Whisk in the eggs until the mixture is smooth. Add the pumpkin puree and whisk until fully combined.

Add the dry ingredients to the wet mixture and fold together until just combined (do not overmix).

Transfer the batter to a piping bag fitted with a large plain tip, or to a resealable plastic bag with a ⅜-inch (1 cm) hole snipped in one corner, and pipe the batter into each cavity in the pan until they are three-quarters full (or simply spoon the batter in). Bake for 15–17 minutes—when they are ready, the tops of the doughnuts will spring back when lightly touched. Let the doughnuts cool in the pan for 5 minutes, then turn them out onto a wire rack.

Meanwhile, to make the pumpkin pie spice sugar, place the sugar and spice in a shallow bowl and mix well.

While the doughnuts are still warm, brush both sides with the melted butter and toss them in the pumpkin pie spice sugar. Return to the racks. Doughnuts are best eaten the day they are made, but can be stored in an airtight container at room temperature for up to 1 day.

Notes: To make the quickest pumpkin puree, you'll need approximately 10 ounces (300 g) of peeled pumpkin (or other winter squash). Cut the pumpkin or squash into cubes and add them to a saucepan with a little water (¼ cup/60 ml to start), cover with a lid and cook over medium heat for 15–20 minutes, until the flesh is very soft. Check it from time to time and add more water if it dries out. When soft, if there is still water in the saucepan, drain it. Stir the flesh with a fork (it should break up easily) until it is completely pureed. This will make about 1 cup (250 g) of pumpkin puree.

To make pumpkin pie spice, combine 2 teaspoons ground cinnamon, 1 teaspoon ground ginger, ½ teaspoon ground allspice, ½ teaspoon ground nutmeg and ⅛ teaspoon ground cloves. Mix well. This quantity makes exactly the right amount for this recipe.

Lazy Spiced Butternut Tiramisu

With a small wedge of winter squash and some impulsively purchased mascarpone in the fridge, this lazy tiramisu was born. Butternut delivers just the right amount of sweet, nutty winter squash flavor, but you could also use kabocha. Canned pumpkin works perfectly, too. There are many elements from a traditional tiramisu missing from this recipe—there are no eggs, no heavy whipping, nor is there cream. To satiate my oft-indolent attitude to cooking, this is a barebones tiramisu, not as rich as the original, but every bit as indulgent. If you have it, you could simply flavor your coffee with the pumpkin pie spice mix on page 351.

SERVES 6–8

2 cups (480 ml) strong brewed coffee or 1 cup (240 ml) Americano mixed with 1 cup (240 ml) water

¾ teaspoon ground cinnamon

½ teaspoon ground ginger

¼ teaspoon ground nutmeg

1 cup (250 g) butternut puree (see page 351 for instructions)

1 pound (450 g) mascarpone

½ cup (100 g) sugar

24 ladyfingers (savoiardi biscuits) (about 7 oz/200 g)

1 tablespoon sugar mixed with ¼ teaspoon ground cinnamon

Pour the coffee into a shallow baking pan. Add the cinnamon, ginger and nutmeg and whisk to combine. Set aside to cool completely.

Place the butternut puree, mascarpone and sugar in a bowl and whisk for about 2 minutes, until combined and thickened slightly.

You'll need a large loaf pan that measures about 9 × 4½ × 2¾ inches (23 cm × 11 cm × 7 cm)—it should be just wide enough to lay a ladyfinger straight across. Quickly dip the ladyfingers into the coffee mixture, allowing excess liquid to drip off. Arrange the ladyfingers in a single layer across the bottom of the loaf pan—it should fit about eight biscuits—then spread one-third of the butternut mascarpone mixture on top. Repeat with the remaining ladyfingers and butternut mascarpone to create two more layers.

To finish, sift the cinnamon sugar all over the top. Cover tightly with plastic wrap and place in the fridge for at least 8 hours or preferably overnight. Cut into slices and serve.

Substitute • ground cinnamon, ginger, nutmeg: 1½ teaspoons pumpkin pie spice (see page 351)

Vegetable swap • butternut puree: sweet potato puree, canned pumpkin puree

Seaweed

"That savory x-factor that makes us crave the next bite"

In 1907, Professor Kikunae Ikeda was eating a bowl of tofu in kombu dashi when he identified another basic taste that was altogether different from sweet, salty, sour and bitter. He deemed this taste *umami* (essence of deliciousness), the fifth taste, changing the way eaters and cooks thought about flavor forever.

Seaweed imparts "meatiness" to meals, that savory x-factor that makes us crave the next bite. Seaweed is one of the most sustainable foods on earth and for that reason alone, we should look to incorporating it more into our daily cooking. It grows very rapidly at sea where other food crops usually don't survive, without any need for fresh water, feed or fertilizer, and reproduces at a phenomenal rate. To start cooking with seaweed, it could be as simple as a basic miso soup with tofu and wakame; this is an easy dish to consume, and it is incredibly nourishing. Or try adding some sea greens into savory oats. Seaweed is an delightful addition to compound butter, which you can melt into pasta or over roasted veggies.

There are many varieties of edible seaweed that are readily found in Asian supermarkets and health-food stores—they are usually sold dried and must be rehydrated before use. Depending upon where you live, you may also be able to find fresh seaweed. Seaweed is best used sparingly. In my daily cooking, I mainly use kombu, wakame, hijiki, dulse, nori and kelp. Kombu can be used to make an easy dashi and is wonderful in broths; add a strip to your bean cooking liquid to make your legumes more digestible. Wakame is an all-rounder that I use in salads and soups. Hijiki is a twig-like sea plant that is also great in salads and stirred into rice; make sure you rinse it well before using. Dulse resembles a leafy, red lettuce and grows wild on the northern Atlantic and Pacific coasts; the salty seaweed has been likened to bacon—to make dulse "bacon," pan-fry whole dulse leaves in olive oil until crisp.

A little dried seaweed goes a long way. About less than a ¼ ounce (5 g) dried wakame rehydrates to over 2 ounces (60 g) of seaweed leaves.

Fish-Free Furikake

Furikake is a Japanese mix of seasonings that is especially made to sprinkle on rice. There are many types of furikake on the market—some have dried wasabi as the main ingredient, while others are made from dried and seasoned shiso, dried egg, bonito fish flakes and even matcha. This is a fish-free furikake, based on nori seaweed and sesame seeds. And while it is wonderful sprinkled on rice, it is also delicious atop udon or ramen noodles, soups, salads, scrambled or boiled eggs, popcorn or avocado toast.

MAKES ABOUT ½ CUP

2 toasted nori sheets (¼ oz/8 g)

¼ cup toasted white sesame seeds

1 tablespoon toasted black sesame seeds

1 teaspoon sea salt flakes

½ teaspoon sugar

Cut the nori into small pieces and place them in a blender or food processor—pulse just four or five times to crush the pieces into chunky crumbs (you could also do this using a mortar and pestle).

Transfer the nori to a bowl, add the sesame seeds, sea salt flakes and sugar and mix to combine. Store in an airtight jar in the pantry for up to 3 months.

Gluten-free and vegan

Vegan Dashi

Dashi is a foundational ingredient in Japanese cooking. The soup stock is infused with a distinct umami flavor, adding richness and depth to countless dishes, such as miso soup, ramen broth, chawanmushi (a savory egg custard) and nimono (simmered dishes), and is often mixed into flour bases for grilled foods like okonomiyaki and takoyaki. Simple and adding a refined elegance to meals, dashi is often made from kombu and smoky katsuobushi (bonito flakes), but can also be created with other ingredients, such as dried shiitake mushrooms. Don't rinse kombu before soaking—the white powdery substance found on the surface occurs as part of the natural drying process and imparts lots of umami flavor. This is an effortless way to make dashi at home.

**MAKES 4–5 CUPS
(1–1.25 LITERS)**

5 × 6-inch (12.5 cm × 15 cm) sheet of dried kombu (10 g)

4 dried shiitake mushrooms

5¼ cups (1.25 liters) filtered water

Place the kombu, shiitake mushrooms and filtered water in a saucepan and set over medium-low heat until it reaches a very low simmer, without boiling. This should take about 10 minutes. Remove from the heat and remove the kombu and shiitake.

The kombu and shiitake can be reused to make one more batch of dashi. Dashi can be cooled and stored in the fridge for up to 1 week or frozen for up to 3 months.

Gluten-free and vegan

Hijiki Baked Rice Wrapped in Nori

People often ask me what my family eats for dinner—if I'm being honest, we frequently eat the dishes featured in my books and columns. We have a varied, unpredictable diet, often led astray by my recipe-testing duties, so the recipes I prescribe are also what we eat. But then there are the meals that are more of an idea, rather than a set formula. This is one of them. You could call this lazy sushi rice rolls, or seaweed rice tacos, but we eat some iteration of this meal at least once a fortnight (which is a lot in our family, as we have a huge repertoire of favorites). It is the dish I turn to when I am craving rice but cannot be bothered to cook up several side dishes. The beauty of this dish is that it requires zero thought, it's nutritious and filling, and it can be topped with whatever vegetables you have on hand. Hijiki adds incredible umami flavor to the rice, and you can add more if you want a more pronounced seaweed taste. Cucumber or raw zucchini are nice toppings, too, but you could also add corn, pan-fried mushrooms, wilted spinach and more. Seaweed snacks, the small sheets of salty, crispy nori, are a staple in our house and they add a fun, cheeky element to this meal. However, if you can't get the snacks, you could also toast a sheet of nori by holding it about 6 inches (15 cm) above a flame, until it smells toasty; cut it into four smaller pieces to wrap the rice.

SERVES 4

¼ cup (6 g) dried hijiki, soaked in 3 cups (720 ml) of hot water

6 cups (900 g) cooked white or brown rice (from 2 cups/400 g uncooked)

2½ tablespoons rice vinegar

4 teaspoons toasted sesame oil

1 teaspoon sea salt

1 teaspoon sugar

1 cup (140 g) shelled edamame

extra-virgin olive oil or neutral oil

Kewpie, regular or vegan mayonnaise

sriracha sauce or hot sauce

Fish-Free Furikake (see page 359; or use store-bought vegan furikake)

4 packs roasted seasoned seaweed snacks

1 avocado, sliced

Preheat the oven to 450°F (230°C).

Drain the hijiki in a fine sieve and rinse with cold water. Drain again, then transfer to a large bowl. Add the rice, rice vinegar, sesame oil, sea salt and sugar and mix to combine. Add the edamame and fold them in.

Drizzle a deep baking pan (about 17 × 12 inches/43 cm × 31 cm) with oil and add the rice mixture, pressing it down so it is spread right to the corners and edges. Place in the oven and bake for 20–25 minutes, until there are a few golden spots on top of the rice. Remove from the oven.

If you're using regular mayonnaise, add a splash of water (just 1–2 teaspoons should do it) to make it more pourable. Spoon or drizzle the mayonnaise (I like Kewpie brand the best) over the rice in a zigzag fashion, and then do the same with the sriracha sauce or hot sauce. Scatter the furikake all over the surface.

Serve with the seaweed snacks and avocado on the side. To eat, place a scoop of rice on a sheet of seaweed, add a slice of avocado and roll it up.

Gluten-free and vegan

Substitute • furikake: toasted white or black sesame seeds • edamame: peas, corn

Vegetable swap • hijiki: spinach, kale

Seaweed, Tofu and Sprout Soup

My mother made tong (soup) every single night, every bowl customized to treat everyday ailments or to promote general health. Her ngaa choy tong (sprout soup), made with crisp bean sprouts or, when available, nutty soybean sprouts, is one of my favorites; lightly savory and clean on the palate. This recipe is an enriched version of this soup, bolstered with the nutrition and savoriness of seaweed and the creamy heartiness of soft tofu. It is a soup that I particularly enjoy ladling over a bowl of rice, as my mother would do—an unfussy meal that both fortifies and comforts.

SERVES 4

1 tablespoon toasted sesame oil

1-inch (2.5 cm) piece of ginger, peeled and sliced

1 garlic clove, finely chopped

4 green onions, white and green parts separated, finely sliced

6⅓ cups (1.5 liters) vegetable stock or Vegan Dashi (see page 360)

¼ cup (15 g) dried wakame

16 ounce (450 g) soft tofu, drained and cut into ¾-inch (2 cm) cubes

3 cups (270 g) soybean sprouts or bean sprouts

4 teaspoons soy sauce or tamari

¼ teaspoon ground white pepper

Heat a large saucepan over medium heat, add the sesame oil, ginger, garlic and the white part of the green onion and sauté for 1–2 minutes, until aromatic and softened. Add the stock or dashi, wakame and tofu and cook for 10 minutes. During this time, the soup will come to a boil; when it does, reduce the heat to medium low.

Add the soybean sprouts or bean sprouts and stir in the soy sauce or tamari and white pepper.

To serve, divide the soup among bowls and scatter with the green part of the green onion.

Gluten-free and vegan

Vegetable swap • wakame: romaine or iceberg lettuce

Seaweed Brown Butter Pasta

Consider this a gateway recipe for seaweed skeptics. The compound butter, spiked with seaweed, is a revelation—deeply savory, with hints of the sea, it is an incredibly versatile ingredient, which can also be served with roasted vegetables or spread onto crusty bread. Dulse is a red lettuce–like leaf that grows wild on the shorelines of the Pacific and North Atlantic Oceans. Sold dried, it is unique in that it can be eaten raw as a snack (a tip from my friends in Nova Scotia). When pan-fried or toasted, it takes on smoky and intensely savory characteristics that are reminiscent of bacon. Browning the butter brings out nuttiness and depth, offering so many layers of irresistible flavor.

SERVES 4

⅓ cup (6 g) dried dulse

8 tablespoons (112 g) unsalted regular or vegan butter, at room temperature

½ teaspoon sea salt

¼–½ teaspoon red pepper flakes

1 pound (450 g) linguine or other long pasta shape

extra-virgin olive oil

2 shallots or 1 yellow onion, finely sliced

2 garlic cloves, finely chopped

3 tablespoons white (shiro) miso

sea salt

handful of grated sharp cheese, for topping (optional)

Fish-Free Furikake (see page 359; or use store-bought vegan furikake), to serve (optional)

Place a small skillet over the lowest heat setting and add the dulse. Toast, stirring often, for 10 minutes, until it is crispy and feels very dry (take care not to burn it).

Place the dulse in a blender or food processor and pulse four or five times until it looks like chunky crumbs (you can also use a mortar and pestle). Slice the butter into smaller pieces and add it to the seaweed, along with the salt and red pepper flakes. Pulse another four or five times until blended—it doesn't have to be completely smooth.

Bring a large saucepan of salted water to a boil and add the pasta. Cook according to the package directions, until al dente. Drain and reserve 1 cup (240 ml) of the pasta cooking water.

Meanwhile, heat a large skillet over medium heat. Drizzle in 1 tablespoon of olive oil, add the shallots or onion and cook for 8–10 minutes, until very soft. Add the garlic and cook for 1 minute, then add the seaweed butter. The butter will foam as it melts—once melted, cook for 2–3 minutes, until it becomes toasty brown, with a rich nutty aroma. Immediately add the miso paste and stir vigorously to combine with the butter (you could use a small whisk to do this if you prefer). Add the pasta, along with ½ cup (120 ml) of the pasta cooking water and toss well to coat. If the pasta needs a bit more moisture, add a little more of the pasta cooking water. Taste and, if required, season with sea salt.

Top with the cheese and furikake, if desired. Serve immediately.

For gluten-free • use gluten-free pasta

Vegan

Vegetable swap • dulse: dried hijiki

Seaweed Scramble

My dad was rarely responsible for cooking dinner. The only time he did so was when my mother was feeling poorly. During these occasions, he always made salmon scrambled eggs. Soft scrambled eggs tangled with the salty, rich, blushed flesh of canned salmon, served with white rice. It was not the most gourmet dinner we ate as kids, but it is a memory we cling to. During the 1980s, canned salmon, especially the red variety that my mother occasionally splurged on, felt like a treat, so a salmon egg scramble was, in many ways, an indulgent meal. This seaweed scramble is my vegetarian take on my dad's signature meal—the seaweed imparts the scent of the sea and a lovely umami flavor. A simple meal full of nostalgia and bittersweet memories.

SERVES 4

8 large eggs

2 teaspoons soy sauce or tamari

sea salt and white pepper

1 heaping tablespoon (5 g) dried wakame, soaked in water for 20–30 minutes

extra-virgin olive oil

1 green onion, finely chopped

toasted sesame oil, to serve

1 tablespoon toasted white or black sesame seeds

white rice, to serve

In a bowl, whisk the eggs until well combined. Add the soy sauce or tamari, season with about 1 teaspoon of sea salt and a few pinches of white pepper and whisk well.

Drain the wakame and squeeze out the excess water. If your wakame is in large chunks, roughly chop. If they are smaller pieces, leave them as is.

Heat a large skillet over medium-high heat. When hot, drizzle with olive oil, add the wakame and stir for 1–2 minutes, until the liquid has evaporated and the wakame starts to char slightly. Pour the egg into the pan, allow to set for 10 seconds, then use a silicone spatula to push the egg around the edge of the pan in a circular fashion, tilting the pan to let the runny egg in the middle run out to the edge. Repeat until the egg is just set with a slightly wet center—this should only take 20–30 seconds. Remove from the heat immediately and transfer to bowls.

Top the scramble with the green onion, a drizzle of sesame oil and the sesame seeds, and serve with white rice.

Gluten-free

Substitute • wakame: hijiki

Vegetable swap • wakame: rehydrated porcini or shiitake mushrooms

Celebration Soup

This soup is inspired by imitation shark fin soup, a dish that was synonymous with childhood celebrations, a signature of wedding banquets, birthdays and Lunar New Year feasts. An ancient dish that originated during the Song dynasty, shark fin soup was served to the elite classes and aristocracy, a decadent banquet dish heralding affluence and status. Shark fin is a cruel delicacy though and, while the barbaric acquisition of shark fin has not been outlawed globally, many families and restaurants have long adopted shark fin–less versions of this soup. Imitation shark fin soup is even a popular street food in Hong Kong and Malaysia. For my version, kelp noodles, the semitransparent noodles made from the jelly-like extract left after steaming edible kelp, team with mung bean vermicelli to provide the robust gelatinous texture that is signature to this soup. I enjoy this soup as a starter or with a bowl of rice.

SERVES 4

4 teaspoons toasted sesame oil, plus more for topping

1-inch (2.5 cm) piece of ginger, peeled and grated

1 garlic clove, grated

6⅓ cups (1.5 liters) vegetable stock

5 dried shiitake mushrooms (about 1 oz/30 g), soaked in 1 cup (240 ml) boiling water for 20–30 minutes

4 teaspoons Shaoxing rice wine

4 teaspoons soy sauce or tamari

2 tablespoons cornstarch mixed with ⅓ cup (80 ml) water

sea salt and white pepper

2 ounces (60 g) mung bean vermicelli, soaked in warm water for 5–10 minutes

3½ ounces (100 g) kelp noodles

1 large egg, beaten

2 green onions, finely sliced, or handful of cilantro leaves

black vinegar, for topping (optional)

Heat a large saucepan over medium-high heat. Add the sesame oil, ginger and garlic and stir for 30–60 seconds, until fragrant. Add the vegetable stock and bring to a boil.

Remove the shiitake mushrooms from their soaking water and squeeze out any excess liquid. Pour the soaking water through a fine-mesh sieve (to remove any grit) into the stock. Finely slice the mushrooms and add them to the soup, along with the Shaoxing rice wine and soy sauce or tamari. Cover and simmer over low heat for 10 minutes.

Stir the cornstarch so it's well combined with the water and pour it into the soup. Increase the heat to medium and stir until the soup is thickened. Taste and season with sea salt, if needed, along with about ¼ teaspoon of white pepper. Drain the mung bean vermicelli and add to the soup, along with the kelp noodles. Cook for about 2 minutes, until the vermicelli are translucent. Slowly pour the egg into the soup and allow it to set for 15–30 seconds before stirring gently to disperse.

Ladle the soup into four bowls and top each with the green onion or cilantro leaves, a few drops of sesame oil and black vinegar, if desired.

For gluten-free • omit the Shaoxing rice wine

Veganize • omit the egg

Substitute • dried shiitake mushroom: any variety of fresh mushroom • mung bean vermicelli: sweet potato starch noodles

Vegetable swap • kelp noodles: 1 heaping tablespoon (5 g) dried wakame, soaked in water for 20 minutes

Triple Treat Salad

The vaguely named Triple Salad at Spicy Village, a beloved pocket-sized eatery in Chinatown, Manhattan, is one of my favorite dishes in the city. It's a very simple dish of long, crunchy strips of seaweed, twisted with firm tofu and crisp chunks of cucumber, tossed in a salty, slightly spicy dressing. I admire the restraint shown in this dish, each modest mouthful replete with exciting textures and unmistakable umami. This salad is my ode to triple salad—it can be eaten as a side dish, or with a bowl of rice or noodles as a full meal.

SERVES 4 AS A SIDE

neutral oil

14 ounces (400 g) extra-firm tofu, cut into slices about ¼ inch (6–7 mm) thick

sea salt and white pepper

1 heaping tablespoon (5 g) dried wakame, soaked in water for 10 minutes

2 Persian (mini) cucumbers (about 7 oz/200 g), diagonally sliced

1 tablespoon toasted white or black sesame seeds

Dressing

2 tablespoons toasted sesame oil

1 tablespoon rice vinegar

2 teaspoons soy sauce or tamari

½–1 fresh Thai red chile, finely chopped

½ teaspoon sea salt

Heat a large skillet over medium-high heat. Add about 1 tablespoon of oil, then add the tofu slices in a single layer (fry the tofu in batches if you need to). Season well with sea salt and white pepper. Pan-fry the tofu for 4–5 minutes, until golden (it doesn't need to be crisp), then flip over and do the same on the other side. Remove from the pan and allow to cool. Slice the tofu slices in half.

To make the dressing, combine all the ingredients in a bowl and stir.

Drain the wakame and squeeze out any excess liquid. Place the wakame in a large bowl, along with the cucumber and tofu, then pour the dressing over the top and toss to combine. Taste and season with sea salt and white pepper. Serve topped with the sesame seeds.

Gluten-free and vegan

Substitute • extra-firm tofu: precooked five-spice tofu

Spinach

"Happy when partnered
with assertive flavors"

In the 16th century, Catherine de' Medici adored spinach so much that, when she left her home in Florence to marry King Henry II of France, she brought along her own cooks who could prepare spinach exactly the way she liked it. Though it could simply be lore, many believe this to be the origins of the culinary term Florentine, which is now used to describe dishes served with spinach.

Spinach is the most versatile of everyday greens, as satisfying cooked as it is raw. It is mellow in flavor, but packs a potent green, grassy, almost chlorophyll flavor that I often crave. Spinach is happy when partnered with assertive flavors. Go rich and creamy with ricotta, feta and eggs, and add acid with lemon juice or vinegar. It always benefits from a hit of garlic and spice. One of my personal favorite vegetable-and-herb couplings is spinach with dill. Often, when I want that pure spinach taste, I will blanch an entire bunch until just wilted but still vibrantly green. Spinach leaves contain a lot of water, so they will cook down dramatically; over 1 pound (450 g) of fresh leaves will wilt to about 1 cup. I then season them with salt, sesame oil and sesame seeds; with rice, it's a simple, bright dinner.

Spinach with Sesame Miso and Soba Noodles

Growing up, it was not unusual for my mother to serve several bundles of greens at dinnertime, presented in stir-fries, tossed with fermented bean curd or blanched with sesame oil. This recipe is a nod to her super-green approach to dinner, a joyful way to devour copious amounts of leafy greens in one sitting. The spinach is quickly blanched and dressed in a nutty and deeply savory sesame-miso sauce, and then tossed with soba noodles. My favorite part of this recipe is pounding the toasted sesame seeds, which releases the earthy perfume of the seeds into the air, enticing my senses. Toasted sesame seeds are key here, as they have a nuttier aroma—I usually buy pretoasted seeds, but you can toast raw sesame seeds very easily at home (see Note below). If you prefer, you can also serve these noodles with a jammy or fried egg on top, or the spinach can be eaten with rice or as a side dish.

SERVES 4

1 large bunch spinach (about 14 oz/400 g), washed well

10 ounces (300 g) soba noodles

¼ cup (35 g) toasted white sesame seeds, plus more for topping

4 teaspoons mirin

1 tablespoon white (shiro) miso

1 teaspoon sugar

1 teaspoon soy sauce or tamari

4 teaspoons toasted sesame oil

2 green onions, finely chopped

Bring a large saucepan of salted water to a boil. If your spinach comes with roots, trim them. Drop the spinach into the water and cook for 45–60 seconds, until wilted. Using tongs, remove the spinach from the water and place in a colander in the sink (keep the boiling water for the noodles). Run the spinach under cold water until completely cool (you can also plunge it into an ice bath if you have ice available). Drain, then squeeze the spinach tightly to remove all the water.

Bring the same pan of boiling water (top it up if you need to) back to a boil. Add the soba noodles and cook according to the package directions, until just al dente. Drain and run under cold water until completely cool. Leave to drain.

Add the sesame seeds to a mortar and pound with the pestle until the seeds are almost ground but still with some texture (it will smell incredible at this stage). Add the mirin, miso, sugar, soy sauce or tamari (straight into the mortar) and mix well. Place the spinach in a large bowl, add the sesame-miso mix and toss very well to combine, coating every strand of spinach. Add the soba noodles to the bowl, along with the sesame oil, and toss to combine.

To serve, top with the green onion and extra sesame seeds.

Note: To toast raw sesame seeds, place them in a dry skillet and toast over low heat, stirring constantly, until they turn golden and start to pop.

For gluten-free • use rice vermicelli

Vegan

Substitute • mirin: rice vinegar mixed with ½ teaspoon of sugar • spinach: kale, Swiss chard • soba noodles: white or brown rice, rice noodles

Spinach and Mint Ruffled Milk Pie

This is my savory take on the Greek dish galatopita, a baked milk pie. The custard is accented with mint and spinach, along with a feta topping that is a firm nod to another Greek favorite, spanakopita. The dish is constructed in stages: the filo is ruffled and loosely rolled, then baked until golden and crispy; the custard is then poured over the pastry and the dish is baked again—the bottom turns into a custardy pudding, while the top remains buttery and crisp. The key to this dish is to give the pastry room to breathe—keep the ruffles and coils loose and space the pastry apart to allow the custard to seep into any gaps and crevices. The filo pastry needs to be completely soft—thaw frozen pastry overnight in the fridge, then take it out of the fridge 30 minutes before using. You can also use frozen spinach. This light, ethereal pie is best served with a salad on the side.

SERVES 4

8 tablespoons (112 g) salted butter, melted

16–18 sheets of filo pastry

1¾ ounces (50 g) feta, crumbled

Spinach and mint custard

4½ ounces (125 g) spinach leaves, washed well

small handful of mint leaves (about ¼ cup packed)

1 garlic clove, roughly chopped

1½ cups (360 ml) oat milk or whole milk

sea salt and black pepper

3 large eggs

Preheat the oven to 350°F (180°C). Grease the bottom and sides of a large baking dish (an approximately 12 × 8-inch/30 cm × 20 cm rectangular dish, or an 8½-inch/22 cm round/oval baking dish or even larger) with a little of the melted butter. You can also use two small baking dishes.

On a clean work surface, take one sheet of filo and brush with butter. Top with another piece of filo and brush with butter again. Using your hands, gently push the long edges toward each other, scrunching them into a long, ruffled strip of dough (it's okay if the filo tears a bit). Roll this ruffled dough into a loose spiral and place it in the center of the baking dish.

Continue with the remaining filo, placing each ruffled spiral around the dough in the center, leaving gaps if you have the room. You should be able to fit about eight spirals in the dish, depending upon the size of your pastry sheets and dish. Don't pack the spirals in too tight, as you want some space for the custard to seep into. Brush the tops of the spirals with butter and bake for 20–25 minutes, until golden and crispy.

Meanwhile, to make the spinach and mint custard, bring a saucepan of water to a boil. Add the spinach and cook for 30–60 seconds, until the spinach is wilted and still bright green. Drain immediately and run under cold water until completely cool. Drain again and squeeze out as much liquid as you can. Roughly chop the spinach.

Add the spinach, mint, garlic, milk and 1 teaspoon of sea salt to a blender or food processor and blend until the mixture is completely smooth. Add the eggs and blend again until smooth. Season with black pepper.

Remove the dish from the oven and gently pour the spinach mixture over the golden pastry, allowing the liquid to seep into all the creases. Scatter on the crumbled feta. Return the dish to the oven and bake for another 20–25 minutes, until the custard is just set.

Allow the pie to cool for about 10 minutes. Best eaten warm.

Substitute • mint: dill • feta: Halloumi

Vegetable swap • spinach: kale, Swiss chard

Notes: Filo pastry sheets vary in size. The brand I use is around 13½ × 8½ inches (34 cm × 22 cm). You may need more or fewer sheets, depending upon their size.

Use a large baking dish to allow the custard to run around the pastry.

Store leftovers in the fridge for up to 3 days, then reheat in the oven.

Spinach and Black Bean Enchilada Bake

This deconstructed enchilada is a weeknight workhorse. A family favorite, this is comfort food that comes packed with leafy greens. Don't be concerned about the mountain of spinach leaves—before baking, it will look like there is too much, but it cooks down considerably. Tortillas are a pantry or freezer staple, an adaptable and transformable ingredient in weeknight cooking—they can be used for layered bakes like this, and for dishes like chilaquiles, quesadillas, quick lunch wraps and as a crunchy topping for soups or salads. For a shortcut here, you could use a store-bought tomato-based pasta sauce and jazz it up with extra garlic, cumin and the spices used below. I like to eat this baked enchilada with a green salad or elote (Mexican grilled corn).

SERVES 4-6

extra-virgin olive oil

24 small (about 5-inch/13 cm diameter) corn or flour tortillas

10 ounces (300 g) spinach leaves, washed well

4 green onions, finely sliced

4 cups (1 lb/450 g) grated cheddar (dairy or vegan)

sea salt and black pepper

1½ cups (250 g) cooked black beans (about one 15 oz/425 g can, drained)

Cumin tomato sauce

extra-virgin olive oil

4 garlic cloves, finely chopped

4 teaspoons cumin seeds

2 teaspoons ground coriander

1 teaspoon smoked paprika

½ teaspoon red pepper flakes

one 28-ounce (800 g) can crushed tomatoes

2 cups (480 ml) vegetable stock

4 teaspoons sugar

sea salt and black pepper

Gluten-free and vegan

Vegetable swap • spinach: kale, Swiss chard

Preheat the oven to 400°F (200°C).

To make the cumin tomato sauce, heat a deep skillet or saucepan over medium-high heat. Add ¼ cup (60 ml) of olive oil, along with the garlic, cumin seeds, coriander, paprika and red pepper flakes. Reduce the heat to medium low and cook for 1–2 minutes, until fragrant. Add the tomatoes, vegetable stock and sugar and season with 1 teaspoon of sea salt and a few turns of black pepper. Cover with a lid and cook for 15 minutes.

Drizzle some olive oil into a 12 × 8½-inch (30 cm × 22 cm) baking dish and add a few tablespoons of the cumin tomato sauce. You will need to divide the remaining sauce over four layers of the bake, so use accordingly. Lay six tortillas over the sauce, overlapping them to cover the bottom of the dish. Top with half the spinach, one-quarter of the green onion, one-quarter of the remaining tomato sauce and 1 cup of the grated cheese. Season with sea salt and black pepper.

For the next layer, lay out another six tortillas, scatter on the black beans evenly, then add one-third of the remaining green onion, one-third of the remaining tomato sauce and 1 cup of grated cheddar. Season again with sea salt and black pepper.

Next, lay out six tortillas, the remaining spinach, half of the remaining tomato sauce, half of the green onion and another 1 cup of grated cheddar, followed by sea salt and black pepper. Depending on how deep your dish is, you may need to gently press down on the tortillas as the uncooked spinach takes up a lot of space. It will cook down, so don't worry if your bake is bulging right to the top of the dish.

Finish with the remaining tortillas, green onion, sauce and cheddar, and season with sea salt and black pepper. Drizzle with olive oil, then transfer to the oven and bake for 30–35 minutes, until golden. Remove from the oven and allow to rest for 10–20 minutes before eating.

Green Curry Spinach and Lentil Soup

Spinach possesses a delicate foliage and has the tendency to melt away into soups or stews, easily eclipsed by other ingredients. But I wanted something more for spinach in this soup—more guts, more distinction. Unapologetically SPINACH. Here, I've achieved this with a simple technique—by pureeing most of the spinach before adding it to the soup, it retains all of its vibrant color, emphatically tinting the entire dish. This soup is fortified by pantry staples—Thai curry paste, lentils and coconut milk—which makes short work of this big-flavored, soul-enriching soup. If you want something more filling, you could serve it with a side of rice, sticky rice or rice noodles.

SERVES 4

extra-virgin olive oil

1 yellow onion, finely diced

1-inch (2.5 cm) piece of ginger, peeled and finely chopped

2 garlic cloves, finely chopped

½ cup (110 g) vegan Thai green curry paste

32 ounces (1 liter) vegetable stock

1 cup (210 g) red lentils

1 teaspoon sugar

sea salt and black pepper

14 ounces (400 g) spinach, washed well and roughly chopped (including any stems)

½ cup basil or cilantro leaves, plus more to serve

one 13.5-ounce (400 ml) can coconut milk

juice of ½ lime

handful of crispy fried shallots

Heat a large saucepan over medium-high heat. Drizzle in about 2 tablespoons of olive oil, add the onion and sauté, stirring constantly, for 2 minutes until softened. Next, throw in the ginger and garlic and stir for 1 minute, until the kitchen smells aromatic. Reduce the heat to medium and add the curry paste, stirring for 2 minutes, until fragrant. Add the vegetable stock, lentils, sugar and 1 teaspoon of sea salt and stir. Cover and cook for 15 minutes or until the lentils are just soft.

Meanwhile, add three-quarters of the spinach, the basil or cilantro, and coconut milk to a blender or food processor and puree for 30–60 seconds, until completely smooth and bright green.

Add the spinach–coconut milk puree and lime juice to the soup and stir for 2 minutes, until heated through. Taste and season with sea salt and black pepper. Turn off the heat and add the remaining spinach leaves (the residual heat from the soup is enough to wilt the spinach).

To serve, divide among bowls and top with extra basil or cilantro leaves and crispy fried shallots.

Gluten-free and vegan

Substitute • Thai green curry paste: Thai red curry paste • red lentils: yellow or green split peas, cooked chickpeas, brown lentils

Vegetable swap • spinach: kale, Swiss chard

Spinach "Boxes"

These oversized spinach dumplings are inspired by Northern Chinese "chive boxes," dough pockets filled with garlic chives, eggs and vermicelli. Spinach is used two ways: first to create an earthy, verdant wrapper; then in the hearty filling. Due to the size of these dumplings, you'll need to make your dough from scratch, as commercial dumpling wrappers don't come large enough. The spinach dough is very simple—just a hot water dough with spinach puree added.

MAKES 12 LARGE DUMPLINGS

neutral oil

2 garlic cloves, finely chopped

1 bunch of spinach (about 7½ oz/200 g), washed well, leaves picked

sea salt

7½ ounces (200 g) extra-firm tofu, crumbled and drained

1 teaspoon soy sauce or tamari

1 teaspoon toasted sesame oil

¼ teaspoon five-spice powder

chili oil or Umami Crisp (see page 27), to serve

Spinach dumpling wrappers

1 packed cup (70 g) spinach leaves, washed well

2½ cups (300 g) all-purpose flour, plus more for dusting

1 teaspoon fine sea salt

about ½ cup (120 ml) boiling water, cooled for 1 minute

To make the spinach dumpling wrappers, begin by making a spinach puree. Place the spinach leaves and ½ cup (120 ml) of water in a small blender or food processor and blitz on high speed until completely smooth. Measure out ¼ cup of the puree and freeze the rest in a small airtight container or zip-seal bag for your next batch of spinach dumpling wrappers, or use in smoothies or soups.

Place the flour and salt in a mixing bowl and whisk to combine (place paper towel underneath the bowl to keep it still when stirring). Add the spinach puree, then slowly drizzle in the just-boiled water, stirring constantly with a pair of chopsticks or wooden spoon until the dough looks shaggy. Use your hands to incorporate all the dry bits of flour into one mass (if the dough is very dry, add more hot water, 1 teaspoon at a time, until it is more workable).

Transfer the dough to a very lightly floured work surface and knead for just 2–3 minutes, until smooth and elastic. Wrap the dough tightly in plastic wrap or place in a zip-seal bag and allow to rest at room temperature for 30 minutes or up to 2 hours. (You can also place the dough in the fridge to roll out the next day. Allow the dough to come back to room temperature before rolling.)

While the dough is resting, make the filling. Place a skillet over medium heat. When hot, add a drizzle of oil and the garlic. Fry for 15–30 seconds, until aromatic, then add the spinach and season with sea salt. Cook for 1–2 minutes, until the spinach is wilted but still bright green. Drain the spinach in a colander and, when cool enough to handle, squeeze the spinach tightly to get rid of as much liquid as possible. Chop the spinach finely and place it in a bowl, along with the tofu, soy sauce or tamari, sesame oil, ¼ teaspoon of sea salt and the five-spice powder and combine well. Taste and adjust with more salt or soy sauce if needed.

Cut the dough into four equal pieces and roll each piece into a thick log. Cut each log into three pieces, giving you 12 pieces in total. Roll each piece into a ball, then cover the balls with a damp tea towel. Working with one ball at a time, use a thin dowel or small rolling pin to roll out the dough into a thin 4–4¾-inch (11–12 cm) round. Ideally, the edges of the round will be a bit thinner than the center—to do this, hold the rolling pin in your dominant hand and roll just the edge of the round, using your nondominant hand to rotate the round a little after each roll, continuing this motion until your round is the desired size. Dust with flour and set aside, covered. Continue with the remaining dough.

To make the dumplings, place a wrapper on a lightly floured work surface and spoon a heaping tablespoon of filling onto one side. Fold the wrapper over, forming a half-moon. Pick the dumpling up and press the edges together to seal it completely. Leave it as is or crimp the edges in a zigzag pattern (you can really crimp these in any way you like), then, holding a dumpling by the crimped edge, press the dumpling onto the work surface to form a flat bottom for frying (see photo next page). Repeat to make 12 dumplings.

Heat a 10–12-inch (25–30 cm) skillet over medium-high heat (I use a well-seasoned cast-iron skillet, but a nonstick or stainless steel pan works, too; just heat until very hot). When hot, add a drizzle of oil and place the dumplings, flat-bottom down, into the oil. Fry for 1–2 minutes, until the bottoms are golden, then carefully add ¼ cup (60 ml) of water and immediately cover with a lid. Cook for 2–3 minutes, then remove the lid and cook for another 30–60 seconds, until all the water has evaporated. Remove the dumplings from the pan and serve immediately with chili oil or umami crisp.

Note: You can also use a stand mixer to make this dough. Add the flour, spinach puree and water to the bowl and, using the dough hook attachment, mix on low speed until the water is incorporated. Increase the speed to medium and continue mixing for 2 minutes, until a dough forms. Transfer the dough to a lightly floured work surface and knead by hand for 1 minute or until the dough ball looks smooth. Wrap it in plastic wrap or a zip-seal bag and rest for at least 30 minutes or up to 2 hours.

Storage: To freeze uncooked dumplings, place them on a tray or plate lined with parchment paper and place them in the freezer. When hard, remove the dumplings from the tray and store them in a zip-seal bag or airtight container. Cook from frozen, do not thaw.

Pictured overleaf ›

Vegan

Vegetable swap • spinach: kale, garlic chives, Asian greens, such as gai lan or choy sum

Spinach "Boxes"

Inspired by Chana Saag

My devotion to Indian saag (made using a mixture of greens) and palak (spinach) dishes runs deep. The spiced, greens-forward sauce is joyous in its celebration of leaves and their ability to power a meal. This creamy coconut spinach with chickpeas is inspired by the wonderful chana saag from a local Indian restaurant, where the chickpeas come bathed in a rich puree of greens and spices. I designed this recipe specifically to be made with frozen spinach, the *coolest* hero of pantry cooking—I use two boxes of frozen spinach in this recipe (the square blocks), which means it is packed with goodness. You also have a lot of options with this recipe—it's a saucy dish, so you could add a third can of chickpeas, or add cubes of tofu, paneer or feta. The quantity is designed for you to have leftovers, so you can make the chana saag fried rice on page 392.

SERVES 4

1 yellow onion, roughly chopped

1-inch (2.5 cm) piece of ginger, peeled and roughly chopped

4 garlic cloves, roughly chopped

1–2 green chiles (jalapeño or serrano), roughly chopped

3 tablespoons (42 g) ghee, butter or vegan butter

1 teaspoon cumin seeds

1 teaspoon garam masala

two 9-ounce (255 g) boxes frozen spinach, thawed

sea salt and black pepper

½ cup (120 ml) vegetable stock

1 cup (240 ml) coconut cream

½ teaspoon chile powder

3 cups (500 g) cooked chickpeas (about two 15 oz/425 g cans, drained)

basmati rice, to serve

Place the onion, ginger, garlic and green chile in a blender or food processor and puree to a paste.

Heat a saucepan over medium-high heat. Melt the ghee or butter, then add the paste and cook for 2–3 minutes, until it's very fragrant and starting to stick to the base of the pan. Add the cumin seeds and garam masala and stir. Add the thawed spinach, along with 1 teaspoon of sea salt. Cook for 4–5 minutes to allow the liquid to evaporate a little, though you don't want it to get completely dry. Season with some black pepper.

Transfer the mixture to a blender or food processor, or use a stick blender to puree the spinach. Once it's relatively smooth, pour it back into the pan and add the vegetable stock, half the coconut cream, the chile powder and chickpeas. Simmer over low heat for 10 minutes.

Taste and season with more sea salt and black pepper, if required. Serve with basmati rice, drizzled with the remaining coconut cream.

Note: To use fresh spinach, you'll need to cook down 2¼ pounds (1 kg) fresh leaves to get the equivalent of 18 ounces (510 g) of frozen spinach.

Gluten-free and vegan

Substitute • coconut cream: coconut milk, cream

Vegetable swap • frozen spinach: fresh spinach (see Note), kale, Swiss chard

Chana Saag (or Any Leftover Curry) Fried Rice

Curries are the most fruitful leftovers because their flavor improves with a day or two in the fridge, when they can be transformed into something completely different (see the Sweet Potato Panang Curry Pizza on page 402). This fried rice recipe came about using the leftovers from my local Indian restaurant— a container of basmati rice and a small portion of chana saag, thrown together in a wok, emerging as a dish with strong Indo-Chinese fried rice vibes. Some eggs, ginger and peas bring this unconventional dish back to my roots. You could make this dish with any leftover curry.

SERVES 4

4 large eggs

sea salt and white pepper

neutral oil

1-inch (2.5 cm) piece of ginger, peeled and finely chopped

4 cups (600 g) cold or leftover rice, preferably basmati

1 tablespoon soy sauce or tamari

generous 1 cup (150 g) frozen peas (no need to thaw)

1 cup (150 g) leftover Chana Saag (see page 391) or any leftover curry

2 green onions, finely sliced

Crack the eggs into a bowl and add about ½ teaspoon of sea salt. Whisk until well combined.

Heat a wok or large skillet over medium-high heat. When hot, drizzle in about 1 tablespoon of oil and pour in the eggs. Move the eggs around with a silicone spatula, cooking for 30–60 seconds, until just set. Break up the egg slightly and remove from the pan. Set aside.

Heat another 2–3 tablespoons of oil in the pan and add the ginger, frying for 20 seconds to flavor the oil. Add the rice and fry, breaking it up with a wooden spoon, for about 2 minutes. Add the soy sauce or tamari and 1 teaspoon of sea salt and toss, then add the egg, frozen peas and leftover curry. Stir-fry for 3–4 minutes, until everything is heated through. Turn off the heat and add a pinch of white pepper and season with more sea salt, if needed. Stir in the green onion and serve immediately.

Gluten-free

Veganize • omit the eggs

Substitute • leftover chana saag: fresh or frozen spinach

Spinach and Pandan Chiffon Cake

My mother never baked when I was growing up, but luckily for me she had friends who did. Every now and then, as an after-school treat, Aunty would bring me a piece of fluffy, diaphanous chiffon cake, iridescently green, ethereal in appearance and flavor. I fell in love with chiffon cakes as a child and I have often thought that if I ever had a cake shop, perhaps it would only sell dainty chiffon cakes, in a mélange of colors, imbued with pandan, orange, matcha, coffee, chocolate, lavender and hojicha. There might even be a vibrantly green-hued chiffon in that lineup, infused with spinach of all things; not your average chiffon. This would be the recipe.

SERVES 8–10

1⅔ cups (200 g) all-purpose flour or gluten-free all-purpose flour

2 teaspoons baking powder

2½ tightly packed cups (150 g) spinach leaves, washed well

8½ tablespoons (125 ml) neutral oil

10 large eggs, separated

1½ cups (190 g) powdered sugar

¾ cup (180 ml) coconut milk

1 teaspoon pandan essence (see Note)

1 teaspoon cream of tartar

Preheat the oven to 350°F (180°C).

Lightly oil the bottom of an angel food cake pan (preferably the type with legs). Do not oil the sides or the middle spout as this will prevent the cake from rising.

In a bowl, whisk together the flour and baking powder.

Add the spinach and oil to a blender or food processor and puree until it is as smooth as you can get it—you may still see tiny chunks of spinach, which is okay. Set aside.

Place the egg yolks and one-third of the powdered sugar in a bowl and whisk (a handheld whisk is fine) until thick and creamy. Whisk in the coconut milk until combined. Add the flour mixture, a little at a time, until just combined. Fold in the spinach oil and the pandan essence.

Meanwhile, in a stand mixer with the whisk attached or using electric beaters, beat the egg whites on high speed until white and foamy. Reduce the speed to low and add the cream of tartar and the remaining powdered sugar, 1 tablespoon at a time, then increase the speed to high and whisk to firm peaks.

Fold half of the beaten egg whites into the egg yolk and flour mixture to loosen it up. Then, gently fold this loosened mixture back into the remaining egg whites, making sure to fold gently, as you don't want to knock too much air out of the batter.

Pour the batter into the prepared pan. Gently tap the pan on the kitchen counter to break up any large air pockets.

Bake for 15 minutes, then reduce the oven temperature to 325°F (160°C) and bake for an additional 45 minutes or until a knife inserted into the cake comes out clean.

Take the pan out of the oven and invert the finished cake, while it is still in the pan. Let it cool completely upside down. Once cooled, run a knife around the edges of the cake pan to release the cake, then remove from the pan. Serve bottom-side up.

Note: Pandan essence (it also comes as a powder) is available at Asian grocery stores that specialize in Thai and Southeast Asian ingredients, or online.

Gluten-free

Substitute • pandan: vanilla extract or omit (see Note)

Sweet potato

"Brings a cool confidence and
quiet swagger to the plate"

Ray Charles once passionately sang that he was on cloud nine, simply due to sweet potato pie. It is no wonder that the humble sweet potato elicits such an ardent serenade. There is something incredibly special about sweet potato—it brings a cool confidence and quiet swagger to the plate.

My mother shared Ray Charles's sweet potato fervor. When the craving hit, she would jump up from her chair, struck by sudden inspiration, and declare that she needed faan syu (sweet potato). Retreating to her makeshift pantry in the laundry room, she would pick out a handful of fist-sized sweet potatoes. She preferred small ones, which meant she could cook them whole, quickly. She wrapped them in foil, skin on, and roasted them in her countertop oven until the flesh was tender. We ate them without adornment, peeling back the scorching foil and skin and devouring the creamy flesh.

Sweet potatoes are naturally sugary-sweet, and so replete with earthy nuttiness that little embellishment is required. Yet, they are also very receptive to flavor pairings—I love to pair them with salty things like olives, feta and hard cheese, spicy sauces and cilantro, earthy herbs, such as rosemary and sage, maple-spiced butter and warming spices.

There are hundreds of varieties of sweet potato, with skin and flesh that ranges from deep purple and reddish-purple to yellow, cream and white. One of my favorite varieties is Japanese sweet potato (satsumaimo), which has a red-toned purplish skin and a pale-yellow flesh that is creamy, starchy, nutty and sugar-sweet; the texture is fluffy, resembling a dense cake. The Okinawan sweet potato is also a special variety—mildly sweet with notes of honey, it has beige skin and a bright purple flesh, which stays that way after cooking.

Sweet Potato Panang Curry

Panang curry is distinct from other Thai curries—sweeter and creamier, it has a sophisticated spice layer that is punctuated with tanginess. Galangal is traditional but I most often use ginger because that is what I have on hand. As with most homemade spice pastes, the list of ingredients may look long, but they are mostly things we keep in our pantry, and making it is as easy as gathering and blending. This recipe is great for meal prepping—keep 2 cups of the curry aside to use for the Sweet Potato Panang Curry Pizza on page 402.

SERVES 6

neutral oil

1 yellow onion, cut into thin wedges

one 13.5-ounce (400 ml) can coconut milk

1½ cups (360 ml) vegetable stock

1¾ pounds (800 g) sweet potatoes, peeled and cut into 1-inch (2.5 cm) pieces

4 teaspoons soy sauce or tamari

¼ cup (45 g) brown sugar

sea salt

juice of 1 lime, plus wedges to serve

7 ounces (200 g) canned baby corn, drained

4½ ounces (130 g) canned bamboo shoots, drained

5 ounces (150 g) snow peas, trimmed

handful of roasted peanuts, chopped

handful of cilantro leaves

rice or noodles, to serve

Panang curry paste (makes 1½ cups)

4–8 dried red chiles

3 lemongrass stalks, tender white parts only, roughly chopped

1-inch (2.5 cm) piece of ginger or galangal, peeled and roughly chopped

4 garlic cloves, roughly chopped

3 shallots, roughly chopped

6 makrut lime leaves, roughly sliced

½ bunch (1 packed cup) cilantro leaves

1 teaspoon coriander seeds or ½ teaspoon ground coriander

1 teaspoon cumin seeds or ½ teaspoon ground cumin

¼ cup (40 g) roasted peanuts

1 teaspoon sea salt

¼ cup (60 ml) neutral oil

Gluten-free and vegan

To make the panang curry paste, first soak the chiles in hot water for at least 15 minutes. Drain the chiles and place them in a blender or food processor. Add the remaining ingredients, except the oil, and blend or process until you have a chunky paste. Drizzle in the oil and blend again until mostly smooth.

Heat a large skillet over medium-high heat. Add 1–2 tablespoons of oil and the onion, then reduce the heat to medium and sauté for 4–5 minutes, until soft. Add half the curry paste (see Note) and fry for 2 minutes, until aromatic. Add the coconut milk, vegetable stock and sweet potato, cover with a lid and cook for 20 minutes. Add the soy sauce or tamari, brown sugar, 2 teaspoons of sea salt and the lime juice and stir. Add the baby corn, bamboo shoots and snow peas and stir to combine. Turn off the heat immediately. Taste again and season with more sea salt, sugar or lime, if needed.

To serve, scatter the curry with the peanuts and cilantro leaves and serve with a wedge of lime, alongside rice or noodles.

Note: If we are going to the trouble of getting our blender or food processor out, let's go bulk. This paste recipe makes enough for two curries; keep the unused portion in an airtight container or zip-seal bag in the freezer for up to 3 months (thaw before using).

Sweet Potato Panang Curry Pizza

When life gives you leftover sweet potato panang curry (or any veggie curry, for that matter), make pizza. Curry is not an obvious pizza topping, and some may scoff at the concept, but it is a meal that I often ate at a local restaurant in Sydney, an inspired dish that beautifully showcased how two disparate food genres could come together. The curry "topping" here can be used on any pizza crust—whether you like to make your own dough, use store-bought fresh dough, or just a basic supermarket pizza crust. You'll need about 2 cups of curry for this pizza, but a bit more or a little less works, too; just make sure you don't add too much liquid, which will make the crust soggy. Other leftover curries work, too, particularly vegetable korma or saag paneer (or try it with my Inspired by Chana Saag recipe on page 391).

MAKES ONE 12-INCH (30 CM) PIZZA

extra-virgin olive oil

1 pound (450 g) fresh pizza dough (or 12-inch/30 cm store-bought pizza crust)

2 cups Sweet Potato Panang Curry (see page 400) or any leftover curry

7 ounces (200 g) mozzarella or bocconcini, sliced or torn

sea salt and black pepper

handful of basil leaves

pinch of red pepper flakes

Preheat the oven to 450°F (230°C) for fresh dough or 425°F (220°C) for a prebaked pizza crust.

Drizzle a sheet pan with olive oil. If you're using fresh dough, place it onto the pan and coax and pull it into a 12-inch (30 cm) round. If you're using a prebaked pizza crust, place it on the pan. Spread the curry evenly over the crust. Top with the mozzarella or bocconcini and season generously with sea salt and black pepper. Bake for 20–25 minutes for fresh dough and 10–12 minutes for a prebaked pizza crust, until the cheese is golden and bubbling.

Top with the basil leaves and red pepper flakes. Let sit for 5–10 minutes before slicing.

For gluten-free • use a gluten-free pizza crust

Veganize • use vegan mozzarella or other vegan cheese

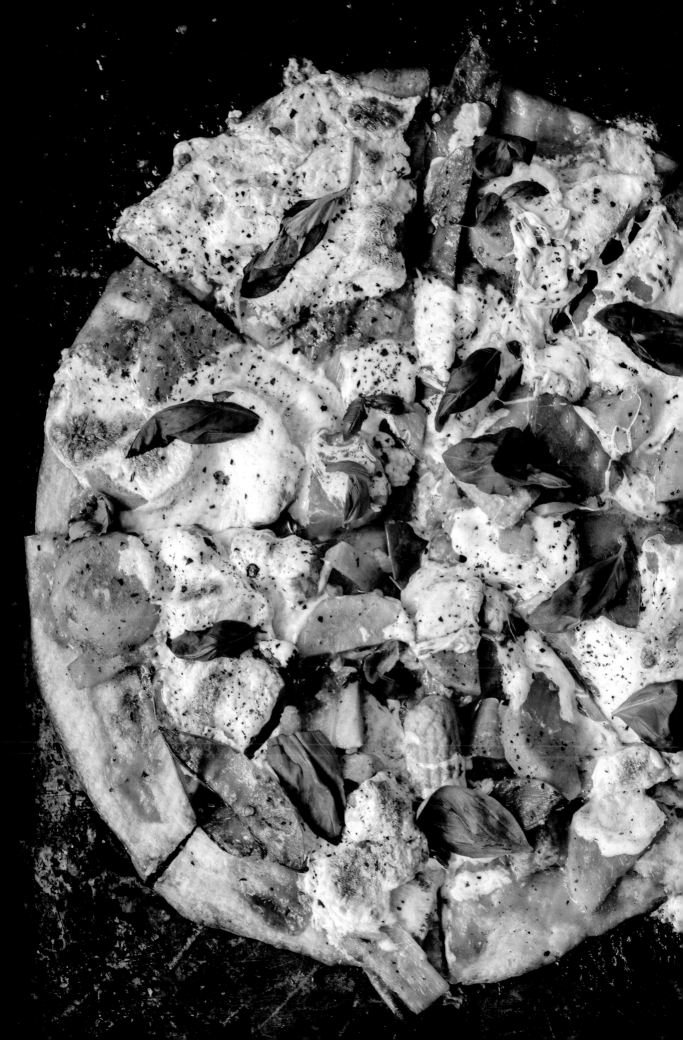

Hasselback Sweet Potatoes with Garlicky Caper and Thyme Oil

Hasselbacking, the technique of slashing vegetable flesh not-quite-all-the-way through in thin, even layers, creates more surface area for crispy textures, while also opening up perfect little slots for seasonings to seep into. This garlicky caper and thyme oil is designed to enhance all the natural attributes of sweet potato, bringing a briny tang that brightens the creamy flesh. This dish is unashamedly garlicky, so use less if you would like a more mellow flavor. This is an attractive main for the holiday table.

SERVES 4

4–6 purple or orange sweet potatoes (about 9 oz/250 g each), scrubbed

3–4 thyme sprigs

extra-virgin olive oil

sea salt and black pepper

1 cup (200 g) Puy (French) or brown lentils

5 garlic cloves, finely sliced

3 tablespoons capers, rinsed and roughly chopped

2–3 strips of lemon peel

parsley leaves, for topping

Preheat the oven to 400°F (200°C).

Using a sharp knife, slice the sweet potatoes at scant ¼-inch (4–5 mm) intervals, slicing only two-thirds of the way through so that the potato still holds together. Place the potatoes on a sheet pan. Tear up one thyme sprig and scatter it over the top or, if you can, insert it into a few of the slits. Drizzle with olive oil and season with sea salt and black pepper. Roast for 35–40 minutes, until the potatoes feel completely soft and the tops are golden.

Meanwhile, bring a saucepan of salted water to a boil and add the lentils. Cover, then reduce the heat to medium low and cook for 20–25 minutes, until the lentils are just tender. Drain.

To make the garlicky caper and thyme oil, place ½ cup (120 ml) of olive oil, along with the garlic, capers, lemon peel, remaining thyme sprigs and 1 teaspoon of sea salt, in a small saucepan. Warm over medium-low heat until the oil starts to bubble, 3–5 minutes. Reduce the heat to the lowest setting possible and continue to cook for 2–3 minutes, watching over it constantly to make sure the garlic doesn't burn. Remove the pan from the heat immediately and pour the oil into a heatproof bowl. Set aside to cool for 5–10 minutes.

Place the lentils on a plate and arrange the sweet potatoes on top. Spoon as much or as little of the garlicky caper and thyme oil on top as you like, allowing some to drizzle down into the lentils. Scatter with parsley and serve.

Note: Leftover garlic and thyme oil can be used to drizzle over other roasted vegetables or to finish soups or pasta dishes.

Gluten-free and vegan

Substitute • lentils: cooked chickpeas, black-eyed peas, quinoa

Vegetable swap • sweet potato: large potato, carrot

Roast Sweet Potato Wedges with Ají Verde

Sweet potato–led dishes frequently border on being too sweet, crying out for contrast and opposition. In this dish, balance is restored with the help of ají verde, an iconic spicy green sauce from Peru. Traditionally made of ají amarillo paste (yellow chile), ají verde is often served with grilled meat and vegetables, but I consider it a handy everyday sauce that can be served on salads, soups or any dish that needs a spicy edge. The sweet potatoes are soaked beforehand (like in the Crispy Potato Wedges on page 328), which ensures they get extra crispy, with an internal flesh that is soft and tender. I enjoy the texture of leaving the skin on, but peel them if you prefer. If you would like a more substantial meal, add some legumes or a grain.

SERVES 4

2 pounds (900 g) small sweet potatoes

extra-virgin olive oil

sea salt and black pepper

handful of cilantro leaves

Ají verde (makes ¾ cup)

½ cup (125 g) regular or vegan mayonnaise

1 garlic clove, roughly chopped

1 jalapeño or fresh Thai green chile, roughly chopped

1 cup cilantro leaves

juice of ½ lime (about 1 tablespoon)

Wash and scrub the sweet potatoes (leave the skins on). Cut each sweet potato in half lengthwise, then cut each half lengthwise into quarters—you'll end up with eight wedges per sweet potato; make sure they are about the same thickness and size. Place in a bowl and cover with hot water for 10 minutes.

Preheat the oven to 400°F (200°C). Line two sheet pans with parchment paper.

Drain the sweet potato wedges and pat them dry with paper towel. Place them on the prepared pans, drizzle with olive oil, season well with salt and black pepper and, using your hands, toss until they are well coated. Lay the wedges out, one cut side down, and place the pans in the oven. Roast for 25–30 minutes, flipping halfway through, until both cut sides are golden and crispy.

Meanwhile, to make the ají verde, combine all the ingredients in a blender or food processor and whiz until smooth and the sauce has a light green tint.

To serve, place the sweet potato wedges on a plate and either spoon the ají verde over the top or serve the sauce on the side. Top with the cilantro leaves.

Gluten-free and vegan

Vegetable swap • sweet potato: carrot, butternut squash, eggplant

Sweet Patatas Bravas Salad

Sweet potatoes are given the patatas bravas treatment, the classic and much-loved Spanish tapas dish. The salsa brava, the fiercely flavored smoky sauce, is traditionally made with hot pimentón (Spanish smoked paprika), but here I use smoked paprika and add some chile powder for heat. I love the miscellany of robust flavors in this dish—the smoky, spicy red sauce and the garlicky mayonnaise are full of umami goodness, bringing out the savory side of the sweet potatoes. Canned tomatoes make this sauce pantry-friendly and quick, with a richer tomatoey flavor, while the lemony garlic aioli introduces welcome creaminess.

SERVES 4

1 ¾ pounds (800 g) sweet potatoes, peeled and cut into ¾-inch (2 cm) cubes

extra-virgin olive oil

sea salt and black pepper

1 cup (200 g) pearl barley

handful of parsley leaves

½ cup toasted almonds, chopped

Bravas sauce

4–5 whole peeled tomatoes (from one 14.5 oz/411 g can)

3 garlic cloves, roughly chopped

1 small shallot, roughly chopped

2 teaspoons smoked paprika

½ teaspoon chile powder

Garlic aioli

⅓ cup (80 g) regular or vegan mayonnaise

1 garlic clove, grated, or ½ teaspoon garlic powder

¼ teaspoon sea salt, or more to taste

2 teaspoons lemon juice

Preheat the oven to 400°F (200°C).

Place the sweet potato on a sheet pan and drizzle with olive oil. Season with sea salt and black pepper and roast for 20–25 minutes, until the sweet potato is golden and tender.

Meanwhile, place the pearl barley in a saucepan with 3 ¼ cups (780 ml) of water. Add 1 teaspoon of sea salt and bring to a boil over medium-high heat. Reduce the heat to low, then cover and cook according to the package directions, until just tender. Drain and set aside to cool slightly.

To make the bravas sauce, drain the whole peeled tomatoes (save the liquid for another use) and place them in a blender or food processor, along with the garlic, shallot, smoked paprika and chile powder. Puree until completely smooth. Place a small saucepan over medium-low heat, add 1–2 tablespoons of olive oil, along with the bravas sauce, and stir to combine. Simmer for 6–8 minutes, stirring every now and then, until the sauce has thickened slightly and the flavors have melded.

To make the garlic aioli, combine the ingredients in a small bowl.

Combine the sweet potato, pearl barley, parsley and about three-quarters of the bravas sauce and fold to coat the potato. To serve, drizzle with the remaining bravas sauce, top with garlic aioli and scatter with the almonds. Serve warm or at room temperature.

Do ahead: Make the bravas sauce up to 24 hours ahead and keep, covered, in the fridge. This allows the flavors to meld further.

For gluten-free • use quinoa, chickpeas or lentils

Vegan

Substitute • pearl barley: farro, quinoa, chickpeas, lentils • canned tomatoes: 3–4 fresh tomatoes, peeled • shallot: small yellow onion

Vegetable swap • sweet potato: potato, cauliflower

Sweet Potato Rendang

Rendang is a dry curry with origins in Indonesia and Malaysia. It is traditionally made with beef that has been cooked low and slow in a heavily perfumed mélange of coconut, lemongrass and alliums. Sweet potato is not the usual rendang ingredient, but it adds a smooth mildness that tempers the punchy sauce. This recipe is faithful to traditional rendang recipes and techniques—a robust spice paste of shallots, garlic, lemongrass and ginger (galangal is also used traditionally) is cooked down until it caramelizes and clings onto the sweet potato. The resulting curry-like stew is spicy, sweet and tangy. Classic rendang includes kerisik, a fried coconut paste that is buttery and creamy. I cheated by using toasted shredded coconut, but if you have kerisik, please use it.

SERVES 4

¼ cup (60 ml) neutral oil

1 cinnamon stick

¼ teaspoon whole cloves or ⅛ teaspoon ground cloves

2 star anise

¼ teaspoon ground cardamom or 2 cardamom pods, smashed

1 lemongrass stalk, white part only, cut into 2-inch (5 cm) pieces and smashed

2 pounds (900 g) sweet potatoes, peeled and cut into chunks or discs ¾–1¼ inches (2–3 cm) thick

1 cup (240 ml) coconut cream

4 teaspoons tamarind paste

½ cup plus 1 tablespoon (45 g) unsweetened shredded coconut

5 makrut lime leaves, finely sliced

2 tablespoons brown sugar

2 teaspoons sea salt

white or brown rice, to serve

handful of cilantro leaves, to serve

Rendang spice paste

4 shallots (about 7 oz/200 g), chopped

1½-inch (4 cm) piece of ginger or galangal (about 1 oz/30 g), peeled and chopped

2 lemongrass stalks, tender white parts only, roughly chopped

6–8 dried red chiles, soaked in warm water for 10 minutes, drained

4 garlic cloves, roughly chopped

Gluten-free and vegan

Vegetable swap • sweet potato: potato, mushrooms

To make the rendang spice paste, place all the ingredients in a blender or food processor and blend until you have a thick paste. Alternatively, you can use a mortar and pestle to pound all the ingredients together.

Place a large saucepan or Dutch oven over medium-high heat. Add the oil, along with the spice paste, and cook for 2 minutes, until fragrant. Add the cinnamon, cloves, star anise, cardamom and lemongrass, then reduce the heat to medium low and stir for 2–3 minutes, until the paste is starting to caramelize. Add the sweet potato and stir for 2 minutes to combine. Add the coconut cream and tamarind paste, along with 1 cup (240 ml) of water. Stir, then cover with a lid and simmer over low heat for 10 minutes, until the sweet potato has softened a little.

Meanwhile, heat a small skillet over medium heat. Add the shredded coconut and stir constantly for 3–4 minutes, until golden.

Add the toasted coconut, makrut lime leaves, 1 tablespoon of the brown sugar and 1 teaspoon of sea salt to the sweet potato mixture. Stir, then cover again and cook over low heat for another 18–20 minutes, until the sweet potato is completely tender and the liquid has thickened. Add the remaining 1 tablespoon of brown sugar and 1 teaspoon of sea salt. The rendang should be spicy, sweet and rich. Serve with white or brown rice, topped with cilantro leaves.

Note: If you prefer less spice, remove the seeds from the dried red chiles before soaking them.

Sweet Potato and Black Sesame Marble Bundt

This cake is a triumphant combination of opposites, sharply contrasting flavors and colors that both complement and highlight one another. One part is delicately moist thanks to the sweet potato, the other part dense, nutty and earthy, courtesy of the black sesame. While visually impressive, this is a simple cake to make, and fun, too—the two batters mingling and swirling together to create a dramatic marbling effect. Special enough to serve for a celebration, but also easy enough to bake for the family for afternoon tea, this cake falls into my favorite category of desserts—not too sweet. Black sesame paste, sometimes called black tahini, can be found at Asian or Middle Eastern supermarkets (it's also easy to find online), but if you are unable to source it, you could use regular tahini, adding a tablespoon of cocoa powder to deepen the color and add a chocolatey edge.

SERVES 6–8

1 pound (450 g) sweet potatoes, peeled and cut into ¾-inch (2 cm) pieces

1¾ cups plus 2 tablespoons (225 g) all-purpose flour

2 teaspoons baking powder

½ teaspoon sea salt

1 cup plus 1½ tablespoons (220 g) sugar, plus more for dusting

9 tablespoons (126 g) unsalted butter, melted

2 large eggs

2 teaspoons vanilla extract

½ cup (150 g) black sesame paste (black tahini)

¼ cup (60 ml) whole milk, oat or soy milk

powdered sugar, for dusting

For gluten-free • use cup-for-cup gluten-free all-purpose flour

Veganize • use flax eggs (see Cook's Notes page 30), vegan butter and nondairy milk

Substitute • black sesame paste: Chinese sesame paste, tahini

Vegetable swap • sweet potato: winter squash, parsnip

Pour ¾–1¼ inches (2–3 cm) of water into a saucepan or deep skillet and bring to a boil. Add the sweet potatoes to a steaming basket, then place the steamer in the pan, making sure that the water doesn't touch the bottom of the steamer. Cover and steam for 10 minutes or until the sweet potatoes are completely soft. Remove the sweet potatoes from the steamer and transfer to a bowl. Mash until completely pureed.

Preheat the oven to 350°F (180°C).

Place the flour, baking powder and salt in a bowl and whisk together to combine well.

In another bowl, combine the sugar and melted butter and whisk until blended. Whisk in the eggs, one at a time, followed by the vanilla. Fold in the flour mixture, one-third at a time, stirring well after each addition.

Divide the mixture in half, separating it into two bowls (I just eyeball this, though you can weigh it if you like). To one bowl of batter, add the mashed sweet potato and fold until combined. To the other bowl of batter, add the black sesame paste and milk and fold until combined.

Prepare your Bundt pan right before you are ready to fill it—this prevents the oil from running to the bottom of the pan. Grease a 10–12 cup capacity Bundt pan with cooking spray, making sure to pay extra attention to any details and crevices in your pan, then dust with granulated sugar. Shake the pan to evenly distribute the sugar, then remove any excess sugar by tipping the pan upside down over the sink (you can also use an 8½-inch/22 cm springform pan or large 10 × 5-inch/25 cm × 13 cm loaf pan lined with parchment paper).

Add spoonfuls of the two batters alternately to the Bundt pan, distributing it evenly. Run a single chopstick or knife through the mixture to create a marbled effect.

Bake in the middle of the oven for 1–1¼ hours. Start checking the cake for doneness at the 1 hour mark. Insert a toothpick or bamboo skewer into the cake and if it comes out clean, it is ready.

Leave the cake in the pan on a wire rack to cool for 10 minutes, before turning out to cool completely. Once cooled, dust the cake with a little powdered sugar.

Sweet Potato Spiral Mantou

Mantou are plain steamed Chinese buns. The dough is similar in texture and taste to the one used for char siu bao, but mantou are traditionally filling free. They are eaten as a snack, either steamed or deep-fried. Here, I've added sweet potato to the dough to give a hint of sweetness and color, and have also snuck in a thin layer of sweet potato and coconut paste. To top it off, dip the mantou into sweetened condensed milk, which is a traditional way of serving them.

MAKES 12

½ teaspoon active dry yeast

½ teaspoon granulated sugar, plus another ¼ cup (50 g)

7 tablespoons (100 ml) warm water (90°–110°F/32°–43°C)

1 large sweet potato (about 10 oz/300 g), peeled and cut into ½-inch (1.5 cm) pieces

2 cups plus 1½ tablespoons (250 g) all-purpose flour, plus more if needed and for dusting

4 teaspoons neutral oil

2½ tablespoons brown sugar

5 tablespoons (25 g) unsweetened shredded coconut

sweetened condensed milk, to serve (optional)

Veganize • omit the sweetened condensed milk or use sweetened condensed coconut milk

Vegetable swap • sweet potato: taro, butternut squash

In a small bowl, combine the yeast, the ½ teaspoon of sugar and warm water. Stir and leave for 15 minutes, until puffy and foamy.

Pour ¾–1¼ inches (2–3 cm) of water into a saucepan or deep skillet and bring to a boil. Add the sweet potato to a steaming basket, then place the steamer in the pan, making sure that the water doesn't touch the bottom of the steamer. Cover and steam for 10 minutes or until the sweet potato is completely soft. Remove the sweet potato from the steamer and transfer to a bowl. Mash until completely pureed.

Place the yeast mixture, a heaping ¼ cup (75 g) of the sweet potato, the flour, the remaining ¼ cup (50 g) of sugar and the oil in the bowl of a stand mixer. Knead with the dough hook attachment on low speed until it comes together, then increase the speed to medium and knead for 5–6 minutes, until the dough is smooth and no longer sticky. If the dough still feels sticky, add 1–2 tablespoons of flour. You can also knead the dough by hand—knead for 10–15 minutes, until the dough is smooth and no longer sticky. Leave the dough in the bowl, cover tightly and let it rest for 5 minutes.

Meanwhile, combine the remaining sweet potato with the brown sugar and shredded coconut and stir well to combine.

Prepare 12 pieces of parchment paper to rest the mantou on for steaming. They should be about 2 inches (5 cm) square.

Turn the dough out onto a clean, floured work surface. Sprinkle the top of the dough with flour, too. With your hands, pat and shape the dough into a rectangle before rolling—this makes it easier to roll it into a uniform rectangular shape. Using a rolling pin, roll the dough out into a rectangle that is approximately 14 × 11 inches (35 cm × 28 cm). Spread the sweet potato and coconut mixture across the dough, leaving a ¾–1¼-inch (2–3 cm) border along one of the long sides. Starting from the opposite long side, gently roll the dough into a log, then rest it, seam-side down. Using a sharp, serrated knife, cut the dough log into 12 pieces. Place each mantou, seam-side down, on a square of parchment paper, then leave the mantou, covered with a tea towel, to prove for 30–40 minutes, until they have puffed up a little, about 50 percent more than their original size. Note that the proving time will depend on your kitchen temperature—the dough will prove quicker in a warm temperature and take longer if it's cold. Don't overprove, otherwise the mantou tend to collapse and look flat and wrinkly after steaming.

Prepare your steamer. Add a layer of water to the pan, ensuring that it doesn't touch the bottom of your steaming basket. Working in batches, or with two pans at the same time, place four or five mantou (or however many you can fit without them touching) into the steamer, turning the mantou onto their sides (spiral-side up) to rest on the paper. They will expand when steamed so give them lots of room. Bring the water to a boil, then steam the mantou over medium heat for 10–12 minutes, until puffed. Leave for 2 minutes before lifting the lid so your buns don't collapse due to the sudden change in temperature.

Serve either warm or at room temperature, with sweetened condensed milk, if you like.

Storage: Place the completely cooled mantou into a freezer-friendly container or zip-seal bag. To reheat, place the buns on a steaming rack and steam for 10–12 minutes, until soft. They can also be reheated in the microwave.

Pictured overleaf >

Sweet Potato Spiral Mantou

Taro

"A wonderfully versatile starch, which we should all be eating more often"

Taro look like bearded potatoes and are similarly starchy. Believed to have been one of the earliest cultivated plants, taro is eaten in Africa, Asia, South Asia, Oceanic countries such as Papua New Guinea, Fiji, Polynesia and Hawaii, and the Pacific Islands. In Tonga and Samoa, it is considered a prestige crop, given as gifts and served at feasts. In Japan, taro is called satoimo, and is often simmered in dashi and soy sauce. Poi is a taro paste foundational to Hawaiian cuisine, characterized as one-, two-, or three-finger, which describes its consistency and how many fingers you'll need to scoop it up. In Korea, it is called toran and is cooked in stews or soups. It is called wu tau in Cantonese and is used in both savory and sweet recipes.

My list of favorite taro recipes is long, but I often crave my mother's wu tau gao, a steamed taro cake very similar to lo bak gao (see page 482), and the simple baked taro she often made for lunch, which she served with just a dash of soy sauce and white pepper. And let's not forget the sweet taro coconut soups and taro paste bao from Chinese bakeries.

In everyday cooking, taro is a wonderfully versatile starch, which we should all be eating more often. It can be used as you would a potato—simmered, stewed, roasted, fried or mashed. But while it is reminiscent of potato, it is really unlike any other root vegetable. When cooked, the flesh is dry and firm, yet still soft and custardy. It has a sweet nuttiness that adds lots of flavor to dishes. When boiled, it can feel slightly slimy, but not in an unpleasant way; it adds to the texture of a dish. There are many varieties of taro but the most common are eddoe, which are small, round and hairy, and about the size of a potato, and dasheen, which are larger and elongated, like daikon. Inside, the flesh ranges from white to ivory with streaks of pale purple.

Some people report skin irritation from handling raw taro, due to the presence of oxalic acid crystals, so wear gloves if you are sensitive (I have never experienced any reaction, but best be careful). Also, never eat raw taro!

Taro Gnocchi

While potato gnocchi have a mellow flavor, these morsels are sweet and earthy, and taste unmistakably of taro. The key to good gnocchi is getting your vegetables as dry as possible, which means you can add less flour—this not only gives you a lighter dumpling, but amplifies the flavor of the vegetable. The sage-infused butter and golden pine nuts provide a simple yet stunning sauce, which brings out the nuttiness of the taro. This recipe is easily made vegan by using nondairy ricotta and butter.

SERVES 4

1 pound 7 ounces (650 g) peeled taro, cut into uniform ¾-inch (2 cm) cubes

1⅔ cups (200 g) all-purpose or gluten-free all-purpose flour, plus more if needed

sea salt and black pepper

7 ounces (200 g) regular or nondairy ricotta

4 tablespoons (56 g) salted regular or vegan butter

4 teaspoons extra-virgin olive oil

30–40 sage leaves

¼ cup (35 g) pine nuts

handful of grated hard cheese, such as ricotta salata, parmesan or pecorino (optional)

½ lemon

Place the taro in a large saucepan and add just enough water to cover. Set over medium-high heat, cover and bring to a boil. Reduce the heat to low and simmer for 15–20 minutes, until the taro is fork-tender. Drain and allow to dry out and cool completely, about 10 minutes. Place the taro in a bowl and mash (use a regular masher or potato ricer if you have one), until it is smooth.

In a large wide bowl or on a clean work surface, scatter the flour and 1 teaspoon of sea salt and toss with your fingers to combine. Add the ricotta and mashed taro and, using your hands or a bench scraper, knead just until it comes together (don't overwork it). The dough should feel airy and moist but should hold together nicely. If the dough feels too moist, add more flour 1 tablespoon at a time. If the dough feels dry, add a touch of water.

Bring a large saucepan of salted water to a boil. Divide the dough into four pieces. Take a small ball of the gnocchi dough and boil it to make sure it will hold its shape; if it doesn't, add a bit more flour and try again. When ready, the gnocchi will float to the top.

Pinch off small pieces of dough and roll into ¾-inch (2 cm) balls. If you like, run them along the tines of a fork to create sauce-catching ridges.

Drop 8 to 10 gnocchi at a time into the boiling water. Cook for 1½–2 minutes, until the gnocchi float to the top, then remove with a slotted spoon and place them on a large plate or sheet pan. Cook the remaining gnocchi. Reserve a ¼ cup (60 ml) of the cooking water.

Heat a large skillet over medium-high heat. Add the butter and olive oil and heat until the butter melts and looks foamy. Add the sage leaves and pine nuts and cook for 1 minute, until the leaves curl up and the nuts turn a light golden brown. Add the gnocchi and toss well to coat. Add the gnocchi cooking water, a little at a time, until the buttery sauce looks creamy.

To serve, top with grated cheese (if using), season with sea salt and black pepper and squeeze over some lemon juice.

Gluten-free and vegan

Vegetable swap • taro: potato, sweet potato, winter squash

Taro Puffs

This is a lazy person's wu gok, the ethereal taro croquettes with a crispy lace crust that are served at dim sum. In truth, proper wu gok are tricky to make—the taro dough must be sticky and fried at a specific oil temperature for the skin to crisp up and become flaky. Having tried it a few times at home, I realized that this version is much more my style—not as pretty but still incredibly satisfying. The tender taro dough is simple to make and provides a dreamy, creamy casing for the tofu filling. Resting the dough in the fridge is essential, as it makes it easier to handle and roll.

MAKES 10

1 pound (450 g) taro, peeled and cut into uniform ¾-inch (2 cm) cubes

3 tablespoons (25 g) potato starch or tapioca starch

3 tablespoons (25 g) cornstarch

½ teaspoon baking soda

½ teaspoon five-spice powder

1 teaspoon sea salt

½ teaspoon sugar

pinch of white pepper

¼ cup (60 ml) boiling water

neutral oil

Umami Crisp (see page 27), chili oil or chili crisp, to serve

handful of cilantro leaves, to serve

Tofu filling

neutral oil

1 yellow onion, finely diced

9 ounces (250 g) firm tofu, crumbled

sea salt

½ teaspoon sugar

1 teaspoon toasted sesame oil

2 teaspoons soy sauce or tamari

2 green onions, finely chopped

Gluten-free and vegan

Vegetable swap • taro: potato

Place the taro in a saucepan and add just enough water to cover. Set over medium-high heat, cover and bring to a boil, then reduce the heat to low and simmer for 15–20 minutes, until the taro is completely tender. Drain. Place the taro in a bowl and mash.

In another bowl, whisk together the potato or tapioca starch, cornstarch, baking soda, five-spice powder, sea salt, sugar and white pepper. Add the boiling water and stir well (this cooks the starches). Add the mashed taro and bring together until it is just combined into a soft dough. Cover and place in the fridge for 30 minutes to firm up.

Meanwhile, to make the tofu filling, place a skillet over medium-high heat. When hot, add a drizzle of oil, along with the onion, and cook for 3–4 minutes, until softened. Add the tofu and 1 teaspoon of sea salt and stir for 4–5 minutes, until it starts to turn golden. Turn off the heat and stir in the sugar, sesame oil, soy sauce or tamari and green onion. Taste and, if needed, season with more sea salt. Set aside to cool.

Remove the dough from the fridge and divide evenly into 10 small balls. Working with one ball at a time (keep the rest covered), flatten the dough with your thumbs and fingers to form a round disc, ¼–⅓ inch (6–8 mm) thick. Place 2–3 teaspoons of the tofu filling in the middle, then gather the edges together to seal the filling and use your hands to roll it into an oval shape. Continue with the rest of the dough and filling.

Pour ¾–1¼ inches (2–3 cm) of oil into a deep skillet, wok or small saucepan and heat over medium-high heat. When the oil is hot (test by placing a chopstick or spoon in the hot oil; if it sizzles, the oil is ready), place one or two balls in the oil and fry for 2–3 minutes, until golden on all sides. Place on paper towel to drain.

Serve immediately with umami crisp or chili oil and scatter with cilantro leaves.

Do ahead: The dough can be made a day ahead and stored, tightly wrapped, in the fridge. The filling can be made a day ahead, too.

Serving suggestion: Serve with the sweet chile sauce made for the Taro Curry Puffs on page 429.

Taro Curry

While curries are not common in Chinese cuisine, "curry powder" is used in noodle dishes and to flavor meat, seafood and vegetables. This recipe is based on my mother's signature curry, a saucy, gravy-based dish that is made with just a few ingredients. Her curry did not rely on pastes or aromatics, but was powered quietly yet confidently by S&B brand curry powder, the same spice blend she used for her Singapore noodles. This is a wonderful way to enjoy taro—it becomes sweet and nutty and adds a lot of interest and depth to this unfussy curry. Save leftovers or double the recipe to make the Taro Curry Puffs on page 429.

SERVES 4

neutral oil

1 yellow onion, cut into ¾-inch (2 cm) chunks

2 carrots (about 7 oz/200 g), cut into ¾-inch (2 cm) chunks

1 pound 5 ounces (600 g) taro, peeled and cut into ¾-inch (2 cm) chunks

½ teaspoon sugar

sea salt

4 teaspoons curry powder

2 cups (480 ml) vegetable stock

generous 1 cup (150 g) frozen peas

½ cup (120 ml) coconut cream or coconut milk (optional)

rice, to serve

Heat a saucepan over medium-high heat. Drizzle in some oil, then add the onion and cook for 3–4 minutes, until softened. Add the carrot, taro, sugar, 1 teaspoon of sea salt and the curry powder and stir well to combine. Pour in the vegetable stock and stir, then reduce the heat to medium low and cover. Cook for 15–20 minutes, until the vegetables are tender.

Remove the lid and increase the heat to medium high. Add the peas and stir. Taste and add more sea salt, if needed. Stir in the coconut cream or coconut milk (if using) and cook for another 1 minute.

Serve with rice.

Gluten-free and vegan

Vegetable swap • taro: potato, sweet potato

Taro Curry Puffs

Curry puffs are a legacy of hundreds of years of colonial rule—Portuguese, Dutch and English—in Malaysia and Singapore. Portuguese spice traders introduced the empada—a stuffed pastry—to Southeast Asia in the 1500s but, over the years, the Asian curry puff has evolved to transcend its colonial roots, and recipes now express a family's culinary and cultural identity. Known as karipap and epok-epok in Malaysia, Singapore and Thailand, these pastry pockets can be stuffed with fillings as diverse as sardines, black pepper chicken, grass jelly and durian. Potato curry is also a popular filling, often combined with chicken. This recipe uses the Taro Curry on page 426 as the filling, a wonderful way to use up leftovers or to capitalize on batch cooking. You'll mainly need the solid parts of the curry, so drain most of the liquid, reserving a small amount to keep the filling moist.

MAKES 15–16 PUFFS

2 cups leftover Taro Curry (see page 426), partially drained

2 green onions, finely sliced

1 pound (450 g) puff pastry (thawed in the fridge overnight if frozen)

1 large egg, beaten

handful of nigella seeds and/or black and white toasted sesame seeds, for topping

Sweet chile sauce

4½ tablespoons (55 g) sugar

2½ tablespoons rice vinegar

2½ tablespoons ketchup

¼–½ teaspoon red pepper flakes

1 garlic clove, grated

1 teaspoon cornstarch

½ teaspoon sea salt

Preheat the oven to 400°F (200°C).

Place the curry in a bowl and roughly mash it with a fork until it's chunky but not completely smooth. Add the green onions and stir to combine.

Roll out your puff pastry until it is about 1/16 inch (2 mm) thick (if your store-bought pastry is already rolled thin, then skip this step). Using a 4-inch (10 cm) round pastry cutter, cut out rounds. Working with one round at a time, place about 1 tablespoon of the filling on one side of the pastry, then brush the edge with egg and fold it over to form a half-moon. Press a fork all around the curved edge to seal it. Repeat with the remaining pastry rounds and filling. Place the pastries on a baking sheet lined with parchment paper, leaving about 1¼ inches (3 cm) between the pastries to allow them to expand during cooking. Prick the tops a few times with a fork and brush with egg. Sprinkle with some nigella and/or sesame seeds. Bake for 15–20 minutes, until golden and puffed.

Meanwhile, to make the sweet chile sauce, add all the ingredients to a small saucepan, along with 2½ tablespoons of water. Whisk constantly, over medium heat, until the sauce thickens, then pour into a bowl.

Serve the hot curry puffs immediately with the sweet chile sauce.

Storage: The curry puffs can be baked, cooled, then stored in an airtight container in the freezer for up to 3 months. Reheat in the oven before serving.

Note: Any starchy curry can be used for this recipe. Something mashable like potato, sweet potato, lentils, legumes or tofu all work well.

For gluten-free • use gluten-free puff pastry

Veganize • use vegan puff pastry, replace the egg with nondairy milk

Roasted Taro, Feta and Maple Salad

Roasting taro highlights its nutty, sweet starchiness. The exterior becomes crispy, more robust, a welcome contrast to the creamy, dense interior flesh. This salad plays upon taro's sweet nature, amplifying it with maple syrup, then countering it with salty feta and bright citrus moments. Taro becomes quite dry in the oven, but "rehydrates" when the dressing is added. This is a sophisticated salad, one that celebrates the untapped potential of this starchy staple.

SERVES 4

2¼ pounds (1 kg) taro, peeled and cut into 1-inch (2.5 cm) chunks

extra-virgin olive oil

sea salt and black pepper

7 ounces (200 g) green beans, trimmed and cut into 2-inch (5 cm) lengths

1 lemon, halved

2 tablespoons maple syrup

1 small garlic clove, grated

3½ oz (100 g) feta, crumbled

handful of chives, roughly chopped

Preheat the oven to 425°F (220°C).

Place the taro on a sheet pan, drizzle generously with olive oil and season with sea salt and black pepper. Toss to coat, then place in the oven and roast for 25–30 minutes, tossing halfway through, until the taro is crispy on the outside and tender inside.

Meanwhile, toss the green beans in olive oil and season with sea salt and black pepper. Remove the taro from the oven, add the beans to the pan, and roast for another 7–8 minutes, until the beans are tender and the taro is golden.

In a large bowl (large enough to toss the salad), whisk together 2 tablespoons of olive oil, the juice from one lemon half (about 1 tablespoon), 1 tablespoon of water, the maple syrup and garlic. Add the taro and green beans to the dressing and toss to combine. Add the feta, season with sea salt and black pepper and toss again.

Cut the remaining lemon half into four wedges.

Top the salad with chives and serve with the lemon wedges.

Gluten-free

Veganize • use vegan feta

Substitute • green beans: broccoli, sugar snap peas • maple syrup: honey

Vegetable swap • taro: potato, sweet potato, winter squash

Steamed Black Bean Taro and Mushrooms

My mother loves to steam taro and then serenade them with soy sauce and a sprinkle of white pepper. The sweet, dense flesh is grateful for the hit of salt and spice. This dish is loosely inspired by my mother's steamed taro ways, but with the deeper umami notes of fermented black beans. The sauce can also be used to steam other vegetables, particularly those that absorb flavor enthusiastically—see the vegetable swaps below. As with many rich dishes, this is best served with rice.

SERVES 4

2½ tablespoons fermented black beans, rinsed and drained

1 garlic clove, grated

1 tablespoon soy sauce or tamari

¼ teaspoon red pepper flakes

¼ teaspoon sugar

½ teaspoon sea salt

1 pound 5 ounces (600 g) taro, peeled, rinsed and cut into 1¼–1½-inch (3–4 cm) chunks

1¾ oz (50 g) dried shiitake mushrooms (or about 12 fresh shiitake), rehydrated in water for 30 minutes

1 green onion, finely sliced

toasted white sesame seeds, for topping

toasted sesame oil, for topping

rice, to serve

In a small bowl, mash together the fermented black beans, garlic, soy sauce or tamari, red pepper flakes, sugar and sea salt with a fork.

Place the taro in a bowl. Squeeze the water from the dried shiitake mushrooms and add them to the bowl, too (keep the soaking water to make the Vegan Dashi on page 360). Add the fermented black bean sauce to the bowl and, using your hands or a large spoon, toss until everything is coated. Transfer the mixture to a heatproof dish (thick, sturdy dishes like Pyrex or Corelle work well for this, though I find my Chinese plates like the one in the photo do, too) that is suitable for steaming.

Set up your steamer—I use a steaming basket, which slips inside my deep skillet, or a bamboo steamer, which sits on top of my pan. Make sure you have a lid that will completely enclose everything. You can also use a small stainless steel trivet, which sits inside a deep saucepan, and place the dish or plate directly on top.

Add some water to the pan (making sure it doesn't touch the bottom of the steamer). Add the dish or plate of taro to the steamer, cover with the lid and steam over medium-high heat for 25–30 minutes, until the taro is completely tender. You will need to add more water to the pan during cooking so check it frequently.

When ready, top with the green onion, scatter with sesame seeds and drizzle with sesame oil. Serve with rice.

Gluten-free and vegan

Substitute • mushrooms: tofu

Vegetable swap • taro: potato, eggplant, turnip

Sunday Night Sticky Rice

Growing up, Sunday nights were all about *Countdown*, the iconic Australian music program that aired during the 1980s. Music was a huge part of my life back then (it still is), offering me a bridge to a world that was completely different from my own. It allowed me to dream about what my life could be, where I could travel, the people I could meet. So, on Sunday nights, while I plotted my escape with *Countdown*, my mind lost in the music, it was my traitorous nose that would lead me back to the kitchen, following the perfume of my mother's lo mai faan (sticky rice) wafting from the kitchen . . . the unmistakable scent of reality. Sticky rice can be made in a rice cooker, but here it is steamed, which separates each grain of rice.

SERVES 4–6

6 dried shiitake mushrooms (about 1¼ oz/35 g), rehydrated in water (preferably overnight or for at least 1 hour)

neutral oil

1 shallot or small yellow onion, finely diced

1 pound (450 g) taro, peeled and cut into ⅜-inch (1 cm) cubes

3½ ounces (100 g) marinated, five-spice or extra-firm tofu, finely chopped

½ teaspoon five-spice powder

sea salt and white pepper

4 teaspoons soy sauce or tamari

4 teaspoons Shaoxing rice wine

2 cups (450 g) sticky (glutinous) rice, soaked in water for at least 4 hours or overnight

2 green onions, finely sliced

For gluten-free • omit the Shaoxing rice wine

Vegan

Substitute • dried shiitake mushrooms: fresh shiitake

Vegetable swap • taro: potato

Remove the mushrooms from the soaking water—do not discard the water. Squeeze out the excess liquid from the mushrooms and roughly chop.

Heat a skillet over medium-high heat. Add 1 tablespoon of oil, along with the shallot or onion, and stir for 1 minute, until softened. Add the taro and stir for 2–3 minutes, until softened slightly, then add the mushroom, tofu, five-spice powder, 1 teaspoon of sea salt, a pinch of white pepper, 2 teaspoons of the soy sauce or tamari and the Shaoxing rice wine. Stir to combine, then turn off the heat.

Prepare your steamer—I use a wide, deep skillet and place a bamboo steaming basket on top. You can also place a trivet inside a wide saucepan or skillet and place the steaming vessel right on top. You can steam in a wok if you have a large lid that encloses everything. For the rice, you can use a heatproof shallow bowl, such as Pyrex or Corelle. I use a simple 8½ × 1½-inch (22 cm × 4 cm) round steel cake tin, a vintage piece from my mum's collection.

Drain the rice. Add 1 tablespoon of oil to the steaming vessel and swirl it around so it coats the bottom. Add the rice and, using a spatula, flatten it out. Add ⅓ cup (80 ml) of the mushroom soaking water (you can also use water or vegetable stock). Pile the taro mixture on top of the rice.

Pour about 2 cups (480 ml) of water into the pan and bring to a boil. Once boiling, very carefully transfer your steaming vessel with the rice to the steaming basket or trivet and place it on top of the boiling water. Cover with a lid and steam over medium heat for 30 minutes.

Remove the vessel from the steamer (see Note), then fold the rice to mix it with the savory taro mixture on top. Check that there is still steaming water at the bottom of the pan and add more if needed. Add another ¼ cup (60 ml) of the mushroom soaking water or water to the rice mixture and return it to the steamer for 10–15 minutes, until the rice is tender throughout.

Transfer the rice to a bigger bowl. Add 1 teaspoon of sea salt, the remaining 2 teaspoons of soy sauce or tamari and season with some white pepper. Fold until well combined. Taste and add more sea salt, if needed. Scatter with the green onion and serve.

Note: Be very careful when removing hot plates or bowls from a steamer. I use some handy and inexpensive tongs, which grip the plate and lift it from the steamer—search "hot plate tongs" online.

Taro, Sago and Coconut

Sai mai lo, or sago in a sweetened coconut milk, is a classic Cantonese tong sui, a sweet soup served at the end of a meal. Fruit, such as honeydew, cantaloupe or mango, may be added, but taro is also commonly incorporated and adds a rich, earthy sweetness. I've used coconut milk here, but many Chinese home cooks use evaporated milk or sweetened condensed milk to make the sweet soup. While traditionally served after a meal, I often eat it at breakfast time. It can be enjoyed either hot or cold, so it's handy to make a larger batch, which can be stored in the fridge.

SERVES 4

½ cup (100 g) sago pearls

1 pound (450 g) taro, peeled and cut into ¾-inch (2 cm) cubes

one 13.5-ounce (400 ml) can coconut milk

generous ½ cup (110 g) sugar

Bring a large saucepan of water to a boil and add the sago pearls. Reduce the heat to medium and cook, stirring often, for 10–12 minutes, until the pearls are mostly translucent. Cover and allow to sit for 5–10 minutes, just until the sago is completely translucent. Drain and rinse in cold water, then set aside to drain.

Meanwhile, place the taro in a separate saucepan and just cover with water. Place over medium-high heat and bring to a boil, then reduce the heat to medium and cook for 20–25 minutes, until the taro is tender. Drain.

Place the same pan back over medium heat, add the coconut milk and sugar, and whisk together until combined. Add the taro and sago and stir gently to combine. Serve immediately as a warm soup or allow to cool and serve cold. When cold, the sago sets like a pudding. Store in the fridge for up to 3 days.

Gluten-free and vegan

Substitute • coconut milk: oat milk, soy milk, regular whole milk • sugar: maple syrup, honey

Vegetable swap • taro: mango, cantaloupe or honeydew (no cooking required)

Tomato

"Replete with the scent of earth that
has been kissed by the sun"

The poet Pablo Neruda wrote an impassioned, sensory ode to tomatoes in which he lyrically described the fruit's abundance and singular beauty, comparing it to the sun and lauding its vibrant color and versatility. Few fruits garner the rapture of tomatoes. Encapsulating the promise of the new season, tomatoes are infused with the buoyant spirit of summer, replete with the scent of earth that has been kissed by the sun.

In the summer, we live, we breathe, we inhale tomatoes. Living in New York City, tomatoes embody our emancipation from the cold winter, which invariably drags on for longer than is welcome. Most weekends I visit my local market, sweat building on my brow the moment I step outside, to pick up tomatoes for the week ahead. Heirlooms, baskets of Sungolds, cherries on the vine and tomatoes of all hues—mottled greens, iridescent yellows, blackish purples, classic reds—spill from my bags. With my bounty, I'll make tomatoes with plums and basil, tomatoes with watermelon and feta, tomatoes with peaches and black pepper, tomatoes grated onto bread, countless caprese salads and my "walk away pasta sauce." It is a tomato party and I'm the guest who stays too long.

But it wasn't always like this. My fancy tomato ways were not always my norm. I grew up eating gigantic tomatoes the size of my fist, a blushed-pink tone, that tasted not-quite-of-tomato. But nevertheless, I loved them. I ate them as one would a whole apple, biting straight in, sprinkling salt and white pepper upon the insipid flesh between every mouthful. Nowadays, I still seek them out, the overgrown, tasteless tomatoes of my youth. I find comfort in their underripe flesh and bulging cheeks. There is much connection and joy to be found in tomatoes of all colors, shapes and sizes.

A lesson I learned early in life, and a technique that allows me to eat tomatoes all year round, is to salt them. Salt brings out moisture and concentrates the tomato flavor. Out-of-season tomatoes, and in-season ones, too, benefit from this extra bit of love.

Tomato and Gruyère Clafoutis

Clafoutis, a pudding from the Limousin region of France, is usually made with cherries but often with other fruit, such as berries, apples or pears. This silky pudding also works well as a savory dish, with tangy tomatoes at the helm. I've used Gruyère here as I love its nutty overtones and rich creaminess, but you could also use other cheeses that melt well, such as Comté, fontina, Gouda or brie. Take this tomato dish in another direction by adding some wilted greens (spinach or kale) and feta. It's a fun recipe to experiment with. Tomatoes release a lot of liquid when baked so it's important to let the clafoutis rest when it comes out of the oven, which allows everything to settle and come together.

SERVES 4

2 tablespoons olive oil

1½ pounds (700 g) cherry or grape tomatoes

1 garlic clove, grated

sea salt and black pepper

2–3 thyme sprigs, leaves picked

1 tablespoon red wine vinegar

1 teaspoon sugar

⅔ cup (160 ml) regular whole milk or oat milk

2 large eggs

6½ tablespoons (50 g) all-purpose or gluten-free all-purpose flour

4¼ ounces (120 g) Gruyère, freshly grated

handful of sliced chives or green onions

Preheat the oven to 350°F (180°C). You will need a baking dish or ovenproof skillet that is about 9 inches (23 cm) in diameter (I use a cast-iron skillet, but a rectangular baking dish works, too). Drizzle with 1–2 tablespoons of olive oil and tilt the dish or pan so the oil lightly coats the base and sides.

Place the tomatoes in a large bowl, along with the garlic, 1 teaspoon of sea salt, the thyme leaves, vinegar and sugar. Using clean hands, squeeze the tomatoes until they burst, just enough to allow some of the juices to flow out. Tip this mixture into the prepared dish or pan, and keep the bowl to use again at the next step.

Add the milk and eggs to the bowl and whisk until well combined. Add the flour, Gruyère, about ½ teaspoon of sea salt and a few turns of freshly ground black pepper. Whisk until well combined (some lumps are okay).

Pour the batter over the tomatoes and give the dish or pan a shake so it can settle among the tomatoes. Place on the middle rack of the oven and bake for 35–40 minutes, until the center is just set, with a slight wobble. Remove from the oven and allow to cool for 10–15 minutes before serving—this is important as it allows everything to meld together. Serve topped with the chives or green onion.

Gluten-free

Vegetable swap • tomatoes: kale, corn, mushrooms, zucchini

Walk Away Tomato Sauce with Pici Pasta

During quarantine, with some help from the Pasta Grannies on YouTube (the incredible series created by Vicky Bennison), I mastered malloreddus (sometimes called Sardinian gnocchi), orecchiette and, our family favorite, pici. In some ways, making pici is reminiscent of hand-stretched noodles, uncomplicated and requiring no special equipment other than our hands. My pici recipe uses 100 percent all-purpose flour (mainly for ease, as this is what I always have in my pantry), but often I use a 50/50 mix of all-purpose flour and fine semolina (sometimes called semolina flour)—the semolina adds more of a bite. Pici should be rustic, so don't get caught up on things looking perfect—different lengths and thicknesses are part of the charm. The tomato sauce is intoxicating—charged with flavor, it only requires you to walk away, giving the tomatoes and spices time to transform into a rich sauce.

SERVES 4

4 garlic cloves, sliced

3 tablespoons (42 g) salted regular or vegan butter

¼ cup (60 ml) extra-virgin olive oil, plus more for drizzling

1 tablespoon cumin seeds

1 teaspoon smoked paprika

1 teaspoon sugar

½–1 teaspoon red pepper flakes

1 pound 5 ounces (600 g) cherry or grape tomatoes (I like Sungolds)

sea salt and black pepper

handful of basil leaves

grated cheese of your choice, to serve

Pici pasta

3⅓ cups (400 g) all-purpose flour

½ teaspoon sea salt

2 tablespoons plus 2 teaspoons olive oil

¾ cup (180 ml) warm water

semolina flour, for dusting

Veganize • use vegan cheese to serve or omit

Substitute • all-purpose flour: 00 flour, or a 50/50 mix of fine semolina and all-purpose flour

Heat a large saucepan over low heat. Throw in the garlic, butter, olive oil, cumin seeds, paprika, sugar, red pepper flakes and tomatoes. Cover with a lid and walk away. The sauce will be ready after 1 hour, but you could leave it simmering for longer—up to 1½ hours—as it will get more jammy the longer it cooks. When it's ready, remove the lid and, using a spatula or the back of a wooden spoon, squish the tomatoes against the side of the pan to burst them fully and release all the juices. Season with sea salt and black pepper.

Meanwhile, let's make pici. In a large bowl, whisk together the flour and salt. Add the olive oil and water and, using your hands or a large spoon, mix until the dough looks shaggy—it will be quite dry. Turn the dough out onto a clean work surface and knead for 8–10 minutes, until the dough is smooth. Cover tightly with plastic wrap or place in a reusable zip-seal bag and set aside to rest at room temperature for 30–60 minutes, or up to 3–4 hours (the longer the rest time, the easier it will be to roll the pici). You can also place the dough in the fridge overnight—the next day, bring the dough back to room temperature before rolling.

Place the dough on a clean, dry work surface (make sure there's no flour at all, otherwise it will be impossible to roll). Divide the dough in half, rewrapping the half you're not using, and roll the dough out into a rectangle about 4¾ × 8 inches (12 cm × 20 cm)—it does not have to be exact. Using a knife or pastry cutter, slice the dough into strips a scant ¼ inch (5 mm) wide.

Working with one strip at a time and starting from the middle, start rolling the dough with your hands, spreading your fingers and stretching the dough outward as you roll. If there's an area that's thicker, go over it gently with your fingers to even it out, but it does not have to be uniform. Lay the pasta out flat on a sheet pan and dust with semolina flour to keep it from sticking. You can cook the pici straight away or keep them covered for several hours at room temperature; just make sure they aren't touching and are well coated in semolina flour. Continue rolling the strips of dough into long fat strands. Repeat with the other half of the dough.

Bring a large saucepan of salted water to a boil. Add the pici and cook for 4–5 minutes, until the pasta floats and is al dente.

Using tongs, fish the pici out of the cooking water and toss them straight into the pan with the tomato sauce. Add ½ cup (120 ml) of the pasta cooking water and toss the pici in the sauce until well coated. Transfer the pasta to serving bowls and top with a drizzle of olive oil. Scatter with a few basil leaves and your choice of cheese.

Spiced Tomato Jam

The first few times I visited my husband Ross's childhood home, it was a true culture shock. His upbringing on the bucolic South Coast of New South Wales, tending to cattle, building rabbit traps, playing school sports, was at complete odds with my sheltered, domestic childhood in the suburbs of Sydney. One of the first things I noticed about his parents' home was the abundance of jams and preserves, mostly homemade, in their pantry and fridge. I was intrigued by the seemingly endless options—why did one family need so much jam? This made sense to me when I realized how often they ate sandwiches, a lunchtime staple. Ross was particularly partial to tomato jam, so this recipe is made with him in mind—it is no doubt a little different from the one he grew up eating, with gentle spices of mustard seeds and cardamom adding some curiosity. I've also made this with a 50/50 mix of tomatoes and gooseberries, which adds some sweet tartness; gooseberries are elusive, but if you happen to find them, give them a go in this recipe. I use a mix of yellow and red cherry tomatoes, mainly for color, but you can definitely use all red ones. I like this tomato jam on toast, with an aged cheddar; it will also find a welcome home on a cheese board.

MAKES ABOUT 2 CUPS

2 teaspoons brown mustard seeds

⅛ teaspoon ground cardamom (or seeds from 1 green cardamom pod)

9 ounces (250 g) yellow cherry tomatoes, halved

9 ounces (250 g) red cherry tomatoes, halved

1 cup (200 g) sugar

½ teaspoon ground ginger

¼–½ teaspoon chile powder

2–3 tablespoons lemon juice (from 1 lemon)

Place a saucepan over medium-low heat. Add the mustard seeds and cardamom and toast for 3–5 minutes, until fragrant and the seeds begin to pop. Remove from the heat and set aside to cool.

Place the cherry tomatoes in a bowl and squeeze them vigorously with clean hands until they are thoroughly macerated. Pour the tomatoes into the pan with the mustard seeds and cardamom and add the sugar, ginger, chile powder and lemon juice, then stir to combine. Let sit for 30 minutes.

Place the pan over medium-high heat and bring to a boil, stirring constantly to prevent the tomato mixture from burning. Once the mixture comes to a boil, reduce the heat to medium low and simmer for 10–12 minutes, until the jam is glossy and thickened. Remove from the heat and pour into a sterilized jar (see Note), then allow to cool completely. Store in the fridge for many months.

Note: The quickest way to sterilize jars is to place the jars and lids in a large saucepan and top with water. Place the pan over high heat, bring to a boil and boil for 5 minutes. Using clean tongs, remove the jars and lids from the boiling water and place them upside down on a clean tea towel to dry out. When they are dry, fill them immediately.

Gluten-free and vegan

Vegetable swap • yellow cherry tomatoes: gooseberries, tomatillos

Everything Bread Soup

Canned tomatoes are the true heroes of pantry cooking, a workhorse that powers so many of our most loved family meals. Here, they form a rich umami base for this predominantly leftover-based dish. Like the great Italian bread soup, ribollita, this recipe is a wonderful way of using up stray cuts of bread, leftovers and pantry staples. This soup feels a bit "throw it all in" and, in truth, it is exactly that. It came into being during lockdown, when I baked a lot of sourdough and was constantly left with bread odds and ends. The beauty of lockdown cooking was really the feeling of freedom and the unshackling of rules, by virtue of necessity. In our effort to put a hearty, somewhat nutritious meal on the table several times a day, never wasting whatever food we had on hand, we had to adopt a more open mind to cooking, flavor pairings and meal composition. Meals like this one, which is part pasta dish, part soup, were born. A bread soup with pasta, chickpeas and gochugaru raised no eyebrows. When the world feels precarious, we look to food to comfort and gratify, to fill an emotional hole—this recipe does that in spades.

SERVES 4

¼ cup (60 ml) extra-virgin olive oil, plus more for drizzling

1 yellow onion, diced

2 celery stalks, finely sliced

6 garlic cloves, finely chopped

1 tablespoon gochugaru, plus more to serve

4 teaspoons tomato paste

1 teaspoon sugar

sea salt

1½ cups (250 g) cooked chickpeas (about one 15 oz/425 g can, drained)

one 28-ounce (800 g) can crushed or diced tomatoes

5¼ cups (1.25 liters) vegetable stock

1 bunch of kale

2 teaspoons miso

1 pound (450 g) filled pasta of your choice, such as ravioli or tortellini

5–7 ounces (150–200 g) stale bread, torn

Heat a large saucepan or Dutch oven over medium-high heat. Add the olive oil and onion and cook for 2 minutes, until softened, reducing the heat if the onion starts to brown too quickly. Add the celery and cook for 1–2 minutes, until softened. Add the garlic and gochugaru and stir for 1–2 minutes, until aromatic. Stir in the tomato paste, sugar, 1 teaspoon of sea salt, the chickpeas, crushed tomatoes and vegetable stock, then cover with a lid, reduce the heat to medium and cook for 15–20 minutes, to allow the flavors to mingle.

Prepare the kale by removing the leaves from the stems. Discard the rough and woody ends of the stems (about 1¼ inches/3 cm) and chop up the remaining stems. Roughly tear up the leaves.

When the soup is ready, add the miso paste and stir until it has dissolved. Taste and season with sea salt, then add the filled pasta and chopped kale stems and simmer over low heat for 5 minutes. Add the kale leaves and bread and turn off the heat.

To serve, ladle the soup into bowls and top with a drizzle of olive oil and a few gochugaru flakes.

For gluten-free • use gluten-free bread and pasta

Veganize • use vegan filled pasta or a short pasta shape

Soy-Pickled Tomatoes with Silken Tofu

This is a flavorful, satisfying no-cook dish, a great option for when tomatoes are plentiful and the days are long and too leisurely to contemplate "cooking." This dish is partway between a salad and a dish to be eaten with rice—silken tofu is lavishly draped in tomatoes that have been pickled in a punchy sauce, which is salty, spicy and tart, with just a hint of sweetness. The tomatoes soften while soaking up all the flavors, transforming a block of silky tofu into an exciting meal. The tofu is best served cold, straight from the fridge. For a different take on this dish, and if you only have extra-firm tofu in the fridge, consider serving these pickled tomatoes over thick slices of pan-fried tofu.

SERVES 4

2–3 blocks silken tofu
(about 2 lb/900 g), cold

2 green onions, finely sliced

handful of cilantro leaves

4 shiso leaves, finely sliced (optional)

1 tablespoon toasted white
sesame seeds

Soy-pickled tomatoes

12 ounces (340 g) small tomatoes,
such as cherry or grape, halved

1 garlic clove, grated

2 tablespoons soy sauce or tamari

1 tablespoon black or rice vinegar

1 tablespoon toasted sesame oil

1 tablespoon chili oil

½ teaspoon sugar

To make the soy-pickled tomatoes, place all the ingredients in a bowl and let marinate for at least 10 minutes.

Carefully drain the liquid from the tofu and gently tip the blocks onto a clean tea towel. (Try to keep the blocks in one piece, if possible, but don't worry if they fall apart.) Pat dry with another clean tea towel, removing as much liquid as possible. Transfer the tofu blocks to one large plate or two smaller plates and carefully cut the silken tofu into cubes, without cutting all the way through, so that the blocks stay intact. This creates crevices for the sauce to run into.

Spoon the soy-pickled tomatoes over the tofu and scatter with the green onion, cilantro, shiso leaves (if using) and sesame seeds. Serve immediately on its own or eat with rice.

Do ahead: The pickled tomatoes can be made 24 hours ahead and left to marinate in the fridge overnight. Bring to room temperature before adding to the tofu.

Gluten-free and vegan

Tomato, Watermelon and Feta Salad

In the summer, we eat dead simple tomato salads that involve little more than slicing. There are many iterations of a tomato salad, and in recent years we have started adding fruit. Peaches and nectarines are wonderful and fragrant, providing a tart bite, while cantaloupe imparts an almost-creamy finish. In this salad, I've added sweet and juicy watermelon, which does not take a back seat to the tangy tomatoes. And nor is it designed to. With salty feta and earthy basil thrown in, this is a big, fresh summer salad with bold, confident flavors, one that you will make, remake, adapt and devour all season long.

SERVES 4

¼ small watermelon (about 3 lb 5 oz/1.5 kg)

4 tomatoes (about 1½ lb/700 g)

7 ounces (200 g) feta, crumbled

sea salt and black pepper

extra-virgin olive oil

handful of basil leaves

Slice the watermelon and remove the skin and white rind. Cut the flesh into ¾–1¼-inch (2–3 cm) chunks. Slice the tomatoes, removing the core, and also cut into ¾–1¼-inch (2–3 cm) chunks. Add the crumbled feta, season with sea salt and black pepper and drizzle generously with olive oil. To serve, top with basil leaves.

Gluten-free

Veganize • omit the feta or use vegan cheese and add black olives

Substitute • watermelon: cantaloupe, honeydew, peach, nectarine • basil: mint • feta: fresh mozzarella or bocconcini

Gemista (Stuffed Tomatoes)

The Greek dish gemista, or roasted stuffed tomatoes, encapsulates rustic charm. In Greek, *gemista* means "filled with" and here, succulent and juicy whole tomatoes are filled with herby feta rice, which soaks up all the sweet, tangy flavors of summer's most prized fruit. You could add more vegetables to the rice mix, using up leftover veg from the fridge—eggplant and zucchini would be good additions. Traditionally, stuffed bell peppers are baked alongside the tomatoes, so you could try that, too. Similarly, you could also hollow out eggplant or zucchini halves to use as a stuffing vessel. Opt for heavy tomatoes with a firm flesh here as we don't want them to fall apart in the oven. Even though gemista is a roasted dish, for me it embodies the liveliness of summer produce, a perfect meal to celebrate long, languid days.

SERVES 4

8 large beefsteak tomatoes
(about 4½ lb/2 kg)

2 large russet potatoes (about
1 lb/450 g)

sea salt and black pepper

½ cup (120 ml) vegetable stock
or water

½ cup (120 ml) extra-virgin
olive oil

Herby rice filling

¼ cup (60 ml) extra-virgin olive oil

1 yellow onion, finely diced

4 garlic cloves, finely chopped

¾ cup (150 g) medium-grain rice

½ cup (120 ml) vegetable stock
or water

½ teaspoon sugar

1 teaspoon dried oregano

sea salt and black pepper

½–1 teaspoon red pepper flakes

1 cup chopped dill, parsley or mint
(or a mix)

3½ ounces (100 g) feta, crumbled
(optional)

Gluten-free

Veganize • omit the feta or use
vegan cheese

Vegetable swap • tomatoes: bell
peppers, eggplant, zucchini

Slice the tops off the tomatoes (making a note of which top belongs to each fruit, so you can match them up when baking) and use a spoon to scoop out the flesh and seeds. Transfer the seeds and juice to a bowl, then finely chop the flesh and add it to the seeds and juice. Set aside.

To make the herby rice filling, heat a large skillet over medium-high heat. Add the olive oil, along with the onion, then reduce the heat to medium low and sauté for 8–10 minutes, until the onion is soft and starting to turn golden. Add the garlic and rice to the pan and stir for 4–5 minutes, until the rice is well coated and starting to turn translucent. Add the chopped tomato flesh, seeds and juice, vegetable stock or water, sugar and oregano and season with sea salt and black pepper. Simmer, covered, for 5–7 minutes, until the rice has absorbed most of the liquid but still has a bite (the rice will continue to cook in the oven). The filling should be juicy and not dry at all. If too much moisture has evaporated, add another few splashes of stock or water to loosen up the rice. Turn off the heat and add the red pepper flakes, herbs and feta (if using).

Preheat the oven to 400°F (200°C).

Fill the tomatoes with the rice mixture, about three-quarters full—this allows the rice to expand further in the oven. Cover the tomatoes with their corresponding tops and place them in a baking dish that will fit them snugly. Reserve any remaining rice mixture.

Peel and slice each potato into thick-ish 2-inch (5 cm) chunks (they don't have to be exactly the same size, but similar is ideal). Season the potato with sea salt and black pepper, then place in and around the tomatoes (this helps to keep them upright while in the oven). If you have any remaining rice, place that in the dish, too, around the tomatoes and potato. Carefully pour the stock or water over the tomatoes, potatoes and rice, followed by the olive oil. Cover with foil (or an ovenproof lid) and bake for 45 minutes. Remove the foil and bake for another 45 minutes, until the potato is fork-tender.

Stuffed tomatoes can be enjoyed hot or at room temperature, and are even better the next day.

Tomato and Tofu

My love affair with the Chinese home-style dish tomato and egg began not as a voracious Chinese girl at my mother's dining table, but in 2015, the year our family moved to the United States. Moving countries and leaving my home, my family, but particularly my mother, was the catalyst for a seismic shift in how I regarded my life and my heritage. I began to reach for the small details, the fleeting moments that tethered me, this feisty Chinese-Australian adult living in Brooklyn, to that small timid girl, "tiny number 3" as my dad called me, growing up in the quiet suburbs of southwest Sydney. And as I dug deep, sweeping away the cobwebs of time, I arrived back home, perched at my mother's kitchen table, with a bowl of rice in one hand, chopsticks in the other, piling gee yook biang (Cantonese steamed "pork cake"), shiu dan (steamed water-egg custard) and tomato and egg into my bowl. There are many dishes that stir my culinary nostalgia, but there is something deeply comforting about tomato and egg, a taste of home for the Chinese kids all over the world. This is my latest take on this dish, with all the same flavors, but the egg has been replaced with silky soft tofu. It's only a slight deviation from the original, but the tofu offers a delicate texture and creamy flavor. Same, but different.

SERVES 4

3 large tomatoes (about 2 lb/900 g), such as beefsteak

neutral oil

1 small red onion, cut into thin wedges

1-inch (2.5 cm) piece of ginger (¾ oz/20 g), peeled and finely chopped

¼ cup (40 g) brown sugar

sea salt and white pepper

14 ounces (400 g) silken tofu, drained

white rice, to serve

2 green onions, finely sliced

Umami Crisp (see page 27) or chili oil, for topping (optional)

Set up a large bowl with ice and cold water—this is your ice bath for peeling the tomatoes. Bring a saucepan of water to a boil. Using a small, sharp knife, score a small "x" at the bottom of each tomato, then add the tomatoes to the boiling water. The skin will wrinkle and split—this should take 1–1½ minutes. Remove the tomatoes from the water and drop them straight into the ice bath. Once the tomatoes are cool, lift them out of the water and peel away their skin. Chop the tomato flesh.

Heat a skillet or saucepan over medium-high heat. Add a drizzle of oil, along with the onion and ginger, stir well and cook for 2 minutes, until softened. Add the tomato, then cover, reduce the heat to medium low and cook for 5 minutes. Add the brown sugar and 2 tablespoons of water, then squash the tomato a little to break it up. Cover and cook for another 5 minutes. Season with 1–2 teaspoons of sea salt and a dash of white pepper. Using a large spoon, scoop out large chunks of silken tofu and add it to the tomato. Cook for 2–3 minutes, just until the tofu is warmed through.

Serve with rice, topped with the green onion and umami crisp, if you like.

Gluten-free and vegan

Substitute • tomatoes: canned whole peeled tomatoes (from one 28 oz/800 g can), with a little juice • silken tofu: scrambled eggs

Salted Tomatoes with Tomato and White Bean Dip

There is alchemy when tomatoes meet with salt. The salt draws out flavor and moisture, intensifying the sweetness, tanginess, fruitiness, floralness and umami of this wondrous fruit. For this recipe, use seasonal tomatoes if you can, but if you can only access ones from your local supermarket, the salt will work wonders. This recipe is part dip, part salad, a strong contender for those dip-for-dinner days. The bright, summery vibes of tomatoes run deep in this recipe, a perfect dish to serve with garlic-rubbed sourdough or flatbread to mop up every last drop.

SERVES 4

1 pound (450 g) cherry or other small tomatoes, halved or quartered

1 garlic clove, grated

sea salt and black pepper

extra-virgin olive oil

handful of basil leaves, torn

toasted sourdough or flatbread (see the za'atar flatbread in Smoky Zucchini Dip on page 493), to serve

Tomato and white bean dip (makes about 2 cups)

about 1 cup (5 oz/150 g) cherry or other small tomatoes

2 garlic cloves, peeled

1–2 thyme or oregano sprigs, leaves picked (or ½ teaspoon dried oregano)

sea salt

1½ cups cooked cannellini beans (about one 15 oz/425 g can, drained)

¼ cup (60 g) tahini

2–3 tablespoons lemon juice (from 1 lemon)

1 teaspoon harissa powder or paprika

Preheat the oven to 400°F (200°C).

Place the tomatoes for the dip in a small baking pan. Add the garlic, thyme or oregano leaves and season with a pinch of sea salt. Roast for 10–15 minutes, until the tomatoes are blistered and bursting. Set aside to cool for 5 minutes.

Meanwhile, place the tomatoes for the salad in a bowl, along with the garlic. Sprinkle with 2 teaspoons of sea salt and some freshly ground black pepper. Using a large spoon or your hands, toss to coat. Set aside for 15–20 minutes.

To make the tomato and white bean dip, place the roasted tomatoes, garlic, herbs and all the pan juices in a food processor or blender. Add the cannellini beans, tahini, lemon juice, harissa powder or paprika and season with about 1 teaspoon of sea salt. Puree until smooth.

Finish the tomato salad by drizzling on 1–2 tablespoons of olive oil and scattering with the torn basil leaves.

To serve, smear the dip onto a large plate (or several smaller plates) and top with the salted tomatoes. Serve with toasted sourdough or flatbread on the side, and drizzle everything with one final swig of olive oil.

For gluten-free • serve with gluten-free bread or flatbread

Vegan

Substitute • cannellini beans: chickpeas

Friendships can be forged under the most unlikely of circumstances. Chance, serendipity, proximity, shared interest and collective consciousness can all play their part in bringing people together. Friendships can also be forged from that immutable pang of loss, a shared grieving that is not seen but is felt among those who have lived it.

I met Maria Midões in the winter of 2015, just two months after I had moved to New York. She, too, was a recent transplant, temporarily relocating to New York from Portugal for a photography internship. At the time, Maria was writing for her food blog Nossa Mesa (Our Table), with a tagline of "uma boa história é sempre uma boa receita" (a good story is always a good recipe). She reached out to me via email with a request to feature me in a story. Naturally, I invited her over for salad.

For lunch, we shared a kale Caesar and a salad of charred zucchini with pearl couscous and whipped ricotta, two dishes that I had served at the salad delivery business I had just left behind. Maria took some photos while I cooked. We sat down for lunch at my weathered antique wooden dining table that our family had shipped from Sydney, a wedding gift from my sister that had seen us through three children, three homes and two countries. Though it was our first meeting, our conversation was easy, almost soothing. Maria commented that the salads tasted like something her mother would cook for her. I was flattered. There is no greater compliment than being told your cooking is reminiscent of another's mother.

I felt a visceral connection to Maria that day. Her warmth overwhelmed me. But there was something else that drew me to her. I sensed it, a wistfulness behind that sunbeam smile, a melancholy that threatened to dim her ebullient eyes. I recognized it because I felt it, too. I had long ago made space for that ache that was always in my heart.

Later that day, Maria told me she had recently lost both of her parents.

Ancient Egyptians believed that the heart was an organ of truth—it beats faster when you are feeling nervous, anxious, afraid—working in tandem with the brain to express human emotions. And while our heart can break, it is resilient; even when we lose a huge piece of it, it is able to beat on, and make room for others. That day with Maria, over a table of salads and quiet conversation, my heart made room. And, somehow, it ached a little less.

Arroz de Tomate
(Portuguese Tomato Rice)

Arroz de tomate, or tomato rice, is a foundational dish in Portuguese cuisine, a recipe for which every family will have their unique spin. This recipe belongs to my dear friend Maria Midões, and it is one that she learned from her mother. Having grown up with rice as my daily staple, it is intriguing to learn of the sanctity of rice in Portuguese culture. Like in my family, rice recipes are passed from one generation to another, and for Maria, her memories of childhood are tethered to her family table, feasting on tomato rice with fried fish, octopus rice, freshly caught sea bass, caldeirada de bacalhau (cod fish stew) and finishing off with her grandmother Maria's sweet rice, a rich, eggy rice pudding with a hint of citrus. This tomato rice is accented with kombu, which is a nod to the rich seafood dishes of Maria's family.

SERVES 4

¼ cup (60 ml) extra-virgin olive oil, plus more for drizzling

1 yellow onion, finely diced

3 garlic cloves, finely chopped

2 bay leaves

1 pound 7 ounces (650 g) tomatoes, chopped (keep all the juice)

4 whole cloves

sea salt

1 cup (200 g) Arborio rice

¼-ounce (5 g) piece of kombu

½ cup cilantro leaves, plus more to serve

Heat a large saucepan or Dutch oven over medium heat. Add the olive oil and onion and stir for 2 minutes, until slightly softened. Add the garlic and bay leaves and stir for 1 minute, until fragrant. Add the tomato and all the juice, the cloves and ½ teaspoon of sea salt, and cook for 4–5 minutes, until the tomato has completely softened. Add the rice and stir, then cook for 5 minutes, stirring every now and then, until the rice is plump.

Add 3 cups plus 2 tablespoons (750 ml) of water, 1 teaspoon of sea salt and the kombu and cook, with the lid half on, for 14–15 minutes, stirring every now and then, until the rice is al dente. Remove from the heat, add the cilantro leaves, then cover completely with the lid and allow to steam for 3–5 minutes. Taste and add more sea salt if needed.

Tear up the kombu and stir it into the rice. Top with more cilantro leaves and serve with an extra drizzle of olive oil.

Gluten-free and vegan

Turnip & daikon

"Unique and crammed with flavor"

My favorite Chinese daikon dish is mistakenly called "turnip cake" in English. This misnomer is one of those classic "lost in translation" situations, a common occurrence when trying to accurately describe food (or words) from non-English speaking cultures. Sometimes there are no direct translations.

While I have always thought of turnips and daikons as related, they actually belong to different vegetable families; I guess more family friends than cousins. Still, I have brought them together in this chapter, because sometimes friends can feel like family.

Daikon is actually a type of radish and there are many varieties. The Chinese lo bak resembles an overgrown, plump carrot, with a white body and a light-green tint around the root. The Korean radish is called mu and looks similar to lo bak, but is shorter and rounder. Daikon can be eaten raw, offering a mild, tangy, slightly peppery flavor, with a crisp and juicy texture. When cooked, it becomes tender and sweet.

I was at a farmers' market in Sydney when a vendor encouraged me to try turnips; "just pan-fry them with garlic and butter," he told me enthusiastically. So that is what I did. He was right, just delicious. I have been enamored of turnips ever since.

Turnips don't turn heads the way potatoes do. But they are unique and crammed with flavor. Use them as you would potatoes to bring a different perspective to dishes that you already know. At your local supermarket or greengrocer, you will most likely find the purple-top white globe variety, which is white with purple shoulders. These are good all-rounders and you can use them in all the turnip recipes in this chapter. My favorite variety is Japanese turnip, sometimes sold as Hakurei or Tokyo turnip, which is smaller in size and sweet enough to eat raw, with tender leaves that can be used as salad greens, sautéed or for pesto.

Turnips with Harissa Cashew Cream, Kale and Lemony Breadcrumbs

I am thoroughly charmed by pan-fried turnips—juicy and sweet with a whisper of bitterness, just enough to make every mouthful intriguing. Each element of this salad—the chewy, crispy kale, the crunchy, golden breadcrumbs and the harissa-spiked cashew cream—complements and amplifies the earthiness of the turnips. Any variety of turnip works for this dish—the purple-shouldered turnips, most commonly found in supermarkets, are a good option and their slightly spicier flesh works well with the velvety cashew cream.

SERVES 4

extra-virgin olive oil

6 ounces (180 g) kale leaves (from about 1 bunch), roughly torn

sea salt and black pepper

2 pounds (900 g) turnips, peeled and cut into ¾-inch (2 cm) pieces

handful of parsley leaves

Harissa cashew cream

1 cup (150 g) raw cashews, soaked in boiling water for 15–20 minutes

¾ cup (180 ml) vegetable stock or water

1 small garlic clove, chopped

2½ tablespoons extra-virgin olive oil

2½ tablespoons lemon juice (from 1 small lemon)

1–2 teaspoons harissa (powder or paste), to your preferred spice level

½ teaspoon sea salt

Lemony breadcrumbs

1⅓ cups (80 g) panko breadcrumbs

zest of 1 lemon

2 tablespoons extra-virgin olive oil

1 garlic clove, grated

½ teaspoon sea salt

black pepper

For gluten-free • use gluten-free breadcrumbs

Vegan

Substitute • kale: Swiss chard, gai lan

Vegetable swap • turnip: potato, rutabaga

To make the harissa cashew cream, drain the cashews and add them to a blender or the bowl of a food processor. Pour in the stock or water, along with the garlic, olive oil, lemon juice, harissa and sea salt and puree on high speed until the mixture is very smooth and creamy (if it is too thick, add a few more splashes of water).

To make the lemony breadcrumbs, combine the breadcrumbs, lemon zest, olive oil, garlic and sea salt in a small bowl and season with some black pepper. Heat a small skillet over medium-low heat and add the breadcrumb mixture. Stirring constantly, cook for 3–4 minutes, until the breadcrumbs are golden, then transfer to a plate and set aside.

Heat a large skillet over medium-high heat. Add a drizzle of olive oil, along with the kale leaves, and season with sea salt and black pepper. Reduce the heat to medium and cook the kale for 3–4 minutes, until wilted and vibrantly green, with some golden crispy bits, too. Remove from the pan and set aside.

Drizzle more olive oil into the same pan and add the turnip (depending upon the size of your pan, you may have to cook the turnip in two batches). Season generously with sea salt and cook, turning frequently, for 8–10 minutes, until the turnip is juicy and caramelized.

To serve, dollop some of the harissa cashew cream onto a plate, top with the kale and turnip, then shower with the breadcrumbs and a few parsley leaves. Finish with a final drizzle of olive oil and season with a little sea salt and black pepper.

The Whole Turnip Pasta

This recipe celebrates the turnip, from root to stem, each part treated thoughtfully and with care, each adding a unique element to the final dish. The tops are used in two different ways—first to make a bright pesto, and then as wilted leafy greens—while the turnip bulbs are pan-fried until tender and lightly charred. For this recipe, you'll need a bunch of turnips with an ample head of leafy greens. If you can't find that, and can only access single bulbs, simply substitute the turnip tops with another tender leaf, such as kale, arugula, or spinach.

SERVES 4

1 bunch of Hakurei turnips (4–6 medium turnips with leafy tops), leaves removed and reserved, bulbs peeled

1 pound (450 g) short pasta, such as spirals, farfalle or orecchiette (use gluten-free, if preferred)

2 tablespoons extra-virgin olive oil

sea salt and black pepper

2 garlic cloves, finely chopped

2 tablespoons (28 g) butter or vegan butter

¼ cup (35 g) roasted shelled pistachios, roughly chopped

Turnip greens pesto

3½ ounces (100 g) turnip greens, roughly chopped

2 garlic cloves, roughly chopped

¼ cup (35 g) roasted shelled pistachios, roughly chopped

½ cup (120 ml) extra-virgin olive oil

½–1 teaspoon sea salt

Pick out any discolored leaves from the turnip greens and discard. Wash the leaves well and drain. Roughly chop them and divide into two equal portions. Ideally you will have approximately 7 ounces (200 g) of greens (it's okay to have a bit more)—set aside half for the pesto; the remaining greens will be sautéed. If you don't have enough greens, you can supplement with some kale, spinach or arugula.

To make the turnip greens pesto, add the greens, garlic and pistachios to the bowl of a food processor or small blender. Add 2½ tablespoons of water and blitz to a chunky paste. With the motor running, slowly trickle in the olive oil and blitz until combined but still a little chunky (you can opt for a smoother pesto if you prefer). Season with the sea salt and set aside.

Bring a large saucepan of well-salted water to a boil. Add the pasta and cook according to the package directions, until al dente. Drain and reserve 1 cup (240 ml) of the pasta cooking water.

Meanwhile, cut the turnips in half, then slice each half into six wedges (fewer if the turnip globes are small; more if they are larger). Heat a large skillet over medium-high heat. Drizzle with the olive oil and add the turnip. Season well with sea salt and black pepper and cook, stirring constantly, for 2 minutes or until charred in spots. Reduce the heat to medium, add 1 tablespoon of water, then cover with a lid and cook for 5–7 minutes, until the turnip wedges are tender. Add the garlic, the remaining turnip greens and the butter and sauté for 1–2 minutes, until the greens are just wilted. Turn off the heat.

Add the hot pasta directly to the turnip, along with the turnip greens pesto. Add ¼–½ cup (60–120 ml) of the pasta cooking water, a little at a time, and fold together until the pasta looks glossy and well coated (you can add more pasta cooking water if the pasta looks dry). Top with the pistachios. Serve immediately or at room temperature.

***

Note: Make the pesto your own. Use whatever nuts or seeds you have on hand. Add grated parmesan or pecorino if you like. Nutritional yeast works, too.

Gluten-free and vegan

Vegetable swap • turnip: radish, carrot, beet

Japanese Turnip Curry

Sweet, juicy turnips shine brightly in this Japanese curry. In many ways, it is the perfect vegetable for this dish—its flesh greedily slurps up the spices, becoming achingly tender while still retaining its shape within the rich, saucy stew. While store-bought Japanese curry bricks are an essential pantry item, which will give you a full-bodied dish in a flash, this homemade curry roux is only slightly more involved. Here, I use a good-quality curry powder to deliver maximum flavor quickly. For those looking to make a roux from absolute scratch, using a tailored mix of spices, please refer to the wonderful book *Japanese Home Cooking* by Sonoko Sakai.

SERVES 4

2½ tablespoons neutral oil

1 yellow onion, sliced

2 garlic cloves, finely chopped

1-inch (2.5 cm) piece of ginger, peeled and sliced

1 large or 2 small carrots (about 7 oz/200 g), cut into ¾-inch (2 cm) pieces

2 turnips (about 1 lb/450 g), peeled and cut into ¾-inch (2 cm) pieces

32 ounces (1 liter) vegetable stock or dashi (to make your own, see Vegan Dashi on page 360)

1 teaspoon sea salt

2 tablespoons soy sauce or tamari

1 tablespoon maple syrup or brown sugar

white or brown rice, to serve

Curry roux (makes ¾ cup)

8 tablespoons (112 g) unsalted regular or vegan butter

⅔ cup (75 g) all-purpose or rice flour

3 tablespoons plus 1 teaspoon (35 g) curry powder (I use S&B brand)

4 teaspoons garam masala

¼–½ teaspoon cayenne pepper or red pepper flakes

Gluten-free and vegan

Vegetable swap • turnip: potato, sweet potato

To make the curry roux, place a small saucepan over low heat and add the butter. Allow it to melt completely, then add the flour and whisk until smooth. Cook, whisking constantly, for 10 minutes, until the roux is thickened and a light brown color. Add the curry powder, garam masala and cayenne pepper or red pepper flakes and stir for 30–60 seconds, until well combined. Remove from the heat and set aside.

Heat a large saucepan over medium heat. When hot, add the oil, along with the onion, and cook, stirring, for 4–5 minutes, until softened. Add the garlic and ginger and stir for 1 minute, until fragrant. Add the carrot, turnip, vegetable stock or dashi, sea salt, soy sauce or tamari and maple syrup or brown sugar and stir to combine. Bring to a boil, then cover and simmer for 10–12 minutes, until the vegetables are tender. Reduce the heat to medium low and add half of the curry roux (freeze the rest, see Note below). Stir well and simmer for 6–10 minutes, until thickened and slightly reduced. If the curry looks too thick, you can add a splash of water. Serve with rice.

Note: The curry roux can be frozen. I use half for this recipe and freeze the rest in an airtight container or zip-seal bag for 3–4 months.

Serving suggestion: Make eggplant katsu curry by serving this curry with the Eggplant Katsu on page 186.

Miso Butter–Glazed Turnips with Black Rice

For anyone who has said or thought that they don't like turnips, this is the dish for them. Rich and indulgent, these buttery, succulent turnips are like savory candy, astonishingly easy to eat and will perhaps enslave you to the modest virtues of turnips for life. Black rice is nutty and chewy, with a robust bite that makes it ideal for this warm salad-ish dish. Small Japanese turnips (Hakurei or Tokyo) are preferred for their sweeter, less bitter qualities, but you could also use regular globe turnips, too. If your turnips have tops, wash those well and throw them into the salad.

SERVES 4

1⅔ cups (300 g) black rice

1 teaspoon sea salt

1½ lb (700 g) Hakurei turnips, scrubbed well and cut into wedges ½ inch (1.25 cm) thick

4 tablespoons (56 g) salted regular or vegan butter

2 garlic cloves, grated

¼ cup white (shiro) miso

4 teaspoons maple syrup

2 handfuls of turnip greens, spinach or kale leaves

2 green onions, finely sliced

Place the black rice in a saucepan and add 3 cups plus 2 tablespoons (750 ml) of water and the sea salt. Bring to a boil, then reduce the heat to medium low, cover and cook for 25–30 minutes, until the water has been absorbed and the rice is tender, with a slight chew.

Meanwhile, heat a large skillet over medium-high heat. When hot, add the turnip wedges, 3 tablespoons (42 g) of the butter, the garlic and miso and stir to combine. Add ¼ cup (60 ml) of water and, when the liquid is bubbling, reduce the heat to medium and cover with a lid. Cook for 3–4 minutes, tossing once halfway through, until the turnip wedges are tender, juicy and golden.

Remove the lid, add the remaining butter to the turnip mixture, drizzle with the maple syrup and toss well. Add the greens to the pan, toss for 30 seconds, then turn off the heat.

Combine the black rice with the turnip mixture and toss well. Top with the green onion and serve warm.

Gluten-free and vegan

Substitute • maple syrup: honey or agave • black rice: brown rice

Vegetable swap • turnip: baby potatoes

Turnip Tortilla

Inspired by tortilla española, this recipe replaces potato with juicy turnips. When gently and slowly poached with onions in olive oil, the turnips become even sweeter than usual, losing all hints of bitterness. What I love about using turnips in this dish is their lightness, resulting in a silky, more delicate tortilla. I like to use smaller turnips, such as Japanese Hakurei, in this recipe—they are more tender and cook quicker. Serve either hot or at room temperature alongside a green salad (the Sesame-Infused Kale Salad on page 239 would be a nice accompaniment) for a satisfying meal for breakfast, lunch or dinner.

SERVES 4

¾ cup (180 ml) extra-virgin olive oil

1 small yellow onion, halved and finely sliced

1 pound 7 ounces (650 g) Hakurei turnips, peeled and very finely sliced

sea salt

6 large eggs

Heat a 10-inch (25 cm) skillet over medium heat. Add the olive oil to the pan, along with the onion, and cook for 4–5 minutes, until softened—you don't want the onion to turn golden. Add the turnip and 1 teaspoon of sea salt and fold everything together. Reduce the heat to low and cook the turnip for 20–30 minutes, until completely tender.

Meanwhile, break the eggs into a bowl and add ½ teaspoon of sea salt. Whisk well.

When the turnip is tender, use a spider ladle or a slotted spoon to remove the turnip and onion from the pan, draining off as much oil as you can, then add them to the egg (the egg may scramble a bit but that's fine), folding through to mix well. Pour off all but 1 tablespoon of oil from the pan (reserve this oil for later; see Notes) and return the pan to medium-high heat. Scrape the egg and turnip mixture into the pan and cook, lifting the edge and tilting the pan to let the uncooked egg run underneath, until the bottom and edge of the tortilla are set but the center is still wet, 2–3 minutes.

Using a flexible spatula, slide it under and all around the tortilla to loosen it from the pan. Carefully slide the tortilla onto a large plate (the uncooked side will be facing up). Take the pan and invert it over the plate, then flip the plate so that the uncooked side of the tortilla is now on the bottom of the pan. If the pan is dry, carefully drizzle some of the reserved oil around the edge of the tortilla, lifting the edges with the spatula to let the oil run underneath. Cook for another 2–3 minutes, tucking in the edges, until golden brown. The center of the egg should still be a little runny, but you can cook it for slightly longer if you would like the egg more set.

Slide the tortilla onto a plate and allow to cool for 5–10 minutes before cutting into wedges. Serve warm or at room temperature.

Notes: Store leftover tortilla in the fridge for up to 3 days; return to room temperature before serving.

The reserved frying oil has a lovely turnip-onion flavor and can be used to cook other dishes; alternatively strain it and use to make a salad dressing.

Gluten-free

Vegetable swap • turnip: potato, rutabaga

Roasted Turnips
with Red Onion, Lentils and Wasabi Aioli

Turnips have a natural mild bitterness and spicy undertone, and the same could be said about wasabi. I play with this commonality here, anchoring the dish in these earthy notes, but also counterpunching with lighter, sweeter moments provided by the red onion, leafy greens and herbs. While wasabi often falls into the love-it-or-leave-it basket, pairing it with creamy mayonnaise and garlic neutralizes its nasal-clearing powers. If you're feeling game, try this with a homemade mayonnaise (see Note), but I do understand if this feels like a bridge too far. I use a wasabi powder from my local Japanese grocery store, but you could also use the paste in the tubes that are easily found in larger supermarkets. I suggest adding the wasabi a little at a time, until you find the right potency for you.

SERVES 4

2 pounds (900 g) Hakurei turnips, peeled and halved or cut into wedges ¾–1¼ inches (2–3 cm) thick

extra-virgin olive oil

sea salt and black pepper

1 red onion, sliced into wedges a scant ¼-inch (5 mm) thick

½ cup (100 g) brown or black lentils

2–3 handfuls of spinach or salad greens

handful of cilantro leaves

2 green onions, finely chopped

Wasabi aioli (makes 1 cup)

¾ cup (180 g) regular or vegan mayonnaise (see Note for homemade recipe)

1½–2 teaspoons wasabi powder or paste (according to your taste)

1–2 garlic cloves, grated (according to your taste)

4 teaspoons lemon juice

Gluten-free and vegan

Substitute • lentils: canned chickpeas

Vegetable swap • turnip: potato, rutabaga, beet

Preheat the oven to 400°F (200°C).

Arrange the turnip on a baking sheet, drizzle with olive oil and season with sea salt and black pepper. Roast for 15 minutes. In the meantime, place the red onion in a small bowl, drizzle with olive oil, season with a little sea salt and toss to combine. After 15 minutes, remove the turnip from the oven and add the red onion to the baking sheet. Return to the oven for 10–15 minutes, until the turnip is tender and the red onion is golden. Set aside to cool.

Meanwhile, bring a saucepan of salted water to a boil. Add the lentils and cook for 20–25 minutes, until completely tender. Drain.

To make the wasabi aioli, combine all the ingredients in a small bowl and whisk to combine. It should be salty enough, but if it needs more, taste and season with some sea salt.

Place the turnip and red onion in a large serving bowl and add the lentils. Add about ½ cup (125 g) of the wasabi aioli and toss to combine. Season with sea salt and black pepper. Taste and add more of the wasabi aioli, depending upon how rich you would like the salad. Finally, add the spinach or salad greens, cilantro leaves and green onion and toss again. Serve immediately.

Serving suggestion: Any leftover aioli can be served with roasted veggies—it's especially good with roasted potatoes. Store in an airtight container in the fridge for up to 1 week.

Note: For homemade mayonnaise, in the small bowl of a food processor, high-powered blender or a bowl with a whisk, add 1 egg and blitz/whisk for 20 seconds. Add 4 teaspoons of Dijon mustard, 4 teaspoons of apple cider vinegar or red/white wine vinegar and ½ teaspoon of sea salt and blitz/whisk for another 20 seconds. Scrape down the side of the bowl if you need to. Turn the processor or blender on (or start whisking) and very slowly trickle in 1 cup (240 ml) of neutral oil, a drop at a time at the beginning, until the mixture starts to emulsify. Once it thickens, add the oil in a slow, steady stream. When all the oil has been added, blitz/whisk for 10 seconds longer. Add 4 teaspoons of lemon juice, then taste and adjust the salt and vinegar to your liking. If you're using this homemade mayo recipe for this dish, substitute the Dijon mustard with the wasabi. Makes about 1 cup (250 g). If your mayo splits (it happens), add either 1 teaspoon of mustard or 1 egg yolk to the bowl, then slowly beat it until it becomes emulsified and creamy again.

Daikon with Cold Spicy Noodles

Crisp and juicy daikon pairs delightfully with fiery, slippery cold noodles in this recipe, which is inspired by the Xi'an dish liángpí (literal translation: "cold skin"), a dish of cold wheat or rice noodles doused in a spicy dressing. It is often served with cucumber, which provides a cooling element, but here this job is accomplished masterfully by daikon, which is sweeter, tangier and juicier. A signature of liángpí is chewy and bouncy noodles, so I like to use thick rice or clear glass noodles made from mung bean, potato, sweet potato or tapioca starch, which hungrily absorb the gutsy dressing. The Sichuan peppercorns will give the noodles a tingly zing, but you can omit them if you're looking for something more mellow.

SERVES 4

9 ounces (250 g) daikon, peeled and julienned

2 cups (230 g) bean sprouts

1 pound (450 g) wide rice or mung bean noodles

large handful of cilantro leaves picked and stems finely chopped

Spicy sauce

¼ cup (60 ml) chili oil or chili crisp

4 teaspoons soy sauce or tamari

4 teaspoons black vinegar

2 teaspoons toasted sesame oil

1 tablespoon toasted white sesame seeds

½–1 teaspoon ground Sichuan peppercorns (optional)

½ teaspoon sugar

½ teaspoon sea salt

2 garlic cloves, grated

Bring a large saucepan of salted water to a boil. Add the daikon and blanch for 30 seconds, then add the bean sprouts and blanch with the daikon for 30 seconds longer. Remove the daikon and bean sprouts with tongs and drain. To the same pan of water, add the noodles and cook according to the package directions, until the noodles are tender. Drain the noodles and run under cold water, until they are cool.

Meanwhile, to make the spicy sauce, place all the ingredients in a large bowl and whisk to combine.

Add the daikon, bean sprouts and noodles to the spicy sauce and mix well to coat. Taste and, if you need some more flavor, season with extra sea salt. Add the cilantro and toss again. Serve cold.

Do ahead: The spicy sauce can be prepared a day ahead and kept in the fridge in an airtight container.

Gluten-free and vegan

Substitute • ground Sichuan peppercorns: freshly ground black or white peppercorns

Lo Bak Gao
("Turnip" Cake)

Lo bak gao is a dim sum classic, wheeled around in a cart and fried on the spot. Made of daikon, rather than turnip as its English name suggests, it is a savory steamed cake. The dim sum version will usually feature lap cheong (Chinese sausage), lap yuk (cured pork belly), har mai (dried shrimp) or dried scallops, and is a thin, compressed cake. This homemade version is my mother's recipe, a thicker and more pillowy cake, with a more pronounced daikon flavor. This one is full of umami, with shiitake mushrooms, five-spice powder and green onions. You could also add some finely chopped five-spice tofu, some Chinese preserved vegetables, such as chung choy (salted turnip), or even a few fermented black beans for a flavorful spin. Lo bak gao can be eaten steamed, but most people prefer it pan-fried, with a golden crust.

SERVES 4 AS A LIGHT MEAL

2¼ pounds (1 kg) daikon, peeled

5 dried shiitake mushrooms (about 1 oz/30 g), soaked in 1 cup (240 ml) of boiling water for 30 minutes

neutral oil

½ teaspoon five-spice powder

1 tablespoon sea salt

2 green onions, finely sliced

1 shallot or small yellow onion, finely diced

1 cup (170 g) rice flour (if using fine rice flour, 1 cup is 115 g)

To serve

finely sliced green onion

cilantro leaves

chili oil or chili crisp

toasted white sesame seeds

Lightly spray an 8–8½-inch (20–22 cm) round or square deep pan with neutral cooking spray.

Grate the daikon using the largest holes of a box grater or the grater attachment on a food processor, then set aside. The daikon will release some liquid as you are grating—keep all of this.

Squeeze the shiitake mushrooms to remove any excess liquid and finely chop. Keep the soaking water.

Heat a large saucepan or Dutch oven over medium-high heat. Add 4 teaspoons of oil, along with the mushrooms, five-spice powder and 1 teaspoon of sea salt and stir for 2 minutes. Turn off the heat, add the green onion and stir to combine. Remove from the pan and set aside.

Return the pan to medium-high heat, add 1 tablespoon of oil, along with the shallot or onion, and stir for 2 minutes until fragrant and softened. Add the daikon (and any liquid), 2 teaspoons of sea salt and ⅓–½ cup (80–120 ml) of the mushroom soaking water and cook, stirring constantly, for 10–12 minutes, until the daikon is translucent. The daikon will release more liquid as it cooks, and while some of this will evaporate, the moisture is needed to form the "batter." Add the mushroom mixture, then gradually add the rice flour, a little at a time, stirring constantly until it is a thick and sticky mixture. If the mixture is too thick to stir, just add 1–2 tablespoons of water to loosen it up. The batter should not be too wet; it should be just soft enough to spread into your pan, but still quite sticky. When you can't see any more flecks of flour, transfer the mixture to the prepared pan, patting and smoothing the top with the back of the spoon or a flexible spatula (I often wet my hands and smooth it down with my palm).

Gluten-free and vegan

Set up a wide, deep skillet, Dutch oven or wok with a steaming basket or a trivet (see Note below). Add plenty of water to the pan (making sure it won't touch the bottom of the basket) and place over medium-high heat. Place the pan of turnip cake inside the steaming basket or on the trivet, cover completely with a lid and steam for 1–1¼ hours, until it is set—you will need to refill the pan with water several times during cooking as the water will evaporate. If you have used a slightly different-sized pan, your cake may be slightly thicker or thinner, so you may need to adjust the cooking time. When it's ready, the surface may look a little wet and it may not feel completely firm—that is normal, it will dry out and solidify as it cools. You can eat the lo bak gao now, as a steamed cake. However, if you would like to pan-fry it, proceed to the next step.

Allow the lo bak gao to cool in the pan, then place in the fridge for at least 2 hours or up to overnight.

To remove the lo bak gao from the pan, run a knife or spatula around the edge of the cake to loosen, then turn it upside down onto a cutting board (it should come out in one piece).

Cut the lo bak gao into squares or slices. Heat a large skillet over medium-high heat and, when it's hot, add 1–2 tablespoons of oil. Add the turnip cake to the pan and fry for 2–3 minutes on each side, until golden. Remove from the pan.

To serve, top the lo bak gao with chopped green onion, cilantro leaves, a little chili oil or chili crisp and sesame seeds.

Note: If you don't have a steaming basket or trivet, you can use any metal objects, such as strong pastry cutters or several balls of foil, to balance your pan.

Storage: Keep the lo bak gao in the fridge for 2–3 days, or in the freezer for up to 1 month. To reheat, thaw the frozen turnip cakes first, and pan-fry before serving.

Pictured overleaf ›

Lo Bak Gao ("Turnip" Cake)

Zucchini

"A sunbeam on our plate"

Zucchini has its origins in Mexico, dating from 7000–5500 BCE, when it was an important part of the ancient diet of squash, maize and beans. This trio is known as "the three sisters," and is still a mainstay of Mexican cuisine. In Mexico, squash flowers are often more prized than the fruit, and are used in soups or quesadillas.

A member of the summer squash family, zucchini (known as courgette in some parts of the world) is a sunbeam on our plate, a dazzling star of summer dining. It is 95 percent water, with a mellow flavor that concentrates and becomes sweeter as it cooks and releases moisture. When cooked at high heat—either on the grill or in a very hot pan—it becomes earthy, with a creamy flesh and an irresistible smokiness. Charred or pan-fried, zucchini always benefits from both generous salting and acid, which draws out more sweetness and fruitiness. Red wine vinegar or apple cider vinegar are great options, and lemon works, too. Nowadays, I rarely consume grilled zucchini without a hit of something sour.

When choosing zucchini, size matters. Choose small-to-medium zucchini that are around 6 inches (15 cm) long; larger zucchini may be bitter. Along with the most common black zucchini (the regular green ones), in summer you will find summer squashes of different shapes, sizes and colors. There are golden zucchini; bright yellow "summer squash"; squat pattypan squash with scalloped edges; crookneck squash, which narrows at the top into an elegant curvy neck; a dark-green Italian variety called gadzukes with a star-shaped body; and short pale-green "gray" zucchini, along with others that are yellow, striped or round, plus many more. Taste and texturewise, some summer squashes have less water, or are nuttier or firmer, but they are largely interchangeable, which makes cooking with them in the summer such a seasonal highlight.

Zucchini and Yuzu Bread

When the kids were little, we visited a local café almost every morning. There, while this sleep-deprived mum desperately ingested her skim flat white, the kids fell silent for a few precious moments over a piece of zucchini or banana bread. Now that my kids are teenagers, I can see the deception—these fruit-based "breads" are just cake by another name, a descriptor that carries much less guilt for already-frazzled mums. But whether we want to call them bread, cake or loaf, zucchini is an enduringly excellent addition to these baked goods, ensuring a moist and flavorful crumb. This is zucchini bread, revamped, with the addition of tangy and floral yuzu. If you can't get your hands on yuzu, use grapefruit, lemon, lime or orange juice.

SERVES 6–8

1¼ cups (150 g) coarsely grated zucchini

¾ cup (180 ml) dairy or nondairy milk, such as oat

2½ tablespoons yuzu juice

⅓ cup (80 ml) neutral oil

½ cup (100 g) brown sugar

1 teaspoon vanilla extract

2 cups plus 1 tablespoon (250 g) all-purpose or gluten-free all-purpose flour

1 teaspoon baking powder

½ teaspoon baking soda

½ teaspoon ground cinnamon

1 teaspoon sea salt

Yuzu-walnut glaze (optional)

1 cup (120 g) powdered sugar, sifted

2½ tablespoons yuzu juice

½ cup toasted walnuts, roughly chopped

Preheat the oven to 350°F (180°C). Spray a loaf pan (about 8 × 4 × 2⅓ inches/20 cm × 10 cm × 6 cm) with cooking spray and line with parchment paper.

Press the grated zucchini with paper towels or a clean tea towel to remove some of the moisture. You don't want it to be completely dry, otherwise the loaf won't be moist; you just want to remove any excess.

Place the milk, yuzu, oil, sugar and vanilla extract in a large mixing bowl and whisk to combine.

In a separate large bowl, whisk together the flour, baking powder, baking soda, cinnamon and sea salt.

Add the wet ingredients to the dry ingredients and fold them together until just combined (some lumps are fine, but you shouldn't see any unmixed flour). Fold in the zucchini.

Pour the batter into the prepared loaf pan and bake for 50–55 minutes, until an inserted skewer comes out clean. Remove from the oven and allow the loaf to cool in the pan for 5–10 minutes, before turning out onto a wire rack to cool completely.

If you are making the yuzu-walnut glaze, place the powdered sugar and yuzu juice in a small mixing bowl and whisk until combined. When the cake is cool, pour the icing over the cake and top with the chopped walnuts.

Storage: The unglazed cake can be stored in an airtight container or tightly wrapped at room temperature for up to 1 day, or frozen for up to 1 month.

Gluten-free and vegan

Substitute • yuzu juice: lemon, orange or grapefruit juice

Vegetable swap • zucchini: carrot, parsnip

Smoky Zucchini Dip with Za'atar Flatbread

When peak summer arrives so do the zucchini, en masse. We celebrate this most abundant of seasons with copious batches of this smoky zucchini dip, a recipe that showcases the delicate sweetness and robust richness of seasonal zucchini flesh. This dip is redolent of baba ghanoush, but a sunnier take; blistering the zucchini skin imparts smokiness, while the flesh becomes melty, mingling happily with the tahini and lemon. The za'atar flatbread is one of the easiest and quickest breads you'll make—yogurt is the magic ingredient, providing a nice sourness to the dough. This is a satisfying light lunch, which can also be served with an assortment of crudités, such as cucumber segments, raw asparagus spears, baby carrots, whole radishes, celery stalks and more.

SERVES 4

3 zucchini (about 1½ lb/700 g)

¼ cup (60 g) tahini

zest and juice of 1 lemon
(2½ tablespoons juice)

1 tablespoon extra-virgin olive oil,
plus more for drizzling

1 garlic clove, grated

½ teaspoon sea salt

black pepper

za'atar, for sprinkling

small handful of dill

Za'atar flatbread (makes 6)

2½ cups (300 g) all-purpose flour or
gluten-free all-purpose flour, plus
more for dusting

2 teaspoons baking powder

sea salt

1 cup plus 1½ tablespoons (250 g)
plain or vegan yogurt

¼ cup (60 ml) extra-virgin olive oil

1 tablespoon za'atar

To make the za'atar flatbread, combine the flour, baking powder and 1 teaspoon of sea salt in a bowl and whisk until combined. Add the yogurt and stir together until a stiff dough forms (it will look very dry, that is normal). On a lightly floured surface, knead the dough until soft and slightly sticky (it won't be completely smooth). Dust your surface with a touch more flour, place the dough on top, then cover with an upturned bowl (the one you used for mixing is fine) and let rest for 30 minutes.

Meanwhile, heat a heavy (cast-iron) skillet over medium-high heat. Add the whole zucchini to the dry pan and char, turning constantly, until the skins are blackened all over and the insides are tender. This should take 15–20 minutes. You can also blister the skins on an outdoor grill or under a hot broiler, but keep a close eye on them to prevent burning. If the skins are black but the flesh is not yet completely soft (test it by squeezing the thick end of the zucchini with your fingers), place the zucchini in a preheated 400°F (200°C) oven and roast for 5–10 minutes, until they feel very soft. When completely soft, slice the zucchini in half lengthwise and scoop out the creamy flesh, avoiding any of the blackened skin. Place the flesh in a bowl and stir with a fork—the flesh should break up easily. Add the tahini, lemon zest and juice, olive oil, garlic and sea salt and season with black pepper. Set aside.

Make a za'atar oil for the flatbread by combining the olive oil, za'atar and ½ teaspoon of sea salt in a small bowl.

Place the flatbread dough on a floured surface and divide it into six balls. Roll each ball into a 6½–6⅔-inch (16–17 cm) round. Brush each side with the za'atar oil. Heat a skillet over medium-high heat until it is smoking hot, then add the flatbreads to the pan, one at a time, and cook for 30–60 seconds each side until puffed up and charred.

To serve, place the zucchini dip on a plate, drizzle with olive oil, sprinkle with za'atar and scatter with the dill. Serve alongside the za'atar flatbread.

Gluten-free and vegan

Fried Zucchini Pasta

In early 2021, after 12 months of being at home, Americans became obsessed with Stanley Tucci's show *Searching for Italy* and, specifically, his fried zucchini pasta. On the stunning Amalfi Coast, an area that holds a special place in my wandering heart, Stanley grilled a local chef about how to make his favorite fried zucchini pasta, a dish he apparently tries to replicate at home weekly. My interest was piqued, my mind immediately churning with ideas of how to create this dish for myself. In the weeks after, spaghetti alla Nerano blew up on social media. Everyone was frying mounds of zucchini and tucking into this sun-kissed bowl of pasta. Such was my joy at seeing so many devouring this often-underappreciated vegetable, I had to give my take on this now-famous zucchini dish; not completely faithful to the Italian way, but with a few of my own quirks. The traditional dish is topped with provolone, but I've left this optional as I quite like this unadorned, bare.

SERVES 4

extra-virgin olive oil

8 zucchini (about 3½ lb/1.6 kg), trimmed and finely sliced

sea salt and black pepper

1 pound (450 g) bucatini or other long pasta

6 garlic cloves, finely chopped

3 tablespoons (42 g) regular or vegan butter

handful of basil leaves

¼ cup toasted pine nuts

To serve (optional)

juice of ½ lemon

grated provolone

Heat a deep saucepan over medium-high heat and add 1–1¼ inches (2–3 cm) of olive oil. Insert a wooden chopstick or spoon into the oil and, when it sizzles aggressively, the oil is hot enough. Working in batches, add a handful of zucchini slices at a time and fry, tossing every now and then, until golden—this should take 3–5 minutes for each batch. Remove with a slotted spoon and drain in a colander. Sprinkle with sea salt. Continue with the remaining zucchini. When all of the zucchini has been fried, set aside.

Meanwhile, bring a large saucepan of salted water to a boil and add the pasta. Cook according to the package directions, until al dente. Drain the pasta, reserving about 1 cup (240 ml) of the pasta cooking water.

Heat a large skillet over medium heat and add 2–3 tablespoons of olive oil, along with the garlic. Stir for 30–60 seconds, until fragrant, then throw in all the fried zucchini. Cook, stirring frequently, for 2–3 minutes, until the zucchini starts to break apart and become jammy. Add the pasta to the pan, along with ½ cup (120 ml) of the pasta cooking water, and, using tongs, toss to coat the pasta with the zucchini. Add the butter and season well with two or three big pinches of sea salt, plus some black pepper. Give the pasta another toss.

Top the pasta with the basil leaves and toasted pine nuts. If you like, serve with a squeeze of lemon juice and some grated provolone.

For gluten-free • use gluten-free pasta

Vegan

Zucchini and Kimchi Stew

This recipe is partway between two incredible Korean dishes: gochujang hobak jjigae, a spicy zucchini stew, and kimchi soondubu jjigae, a kimchi and soft tofu stew. Jjigae is a Korean stew that is typically made with meat, seafood or vegetables, cooked in a broth seasoned with the fermented flavors of gochujang, doenjang, ganjang or saeujeot. The addition of zucchini adds freshness and sweetness, while the punchy flavor of kimchi marries all the ingredients together. I cook the zucchini minimally in this dish, so it retains a bright crunch.

SERVES 4

neutral oil

1 yellow onion, finely sliced

2 garlic cloves, finely chopped

2 cups (400 g) regular or vegan kimchi, roughly chopped

3 green onions, sliced into 1-inch (2.5 cm) segments, white and green parts separated

1 teaspoon sugar

2 teaspoons sea salt

4 teaspoons gochugaru

2½ tablespoons gochujang

2 teaspoons toasted sesame oil

32 ounces (1 liter) vegetable stock or dashi (to make your own, see Vegan Dashi on page 360)

1 block of soft tofu (about 14 oz/400 g), sliced ¾-inch (2 cm) thick

1–2 zucchini (about 7 oz/300 g), trimmed, halved lengthwise and cut into half-moons ⅜-inch (1 cm) thick

white rice or glass noodles, to serve

Heat a large saucepan over medium-high heat and, when it's hot, drizzle in 1–2 tablespoons of oil. Add the onion and cook for 2–3 minutes, until softened. Add the garlic and kimchi (if your kimchi has brine, it's okay to add up to ¼ cup of that, too) and the white part of the green onion, and cook for 2–3 minutes, until the kimchi is starting to stick to the base of the pan. Add the sugar, sea salt, gochugaru, gochujang, sesame oil and vegetable stock or dashi. Cover and cook for 10–12 minutes, until fragrant.

Reduce the heat to medium and add the tofu (it will likely break up and that is fine), zucchini and green part of the green onion and simmer, uncovered, for 5–7 minutes, until everything is hot.

Ladle the stew into bowls and serve alongside rice or glass noodles.

Serving tip: When you add the tofu and zucchini, you can also break some eggs into the stew and allow them to poach in the spicy liquid. I usually allow 1 egg per person.

Gluten-free and vegan

Substitute • gochugaru: 1–2 teaspoons red pepper flakes or chile powder (to your liking)

Vegetable swap • zucchini: mushrooms

Zucchini, Dill and Tahini Soup

The mellow side of zucchini may preclude you from considering it for soup, but it is this very gentility that shines in this recipe. There are a lot of assertive flavors vying for attention here—the grassiness of dill, the brightness of lemon, the bitter earthiness of walnuts and the nuttiness of tahini—and even with all these ingredients in play, it is the quiet sweetness of the zucchini that glows brightest. This is the elegant power of vegetables, to always dazzle, even among the most confident of company. Zucchini for the win here.

SERVES 4

extra-virgin olive oil

1 yellow onion, finely diced

3 garlic cloves, finely chopped

2 thyme sprigs, leaves picked

2 large zucchini (about 1 lb/450 g), trimmed and cut into ⅜-inch (1 cm) thick discs

32 ounces (1 liter) vegetable stock

1 cup whole walnuts

sea salt and black pepper

3 tablespoons lemon juice (from about 1 lemon), plus more to serve

1 bunch of dill (about 1 oz/30 g), leaves and stems

¼ cup (60 g) tahini, plus more for drizzling

toasted white sesame seeds, for topping

Heat a large saucepan over medium-high heat. Add 2 tablespoons of olive oil, along with the onion, and cook, stirring, for 2–3 minutes, until softened (if the onion starts to color, reduce the heat). Add the garlic and thyme leaves and toss for 1 minute. Add the zucchini and stir for 2 minutes, just to soften it slightly (try to prevent it from getting too much golden color). Next, add the vegetable stock and walnuts, along with about 1 teaspoon of sea salt and a good grind of black pepper. Bring to a boil, then cover with a lid, reduce the heat to medium and simmer for 10 minutes.

Transfer the soup to a blender or food processor (or use an immersion blender). Add the lemon juice, three-quarters of the dill leaves and all the stems (reserve the remaining leaves for topping) and the tahini and puree the soup until completely smooth. Taste and season with more sea salt and black pepper.

Ladle the soup into bowls and top with the remaining dill leaves, some sesame seeds, a squeeze of lemon juice, a drizzle of tahini and a few drops of olive oil.

Do ahead: The soup can be made 2 days ahead and kept in an airtight container in the fridge. Reheat on the stovetop and add the toppings just before eating.

Gluten-free and vegan

Substitute • walnuts: cashews, almonds, pumpkin seeds • dill: chives, green onions, parsley, mint

Vegetable swap • zucchini: cucumber

Za'atar Zucchini Ramen Noodles

Za'atar is my daughter Scout's favorite spice blend, so I'm always devising new ways of incorporating it into quick lunches or weeknight cooking. Here, I've come up with a fusion-y recipe, a Scout-approved dish of buttery ramen noodles, topped with za'atar. Za'atar refers to both a wild herb (also called hyssop) and a spice blend. When it comes to the blend, there are many varieties on the market, with different dried herb combinations, some with salt, mint, dried dill or dried orange peel. Try different brands to find your favorite (mine is by New York Shuk). Za'atar is a vegetable lover's pantry essential—it brings vegetables to life, but it works particularly well with milder vegetables like zucchini, delivering tangy, herbal, nutty notes.

SERVES 4

14 ounces (400 g) instant ramen noodles

boiling water

extra-virgin olive oil

2 zucchini (about 1 lb/450 g), trimmed and julienned

sea salt and black pepper

4 tablespoons (56 g) regular or vegan butter, roughly chopped

3 tablespoons za'atar, plus more for topping

1 ounce (30 g) pecorino, parmesan or cheddar, finely grated, or 2–3 tablespoons nutritional yeast

a few mint leaves

Place the noodles in a large bowl, cover with boiling water and soak for 2 minutes. Scoop out ½ cup (120 ml) of the noodle soaking water, then drain the noodles and run under cold water, breaking the noodles up with your hands.

Heat a large skillet over medium-high heat. Add 1–2 tablespoons of olive oil, along with the zucchini and a pinch of sea salt, and stir-fry for 1–2 minutes, until softened. Add the noodles to the pan, along with the butter, za'atar, another pinch of sea salt and a few turns of black pepper and stir for 1 minute, until fragrant. Add about ¼ cup of the noodle soaking water, just enough to loosen the noodles. Cook for 1 minute, then turn off the heat, add half the cheese or nutritional yeast and season well with sea salt. Toss everything together until the cheese melts, adding a bit more of the reserved soaking water if the noodles seem dry.

Transfer to serving plates and top with the remaining cheese or nutritional yeast, another turn of black pepper, more za'atar and a few mint leaves. Serve immediately.

For gluten-free • replace the ramen noodles with rice noodles or rice cakes

Vegan

Substitute • ramen noodles: thick rice, egg, soba or udon noodles

Vegetable swap • zucchini: carrot

Charred Zucchini and Corn
with Basil Caesar-ish Sauce

When charred, zucchini becomes smoky and seductive. Cooking it at a high temperature draws out moisture and concentrates the sweet, earthy flavors. Teamed with crispy, charred corn in this vibrant salad, this dish flies the flag for easy summer eating. If you have a grill, you can cook the zucchini and corn on there to get that smoky char, though cooking on the stovetop will yield excellent, deep flavors, too. I always add a touch of vinegar to my charred zucchini—this really amplifies the sweetness of the fruit. The dressing has an undeniable "Caesar" vibe—acidic and herbaceous, rich with basil, citrus and briny capers. Roll with this feeling and add some crunchy croutons and top with a salty cheese, if you like.

SERVES 4

extra-virgin olive oil

6 small zucchini (about 2 lb/900 g), trimmed and cut diagonally into slices ⅜ inch (1 cm) thick

sea salt and black pepper

2 teaspoons red wine vinegar

3 ears corn (about 2 lb/900 g), husks removed

big handful of mint leaves

big handful of basil leaves

Basil Caesar-ish dressing

4 teaspoons capers, rinsed

1 cup basil leaves

1 garlic clove, roughly chopped

3 tablespoons lemon juice (from 1 lemon)

¼ cup (60 g) tahini

sea salt

Heat a skillet or grill pan over medium-high heat. Drizzle in some olive oil and, working in batches, add the zucchini, season with a pinch of sea salt and a few turns of black pepper and pan-fry for 2 minutes until golden and charred. Flip over and char the other side. Transfer the zucchini to a colander, drizzle with the red wine vinegar and set aside.

Drizzle more olive oil into the same pan and add the corn. Season with sea salt and pan-fry, turning often, for 8–10 minutes, until all sides are slightly charred. When cool enough to handle, slice the kernels off the cobs using a sharp knife.

To make the dressing, add all the ingredients to a blender or food processor and pulse a few times, until it becomes a thick paste. Add ⅓ cup (80 ml) of water and blend or process until smooth. Taste and season with sea salt.

To serve, combine the zucchini, corn, mint and basil leaves. Season with sea salt and black pepper and toss to combine. When ready to eat, drizzle the basil Caesar-ish dressing over the top and serve immediately.

Gluten-free and vegan

Substitute • ears of corn: 2 cups (300 g) frozen corn kernels • tahini: regular or vegan mayonnaise

Vegetable swap • zucchini: broccoli, eggplant

Zucchini Flower Pajeon

Pajeon are savory Korean pancakes. This recipe is based upon one shared with me by New York–based artist and author Erin Jang in my book *Family*. The wonder of pajeon is that they are endlessly adaptable—when Erin first made them for me, hers comprised artfully arranged carrot, bell pepper and zucchini, the vegetables swathed in a light, fragrant batter. Sharing this meal with Erin and her family was a special moment for me and, to this day, I always think of them when I devour these light, crispy pancakes. I love the celestial beauty of zucchini flowers in pajeon—while mellow in flavor, they provide a lovely silkiness. If you don't have the flowers, I also use finely sliced discs of zucchini (but basically any vegetables that are fast to cook will work). There are generally two ways of making pajeon—you can add the vegetables to the pan first, lightly pan-frying before spooning the batter over, or you can mix the vegetables straight into the batter before frying (like I have instructed below). The latter is the slightly easier option, so it really depends on how you want your finished pajeon to look.

MAKES ABOUT FOUR 4¾-INCH (12 CM) OR TWO 8-INCH (20 CM) PANCAKES

1¼ cups (150 g) all-purpose or gluten-free all-purpose flour

2½ tablespoons potato starch or rice flour

1 teaspoon sea salt

½ teaspoon garlic powder or 1 garlic clove, grated

2 teaspoons doenjang or white (shiro) miso

1 cup (240 ml) ice-cold water

12–16 zucchini flowers, stamen/pistils and stems removed

neutral oil

Dipping sauce

2½ tablespoons soy sauce or tamari

4 teaspoons rice vinegar

4 teaspoons maple syrup

2 teaspoons toasted sesame oil

1 teaspoon toasted white sesame seeds

To make the dipping sauce, whisk together all the ingredients in a small bowl. Set aside.

In a separate small bowl, whisk together the flour, potato starch or rice flour and sea salt.

In another bowl, whisk together the garlic powder or garlic, doenjang or miso and cold water.

Combine the wet and dry ingredients and whisk until smooth and lump-free. The mixture should be thick, but just pourable. If it looks too thick or stiff, add another 1–2 tablespoons of cold water. Add the zucchini flowers to the batter and gently fold them in. Don't overmix—the flowers don't need to be completely coated in the batter.

Heat a skillet over medium-high heat and add 1 tablespoon of oil. Add one-quarter of the batter for small pancakes or half of the batter for larger pancakes. Cook for 2 minutes, until golden underneath, then flip over. Cover with a lid, reduce the heat to medium and cook for 2 minutes. Uncover and cook for an additional 1–2 minutes, using a spatula to press the pancake into the pan, until golden and crispy. Repeat with the remaining batter (make sure you increase the heat to medium-high before cooking more pancakes).

Slice into squares or wedges and serve immediately, with the dipping sauce on the side.

Gluten-free and vegan

Substitute • potato starch or rice flour: cornstarch

Vegetable swap • zucchini flowers: 9 ounces (250 g) sliced zucchini, green onions, garlic chives, carrot, bell peppers, cabbage

Ching Ming and the Culinary Rituals of Loss

Every year, on the fifteenth day after the spring equinox (during April), Chinese families gather to honor ancestors who have passed. The Ching Ming (or Qingming) Festival is also called Tomb Sweeping Day, a custom celebrated across many Asian cultures.

Ching Ming is a time of deep reflection. In Chinese culture, caring for our family extends to the afterlife, remembering being a sign of enduring respect. There is deep reverence for the sacrifices of those who have passed; their toil in the past enables us to live as we do in the present.

During Ching Ming, my family visits the resting place of my father and other deceased family members. We sweep and tidy up their resting place. We lay out fresh flowers. My mother cooks for the occasion, bringing an offering of my dad's favorite foods—rice, soy-braised chicken, dried oysters with fat choy (black moss), crispy-skin roast pork, oranges. She sets up an altar, we light incense. We pray and pour small cups of wine onto the ground. We burn joss paper and "hell bank notes" to send money to our loved ones in the afterlife (hell bank notes are papers that look like modern currency; the use of the word *hell* is not negative, it simply refers to the underworld). Around us, the cemetery is bustling with other families gathering to perform their own rituals. Many light firecrackers to alert their ancestors to their presence and to scare away evil spirits. At the end of the ceremony, my mother hands out char siu bao (barbecued pork buns)—this is not traditional, just my mother's ritual because she cannot go long without feeding others.

The culinary canons of grieving have fascinated me for years; that even in death, food is our way to stay connected with lost souls. In Japan, bowls of rice with a pair of chopsticks standing up vertically in them are placed at an altar to represent the Buddhist tradition, which uses chopsticks to separate cremated bones from ashes. In Vietnamese culture, an altar is set up for the deceased, with bowls of rice as part of the offering, signifying the act of sacrificing "white gold" to ensure that crossing over to the afterlife comes with good fortune and no lingering hunger. The Mexican holiday Día de los Muertos (Day of the Dead) is not a day of mourning, but rather a celebration; the sweet pan de muerto (bread of the dead) is an offering to ease the journey to the underworld.

In life and in death, food is a source of immeasurable comfort. It is a symbol of care for the life lost, and a balm for the soul that lives on. And for those of us who survive and thrive, food is a legacy, a way to stay connected to loved ones, past and present.

Acknowledgments

My deepest gratitude goes to my family, for always giving me the latitude to explore, to learn, to follow my own path. I see and appreciate all the sacrifices.

Thank you to my dad, for making the first 15 years of my life count, for fostering my love of food, photography, books, collecting, cheese, encyclopedias and stationery. I never really saw myself in you when I was younger, perhaps because I didn't remember clearly, but the older I get, and the more I pursue this creative life, I see you in everything that I do.

Thank you to my mum for being my mother, my father, my mentor, my role model, my light. You deserve all my enduring reverence and humble appreciation. And clearly, there is no recipe in this book that you haven't touched in some way.

Thank you to my sister, Letty, and my brother, Kerby, who have basically held our home together since I was a teenager. I would not have been able to do the things that I have done without your steadfastness and constancy.

I am incredibly lucky to be surrounded by two of the best publishing teams in the world.

To Lexy Bloom—meeting you felt like I was completing the picture; it is an honor to work with you and a privilege to benefit from your wisdom, vision and kindness.

Thank you also to the hardworking team at Knopf who have supported me and made me feel so welcome—I am humbled to be under your wing.

To my co-conspirator and longtime publisher Mary Small—thank you for your enduring faith in my process. Your belief is the reason my books exist, and your trust has given me the courage to tell my story with heart and candor.

Thank you to everyone at Plum Books and Pan Macmillan Australia. A huge shout-out to Clare Marshall, our trusted captain, who always steers us in the right direction.

Thank you to my copy editors Lucy Heaver (Australia) and Kate Slate (U.S.) for bringing precision to my words. To Daniel New, you are a dream collaborator. Thank you for sharing your art, your vision and your magic with us.

Thank you to the incomparable Judy Linden, for always seeing the best in me— your patience and faith over the years have molded me into the author I am today.

I am grateful to Hannah Davitian and Olga Katsnelson at Postcard PR for handling my story with just thoughtfulness and intention.

Thank you to all the home cooks in the United States and all over the world who steadfastly cook my recipes, buy my books, engage with me on social media and welcome me into your kitchens every day. I feel incredibly lucky to have your trust.

Thank you to Shirley Cai, who brings positivity, warmth and creativity to my days. Thank you to Maria Midões, Leetal Arazi, Betty Liu (for your friendship and Mandarin translations), Kris Warman, Jill Fergus and Jennifer Wong for the kinship and humor you bring to my days. Thank you to Doris Ho-Kane and Yewande Komolafe for sharing your strength, wisdom and kindness.

Of course, I save my biggest thanks for my desert island people—the ones that I would happily be stranded with forever—Rad, Scout, Dash and Huck. I have cherished the unexpected time we have spent together over the past few years—the bonus mealtimes, the movies we have watched, the music we have listened to, the conversations and laughs we have shared. Feeding you four inspired all the recipes in this book. Thank you for being hungry and bold.

With love,

Hetty Lui McKinnon 雷瑜

Index

Also by Hetty Lui McKinnon

To Asia, With Love

Community:
Salad Recipes from Arthur Street Kitchen

Family:
New Vegetarian Comfort Food to Nourish Every Day

Neighborhood:
Hearty Salads and Plant-Based Recipes from Home and Abroad